A CENTURY OF DAILY RECORD LAUGHS

A CENTURY OF DAILY RECORD LAUGHS

compiled by
ROD McLEOD

MAINSTREAM
PUBLISHING

Copyright © Scottish Daily Record and Sunday Mail Ltd, 1994

First published in Great Britain in 1994
by Mainstream Publishing Company (Edinburgh) Ltd
7 Albany Street, Edinburgh EH1 3UG

ISBN 1 85158 667 9

A catalogue record for this book is
available from the British Library

Every effort has been made to contact the illustrators
whose work appears in this book; we apologise if,
by being unable to trace any of the contributors,
we have unknowingly failed to acknowledge
copyright material

The proceeds of this book are being
donated to the **Children's Hospice Appeal, Scotland**

————————

Printed in Great Britain by Scotprint Ltd, Musselburgh

ROD McLEOD is the latest in a long line
of artists to grace the *Daily Record's* pages with his cartoons.
In this book, he casts his eye over the *Daily Record's*
drawings and cartoons since 1895 and chooses
the best of them to celebrate the paper's
centenary in 1995.

CONTENTS

IN THE EARLY DAYS … WELL, AROUND THE TWENTIES 12

ENTER PIP, SQUEAK AND WILFRED 18

BRINGING UP FATHER 21

WE'RE NOW APPROACHING THE THIRTIES … AND THE PACE IS HOTTING-UP 24

ENTER LAUDER, WILLIS AND GORDON 34

AND DONALD DUCK 36

THE DIFFICULT YEARS 38

INTO THE FIFTIES … AND THERE'S NOTHING LIKE AN ELECTION TO
BRING OUT THE CARTOONISTS 46

OR A BUDGET 48

OG, CAPP AND NEILL … A HAT-TRICK OF GOODIES 51

INTO THE SIXTIES WITH THE ADVENTURES OF ANGUS OG 70

THROUGH THE SIXTIES AND INTO THE SEVENTIES 74

FROM THE SEVENTIES THROUGH TO THE NINETIES 85

ROD ON NEWS 86

ROD ON SPORT 91

ANGUS OG 97

A MAN CALLED HORACE 105

PRINCE OF THE PALACE 115

GRANDAD AND THE LAD 119

SHUGGIE AND DUGGIE 124

A Century of Laughs

The cavemen were pretty good at them. Though chiselling out a cartoon meant these early examples weren't able to meet a Daily Record deadline. The Egyptians knew a thing or two about using drawings to trace the progress of society as well. And the much revered Old Masters who painted some of the world's great art treasures were also capable of drawing their subject in something almost qualifying as caricature. But it wasn't until the 1600s that such drawings were actually used as a means of ridicule. Over the centuries since, the cartoon has matured and developed into many different forms. Often those which became the subject of most comment were drawn at periods of great upheaval.

The French Revolution and two World Wars have all been fertile territory for those cartoonists who specialised in politics and current events. The best of them live on long after their creators have departed to the great studio in the sky. People still remember the classic caricature, by the wartime and post war cartoonist Vicky, of premier Harold Macmillan in which he dressed him up as 'Supermac'. Later there was the cartoon created by Jak at the time of the Six Days War in the Middle East. 'Come to Israel and See the Pyramids' was his ironic caption, under a drawing of the major Egyptian tourist attraction! Images like that underline just what a powerful medium cartoons can be, not just in relfecting the imagination of the artists, but reflecting the ideas and opinions of the times. For that very reason, they also became propaganda weapons in states like Stalin's

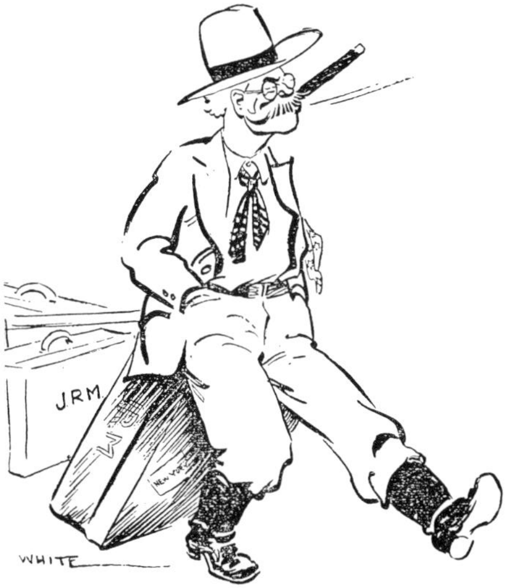
JRM
WHITE

Russia or Hitler's Germany where it was quite literally more than the cartoonist's life was worth to send up the government of the day. Instead, the government would use their pen and wit to send a particular set of signals to the general public. Some people have called cartoons the slang of graphic art, but that almost does them less than justice. Cartoons are often wickedly funny, but at times of tragedy, such as famine, they can also emerge as a poignant and devestating portrait of reality, And, like photographs, can be more powerful and dramatic than the words of the writer which they illustrate.

Most cartoonists would agree that the art of caricature is almost a separate skill. Many very amusing cartoonists have never acquired the difficult knack of portraying a well-known face in such a fashion as to make them instantly recognisable, while using enough exaggeration to add wit and style to the portrait.

Conversely, some of the finest draughtsmen and women in the world have never had any particular facility with jokes!

There is a general belief that the people who make us laugh in our newspapers and magazines through their artwork must be extremely amusing in real life. Not so. It's well known that some of the funniest artists are positively morose around the house .. . ask their spouses!

Very few of the top names would regard themselves as comedians who happen to be able to draw. In fact, in order to find a ready joke in a topical situation you have to have a very particular mindset . . . one which will often let you tie up two apparently unrelated news events,

After the caricature and the topical cartoon came the immense popularity of comic strips, the best of which are laughed at in syndication round the world. Proof positive that there are at least some things the whole world finds funny . Go into any office in the world and you're liable to see a strip of Peanuts, or Andy Capp, or Hagar pinned up. Perhaps because they rely on human weakness and frailty for their subject matter, and there's no shortage of these commodities wherever you look.

Comic strips in essence have become the newspaper soap operas of our time. Readers who got caught up in the West Highland shenanigans of Angus Og would want their daily fix in much the same way that horoscope addicts turn first to that part of the paper.

Over all these cartoon forms, Scotland has had its share of incomparable talents. Bud Neill's gallus Glaswegians became national institutions and went on to become the subject of television documentaries and successful books.

In fact, Bud's immortal Wild West characters, who all, naturally, spoke fluent Glaswegian, even have a statue built in their honour by public subscription. Now, that's staying power.

But it's not just fans who find cartoons so fascinating. For historians they provide a priceless glimpse into different decades, different generations, and different social styles. They tell us a great deal about the life and times in which the artist worked and, just as valuably, about the spirit of the audience. Living would be a much duller business without them.

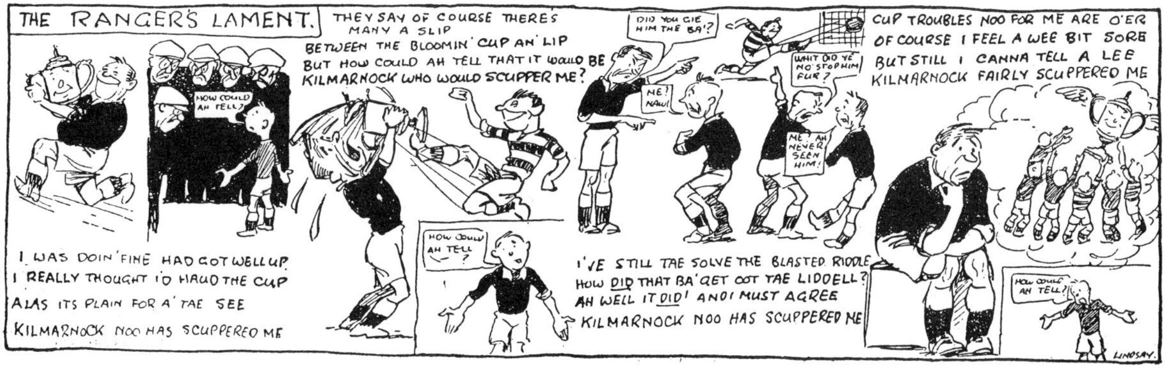
THE RANGER'S LAMENT.
I WAS DOIN' FINE HAD GOT WELL UP
I REALLY THOUGHT I'D HAUD THE CUP
ALAS ITS PLAIN FOR A' TAE SEE
KILMARNOCK NOO HAS SCUPPERED ME
HOW COULD AH TELL?
THEY SAY OF COURSE THERE'S MANY A SLIP
BETWEEN THE BLOOMIN' CUP AN' LIP
BUT HOW COULD AH TELL THAT IT WOULD BE
KILMARNOCK WHO WOULD SCUPPER ME?
HOW COULD AH TELL?
DID YOU GIE HIM THE BA'?
ME! NAW!
WHIT DID YE NO' STOP HIM FUR?
ME? AH NEVER SEEN HIM!
I'VE STILL TAE SOLVE THE BLASTED RIDDLE
HOW DID THAT BA' GET OOT TAE LIDDELL?
AH WELL IT DID! AND I MUST AGREE
KILMARNOCK NOO HAS SCUPPERED ME
CUP TROUBLES NOO FOR ME ARE O'ER
OF COURSE I FEEL A WEE BIT SORE
BUT STILL I CANNA TELL A LEE
KILMARNOCK FAIRLY SCUPPERED ME
HOW COULD AH TELL?
LINDSAY.

In the Early Days . . . well, around the twenties

October 1895, and the *Daily Record* first appeared on the streets of Scotland; a paper without cartoons.

In fact the pages of the new 'Voice of Scotland' looked more like a broadsheet than a tabloid. Early front pages were a mixture of news and adverts; international news jostled with reports from local burgh

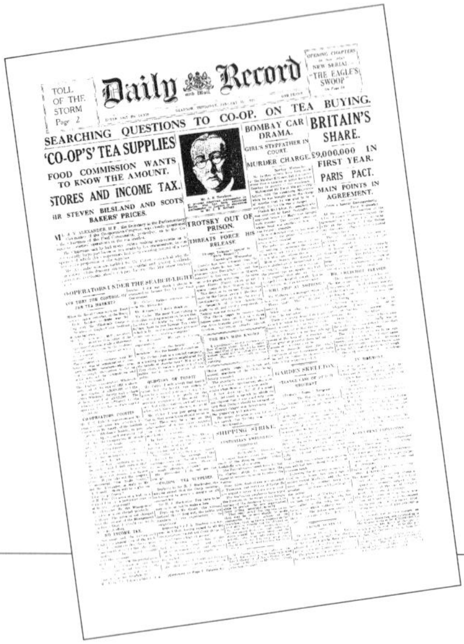
TOLL OF THE STORM Page 2
Daily Record
OPENING CHAPTERS NEW SERIAL "THE EAGLE'S SWOOP"
SEARCHING QUESTIONS TO CO-OP. ON TEA BUYING.
'CO-OP'S' TEA SUPPLIES
FOOD COMMISSION WANTS TO KNOW THE AMOUNT.
STORES AND INCOME TAX.
SIR STEVEN BILSLAND AND SCOTS BAKERS' PRICES.
BOMBAY CAR DRAMA.
GIRL'S STEPFATHER IN COURT.
MURDER CHARGE.
BRITAIN'S SHARE.
£9,000,000 IN FIRST YEAR.
PARIS PACT.
MAIN POINTS IN AGREEMENT.
TROTSKY OUT OF PRISON.
THREATS FORCE HIS RELEASE.
CO-OPERATORS UNDER THE SEARCHLIGHT.
SHIPPING STRIKE.

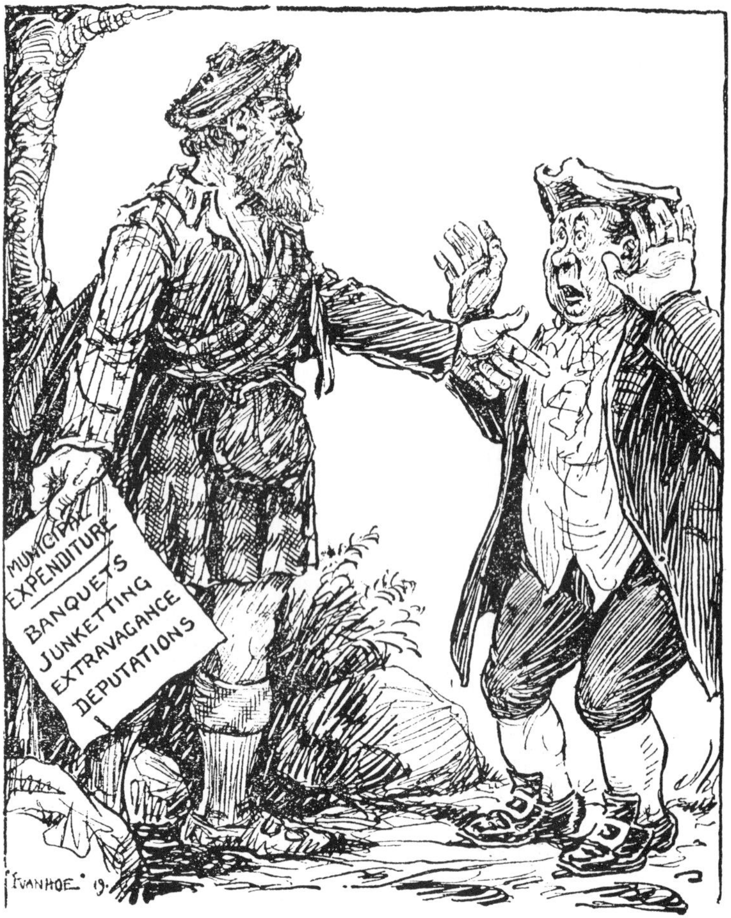
MUNICIPAL EXPENDITURE
BANQUETS
JUNKETTING
EXTRAVAGANCE
DEPUTATIONS
IVANHOE 19.
"Robbed" Roy:—It's high time ye put a stop to this, or maybe we'll ave a hangin' match.
Bailie Nicol Jarvie:—Ah-eh-oh! Ma conscience! Hang a Bailie?

THE THREE-LEGGED RACE.

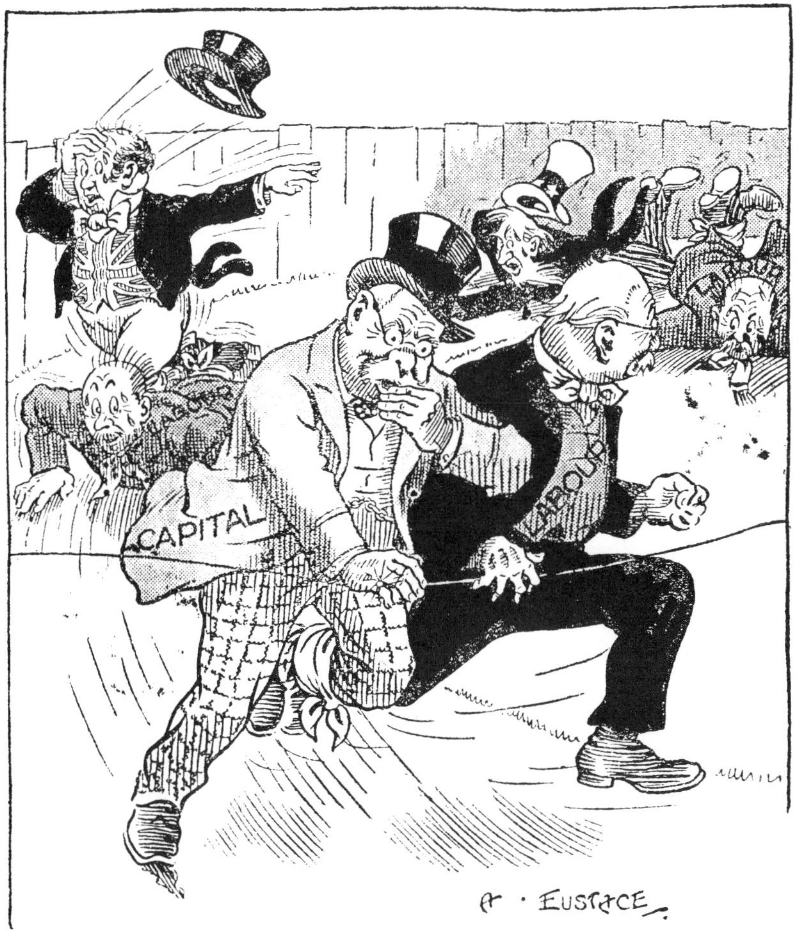
CAPITAL
LABOUR
A · EUSTACE

Fritz:—Stick it, Hans! United we stand, divided they fall!

courts, councils and churches. The motor-car wasn't yet with us so the adverts were mostly for coachmen and grooms. Royal news was pretty scurrilous, revealing what Queen Victoria had for lunch.

Fashion drawings in adverts appeared in the early years but it took time for the illustrators of the day to realise that the newspaper was a natural outlet; somewhere they could express their opinions and exert influence.

The first regular cartoons in the *Daily Record* started

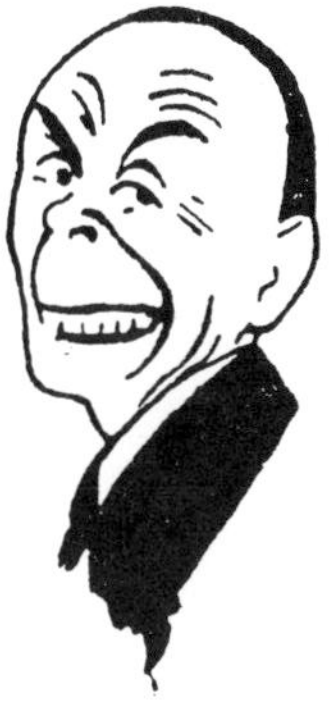

appearing around the 1920s. They were highly realistic and, not surprisingly, they commented on the hot topics of the day. Eustace and Ivanhoe were two artists who pioneered political cartooning in the *Record*, with wonderful

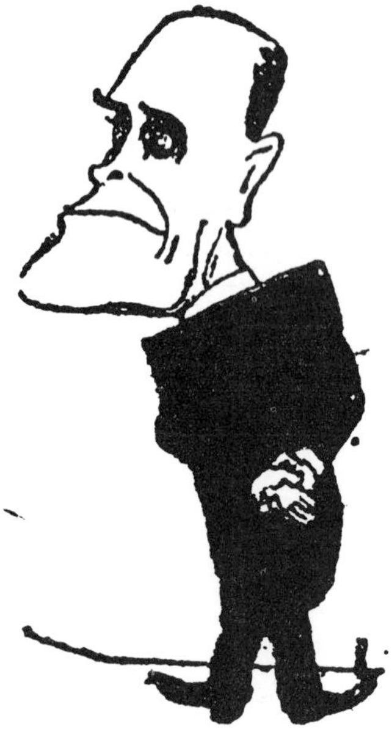

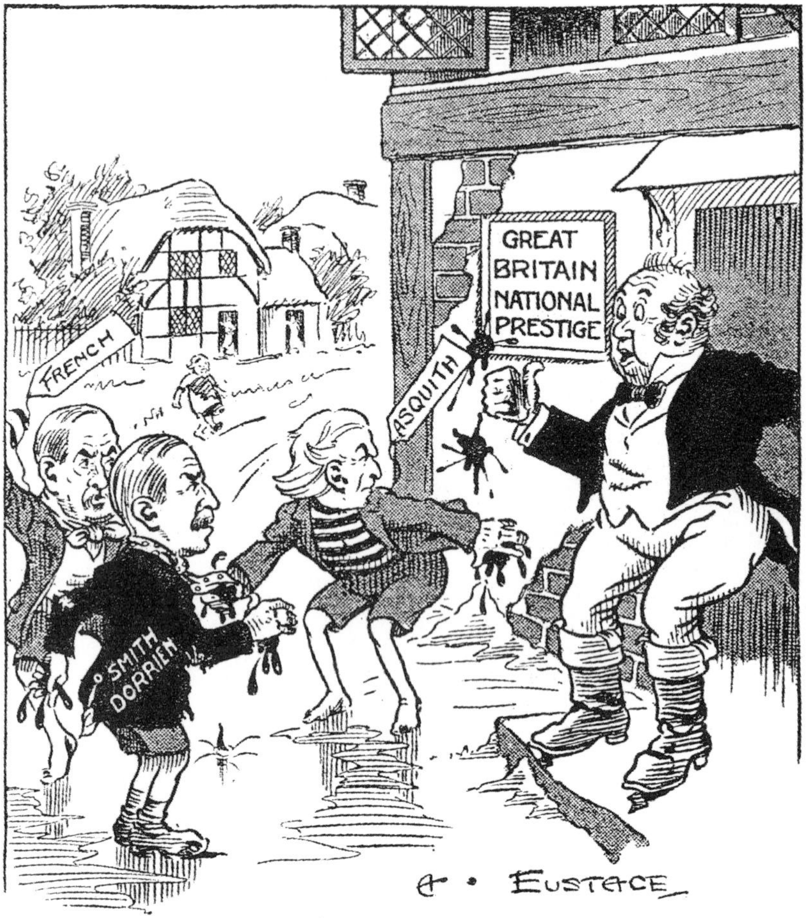
GREAT BRITAIN NATIONAL PRESTIGE
FRENCH
ASQUITH
SMITH DORRIEN
A. EUSTACE

THE MUD-SLINGERS.

John Bull:—"I don't mind you boys slinging mud at each other, but what about my good name-plate?"

The French-Asquith-Smith-Dorrien controversy, according to foreign reports, is simply bringing the good name of Great Britain into disrepute.

THE DANGEROUS "RATE" OF EDUCATION.

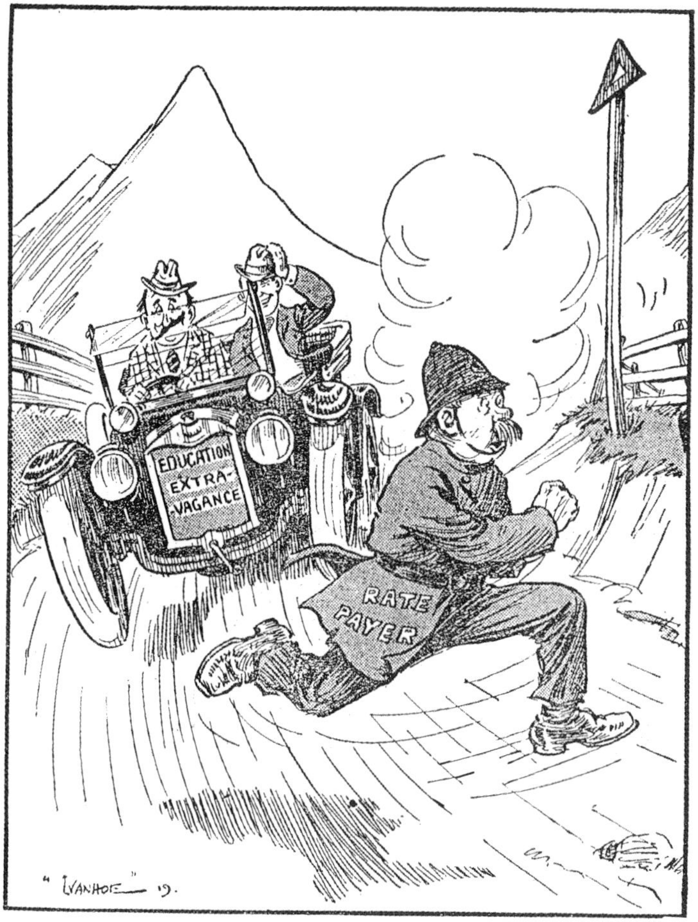
EDUCATION EXTRA-VAGANCE
RATE PAYER
"IVANHOE" 19.

[With apologies to Harry Tate.

The Passenger: But isn't this a fearful rate? The Driver: Not at all. We'll soon make it higher still. The Passenger: But you'll get run in! The Driver: No, but that chap looks like getting run over.—This striking cartoon is reproduced from the "Sunday Mail."

line drawings and witty, if somewhat lengthy, captions.

Jumble and Oddment Sales were often the front page leads in those days. But the first Labour government in 1924 found news stories taking over the front pages and thus the birth of new opportunities for the illustrator/cartoonist. Of course, it's always easier for the cartoonist, when the readers know the story before reading the cartoon. So page one news stories proved a real bonus.

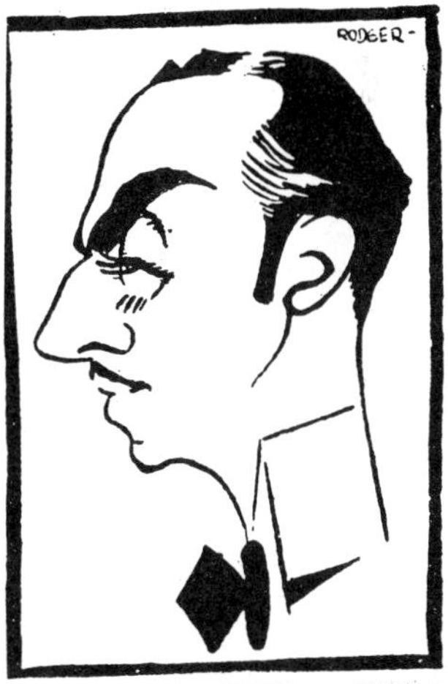
RODGER

FILM FAVOURITES. — William Powell as Rodger sees him.

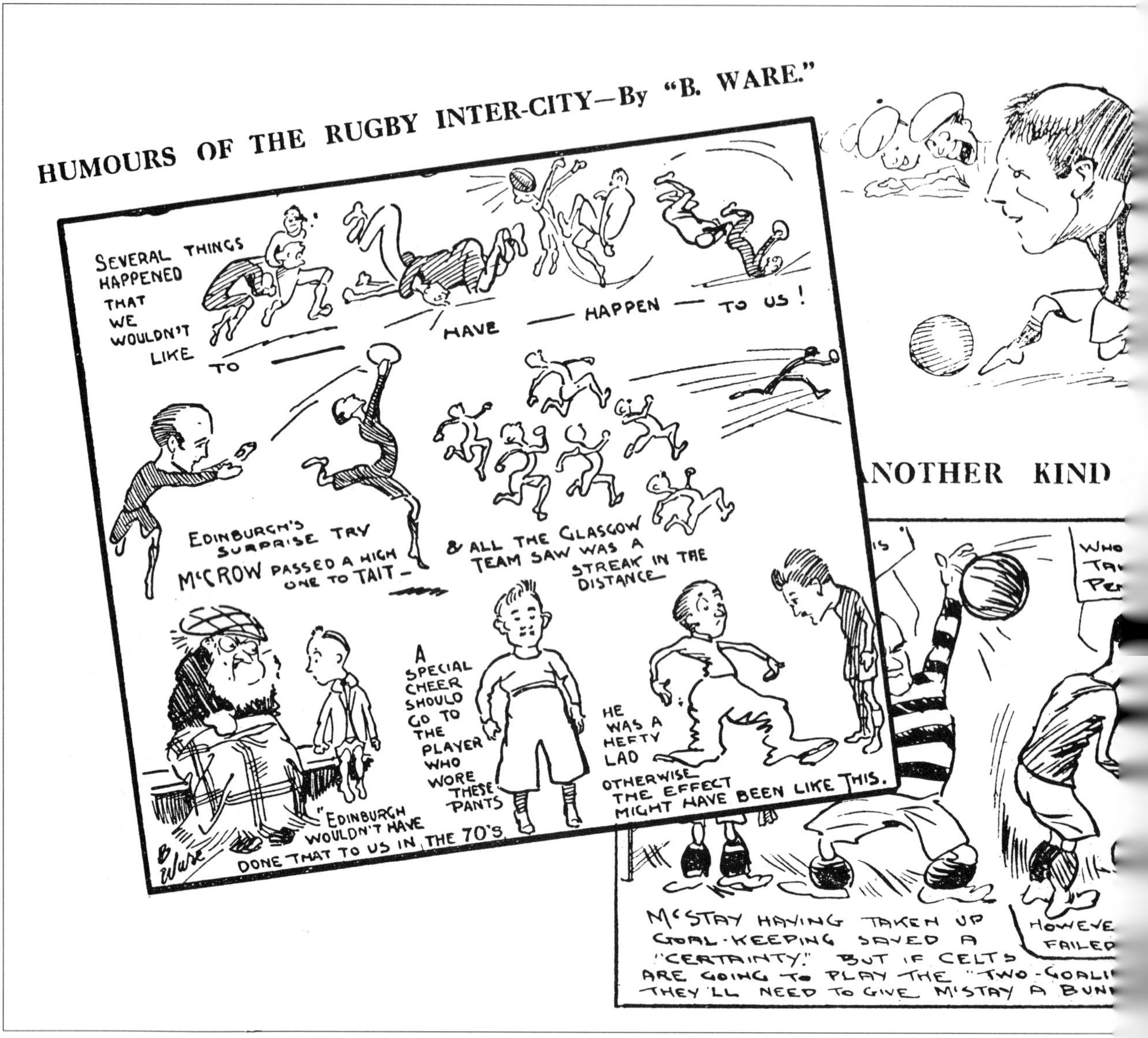
HUMOURS OF THE RUGBY INTER-CITY—By "B. WARE."
SEVERAL THINGS HAPPENED THAT WE WOULDN'T LIKE TO — HAVE — HAPPEN — TO US!
EDINBURGH'S SURPRISE TRY
McCROW PASSED A HIGH ONE TO TAIT—
& ALL THE GLASGOW TEAM SAW WAS A STREAK IN THE DISTANCE
A SPECIAL CHEER SHOULD GO TO THE PLAYER WHO WORE THESE PANTS
HE WAS A HEFTY LAD
OTHERWISE THE EFFECT MIGHT HAVE BEEN LIKE THIS.
"EDINBURGH WOULDN'T HAVE DONE THAT TO US IN THE 70'S
B Ware
ANOTHER KIND
McSTAY HAVING TAKEN UP GOAL-KEEPING SAVED A "CERTAINTY." BUT IF CELTS ARE GOING TO PLAY THE "TWO-GOALI
THEY'LL NEED TO GIVE McSTAY A BUN
HOWEVE
FAILED

A CENTURY OF LAUGHS

While news cartoons gradually emerged in what was normally a 12-page paper, the first sporting cartoons also began to appear. The now traditional Monday morning post-mortem after the Saturday afternoon game began in the *Record*. Under the pen name of 'B Ware', the artist gave an illustrated and amusing round-up of football and rugby to the readers. Individual caricatures were part of the staple diet of both sporting and topical cartoonists at this time.

It's safe to say that these less than flattering cartoon portraits were appreciated more by the readers than the subjects involved!

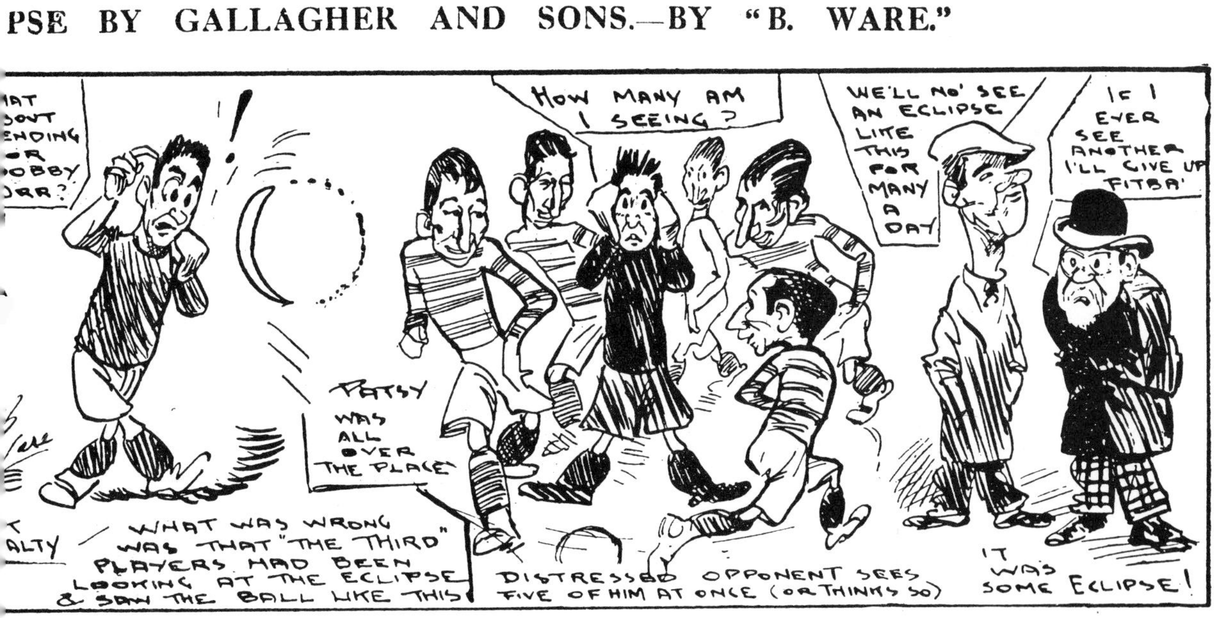
PSE BY GALLAGHER AND SONS.—BY "B. WARE."
HOW MANY AM I SEEING?
WE'LL NO' SEE AN ECLIPSE LIKE THIS FOR MANY A DAY
IF I EVER SEE ANOTHER I'LL GIVE UP FITBA'
PATSY WAS ALL OVER THE PLACE
WHAT WAS WRONG WAS THAT "THE THIRD" PLAYERS HAD BEEN LOOKING AT THE ECLIPSE & SAW THE BALL LIKE THIS
DISTRESSED OPPONENT SEES FIVE OF HIM AT ONCE (OR THINKS SO)
IT WAS SOME ECLIPSE!

Enter... Pip, Squeak and Wilfred

WON'T IT BE LOVELY WHEN WE TOBOGGAN DOWN THE HILL?
YES—IT WILL BE GOOD SPORT!

The *Daily Record*, now firmly established and costing just one penny (a price it was to keep for 20 years), was now in tabloid mode – strong bold pages fighting for Scottish issues. But it never forgot its other duty to entertain its readers. With the number of pages on the increase, the *Record* could devote space to more laughs.

Pip, Squeak and Wilfred, a syndicated cartoon strip (it also appeared in other newspapers), began its run. It featured a dog, a penguin and a rabbit, and although the storylines were sometimes very involved they were always entertaining and sometimes even educational!

MY PETS SEE THEMSELVES AT A XMAS BAZAAR.

BAZAAR
OH COME ALONG PIP—DON'T LET WILFRED SEE US HANGING UP LIKE THAT!
PIP AND SQUEAK CHARMS
PIP AND SQUEAK STALL
PIP AND SQUEAK BISCUITS
PIP AND SQUEAK FOX-TROT
THE BOOK OF THE YEAR
PIP SQUEAK AND WILFRED
MODELS OF PIP AND SQUEAK
HURRY OUT PIP—I FEEL QUITE GIDDY!
SO DO I!
A B Payne

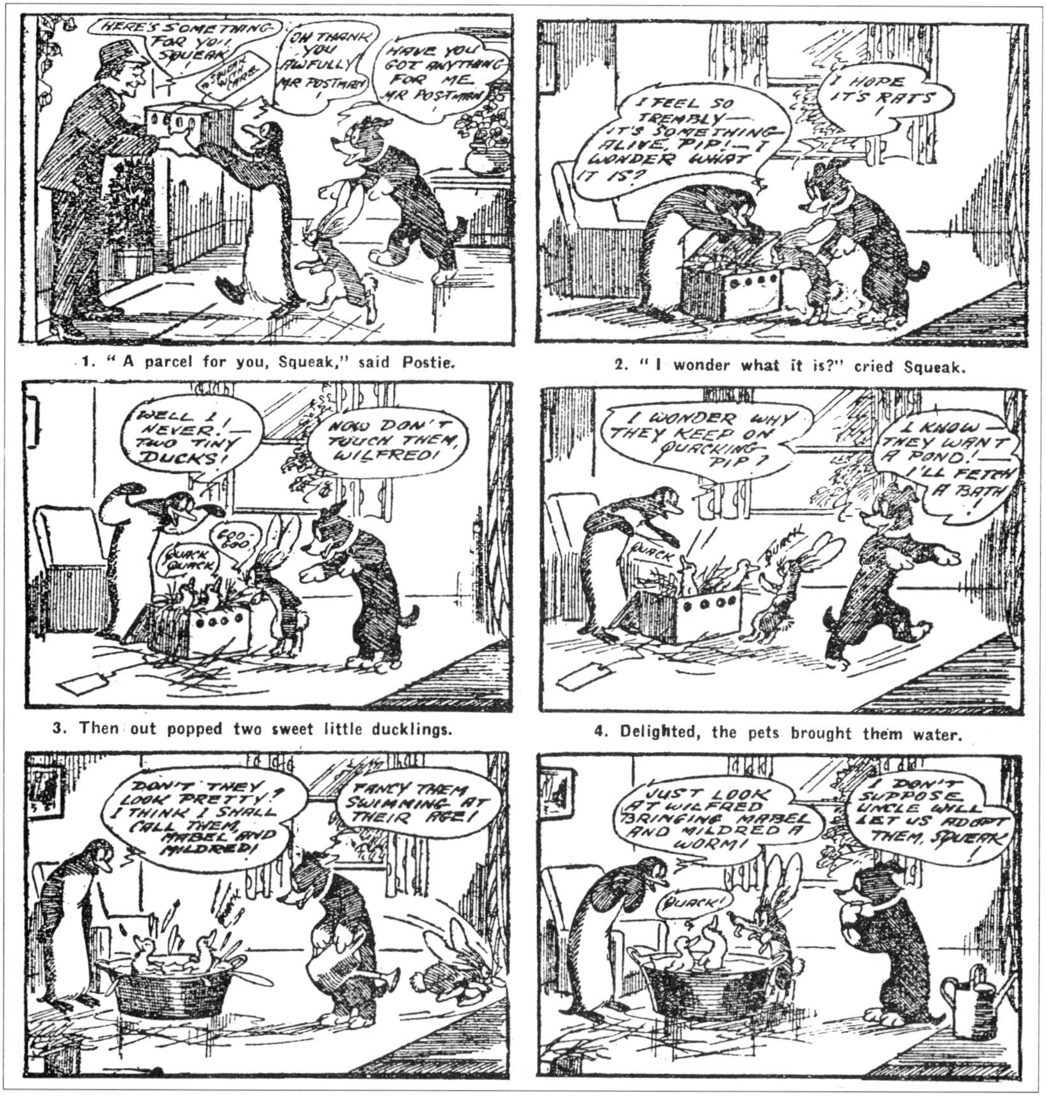
HERE'S SOMETHING FOR YOU SQUEAK!
OH THANK YOU AWFULLY MR POSTMAN!
HAVE YOU GOT ANYTHING FOR ME MR POSTMAN?
I FEEL SO TREMBLY— IT'S SOMETHING ALIVE, PIP!—I WONDER WHAT IT IS?
I HOPE IT'S RATS!
WELL I NEVER!—TWO TINY DUCKS!
NOW DON'T TOUCH THEM, WILFRED!
QUACK QUACK
GOO-GOO
I WONDER WHY THEY KEEP ON QUACKING PIP?
I KNOW—THEY WANT A POND!—I'LL FETCH A BATH!
QUACK
QUACK
DON'T THEY LOOK PRETTY? I THINK I SHALL CALL THEM MABEL AND MILDRED!
FANCY THEM SWIMMING AT THEIR AGE!
JUST LOOK AT WILFRED BRINGING MABEL AND MILDRED A WORM!
I DON'T SUPPOSE UNCLE WILL LET US ADOPT THEM, SQUEAK!
QUACK!

1. " A parcel for you, Squeak," said Postie.

2. " I wonder what it is?" cried Squeak.

3. Then out popped two sweet little ducklings.

4. Delighted, the pets brought them water.

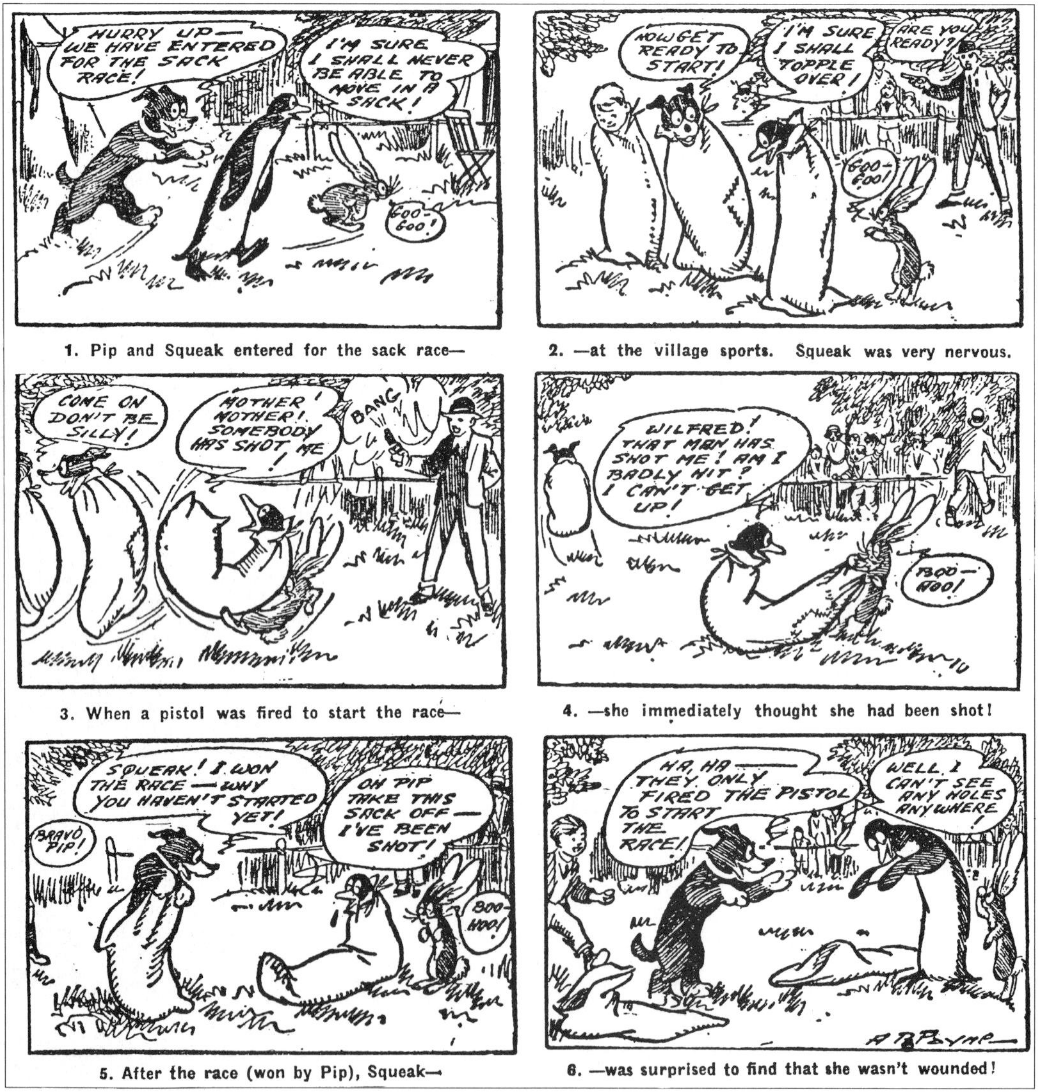
HURRY UP— WE HAVE ENTERED FOR THE SACK RACE!
I'M SURE I SHALL NEVER BE ABLE TO MOVE IN A SACK!
GOO-GOO!
NOW GET READY TO START!
I'M SURE I SHALL TOPPLE OVER!
ARE YOU READY?
GOO-GOO!
COME ON DON'T BE SILLY!
MOTHER! MOTHER! SOMEBODY HAS SHOT ME!
BANG
WILFRED! THAT MAN HAS SHOT ME! AM I BADLY HIT? I CAN'T GET UP!
BOO-HOO!
SQUEAK! I WON THE RACE — WHY YOU HAVEN'T STARTED YET!
BRAVO PIP!
OH PIP TAKE THIS SACK OFF— I'VE BEEN SHOT!
BOO-HOO!
HA, HA— THEY ONLY FIRED THE PISTOL TO START THE RACE!
WELL, I CAN'T SEE ANY HOLES ANYWHERE!

1. Pip and Squeak entered for the sack race—

2. —at the village sports. Squeak was very nervous.

3. When a pistol was fired to start the race—

4. —she immediately thought she had been shot!

5. After the race (won by Pip), Squeak—

6. —was surprised to find that she wasn't wounded!

Bringing Up Father...

Another syndicated strip which started around this time was 'Bringing Up Father'. Distributed by the International Feature Service in America, this beautifully drawn and very popular cartoon featured for almost 30 years in the *Record*. Not really so surprising, because although it was American through and through, its main theme was the battlefield inhabited by husband and wife. Always a winning combination.

The *Daily Record* was by now well established in virtually every household in the land and the cartoon had become a permanent feature in its pages – the topical campaigning illustration on the news or foreign pages, the strips throughout the features pages and the occasional sports commentary at the back.

The cartoon, whether illuminating the main story, appealing to the the common domestic sense of humour, or capturing the essence of the main sporting story of the day, had become an art form in its own right; a part of that indefinable but important package which attracts and keeps reader loyalty.

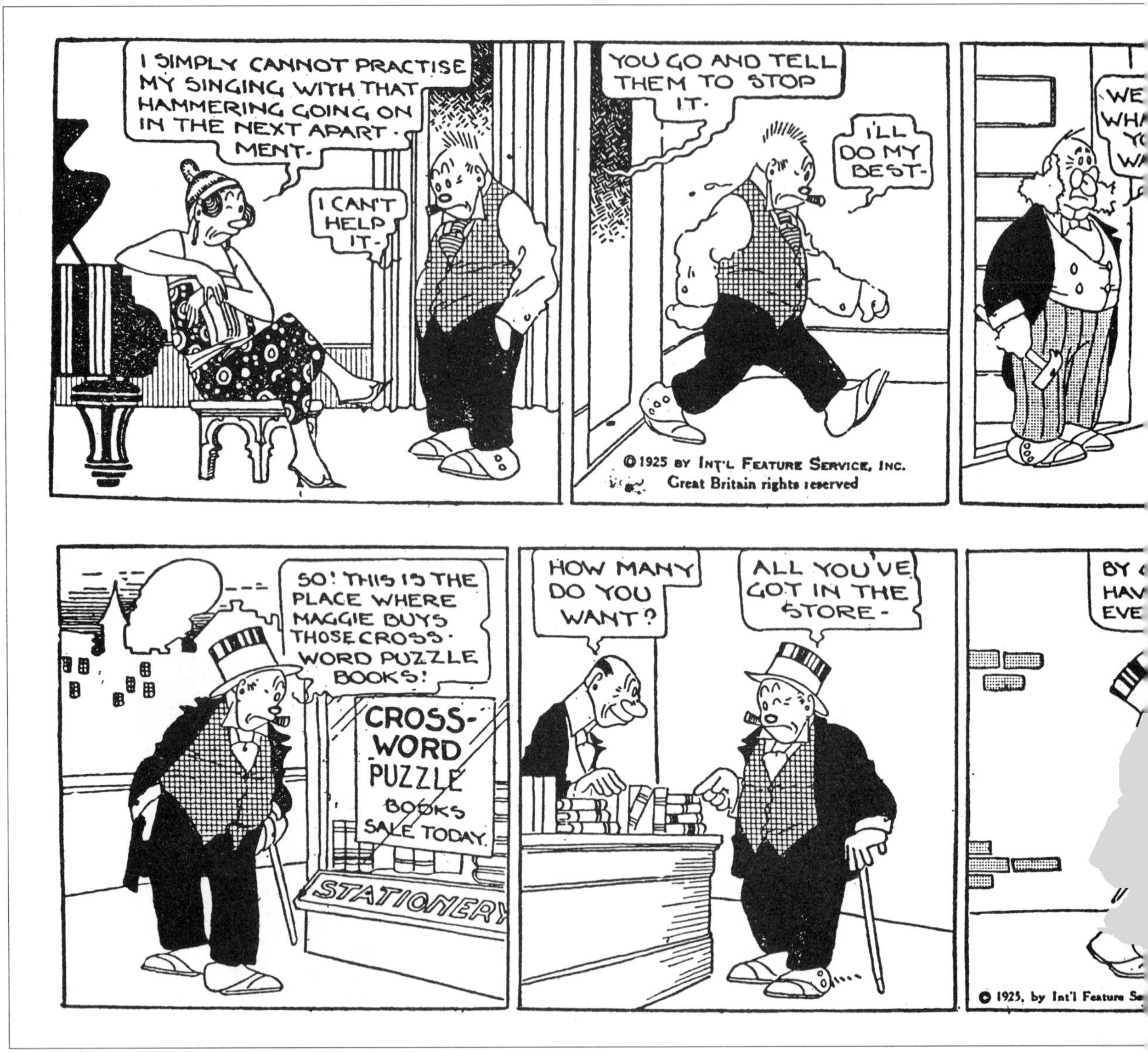
I SIMPLY CANNOT PRACTISE MY SINGING WITH THAT HAMMERING GOING ON IN THE NEXT APART-MENT.
I CAN'T HELP IT.
YOU GO AND TELL THEM TO STOP IT.
I'LL DO MY BEST.
© 1925 BY INT'L FEATURE SERVICE, INC.
Great Britain rights reserved
SO! THIS IS THE PLACE WHERE MAGGIE BUYS THOSE CROSS-WORD PUZZLE BOOKS!
CROSS-WORD PUZZLE BOOKS SALE TODAY.
STATIONERY
HOW MANY DO YOU WANT?
ALL YOU'VE GOT IN THE STORE.

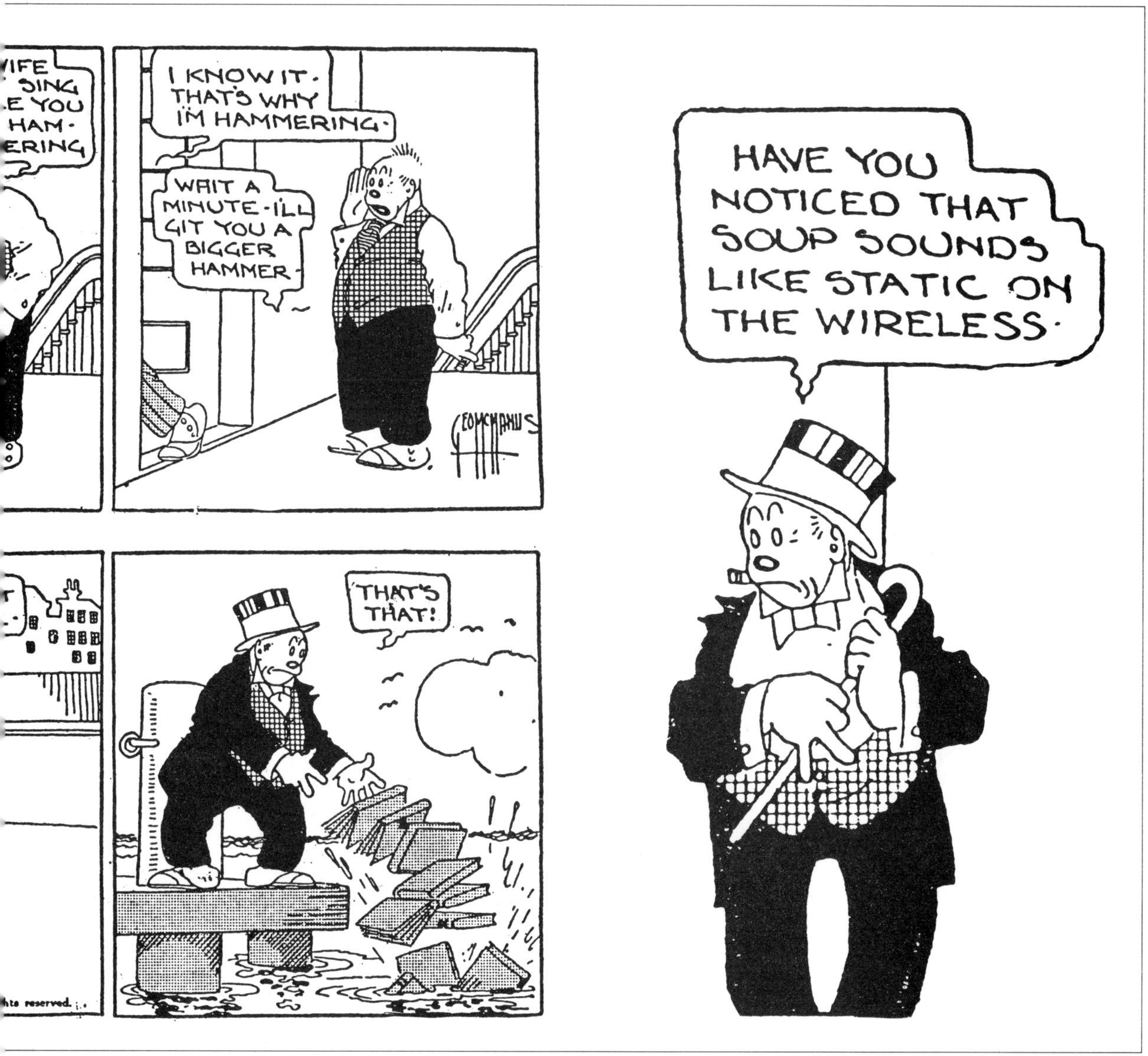
I KNOW IT. THAT'S WHY I'M HAMMERING.
WAIT A MINUTE - I'LL GIT YOU A BIGGER HAMMER.
GEO MCMANUS
THAT'S THAT!
HAVE YOU NOTICED THAT SOUP SOUNDS LIKE STATIC ON THE WIRELESS.

We're Now Approaching the Thirties . . . and the pace is hotting-up

The thirties certainly offered the topical cartoon illustrator plenty of scope. Income tax, national service, international propaganda, war and peace, gave cartoonists Cecil Orr, Rodger and Dzke White loads of subject matter for their pen. All three featured with their up-to-the-minute satirical drawings throughout that troubled decade and beyond.

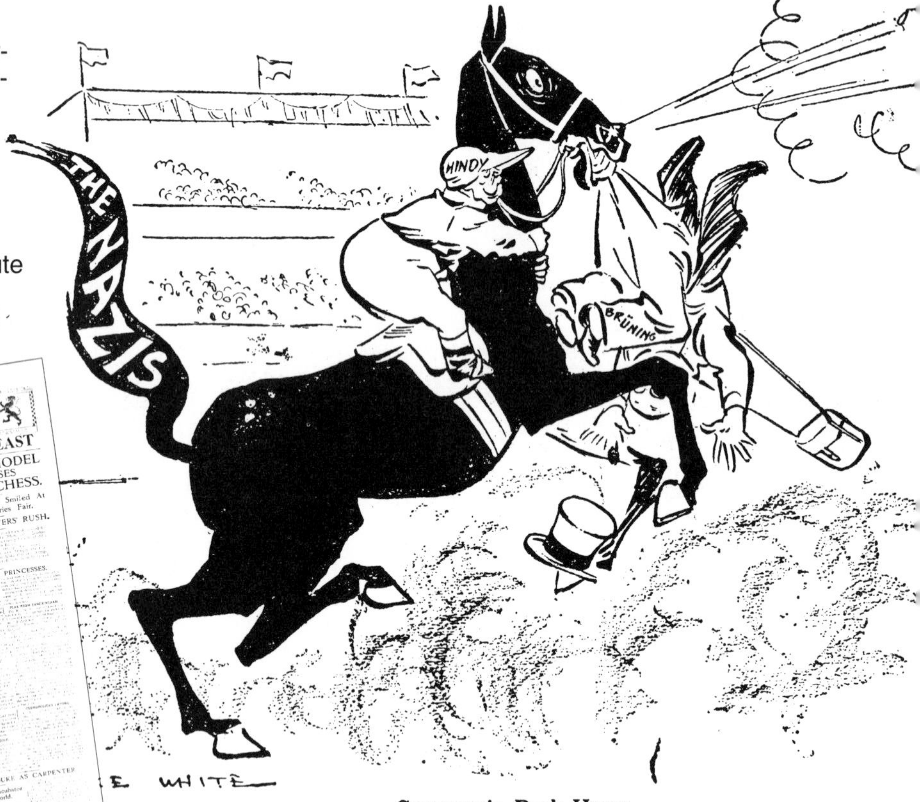
THE NAZIS
HINDY
BRÜNING
E WHITE

Germany's Dark Horse.

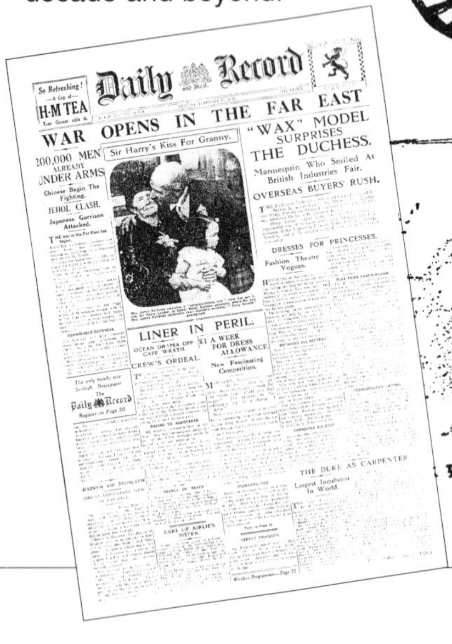

So Refreshing! —A Cup of— H-M TEA Your Grocer sells it.

Daily Record and Mail.

WAR OPENS IN THE FAR EAST

200,000 MEN ALREADY UNDER ARMS

Chinese Begin The Fighting.

JEHOL CLASH.

Japanese Garrison Attacked.

THE war in the Far East has begun.

Sir Harry's Kiss For Granny.

"WAX" MODEL SURPRISES THE DUCHESS.

Mannequin Who Smiled At British Industries Fair.

OVERSEAS BUYERS' RUSH.

DRESSES FOR PRINCESSES.

Fashion Theatre Vogues.

LINER IN PERIL.

OCEAN DRAMA OFF CAPE WRATH.

CREW'S ORDEAL.

£1 A WEEK FOR DRESS ALLOWANCE.

New Fascinating Competition.

The only handy size Scottish Newspaper The Daily Record Register on Page 20

THE DUKE AS CARPENTER

Largest Incubator In World.

EARL OF AIRLIE'S SISTER.

Wireless Programmes—Page 22

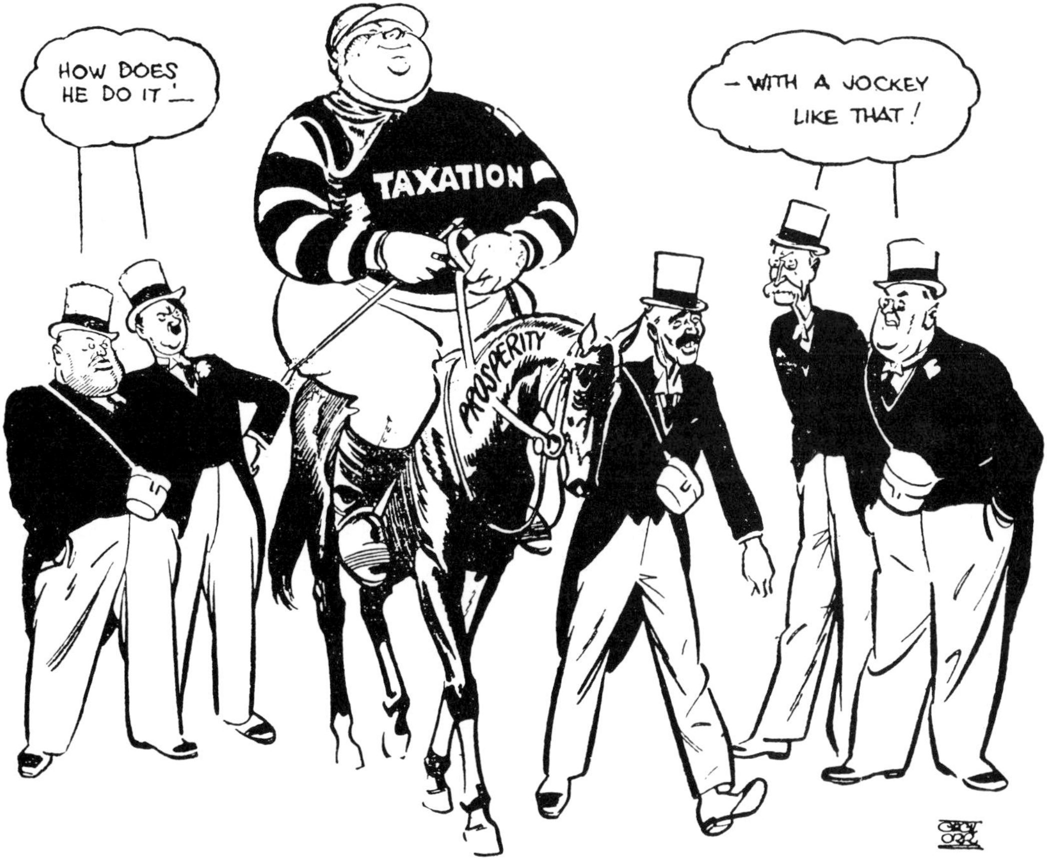
HOW DOES HE DO IT!—
—WITH A JOCKEY LIKE THAT!
TAXATION
PROSPERITY
PROSPERITY

The famous Government-owned Tumbrel isn't the only horse that wins races for them.

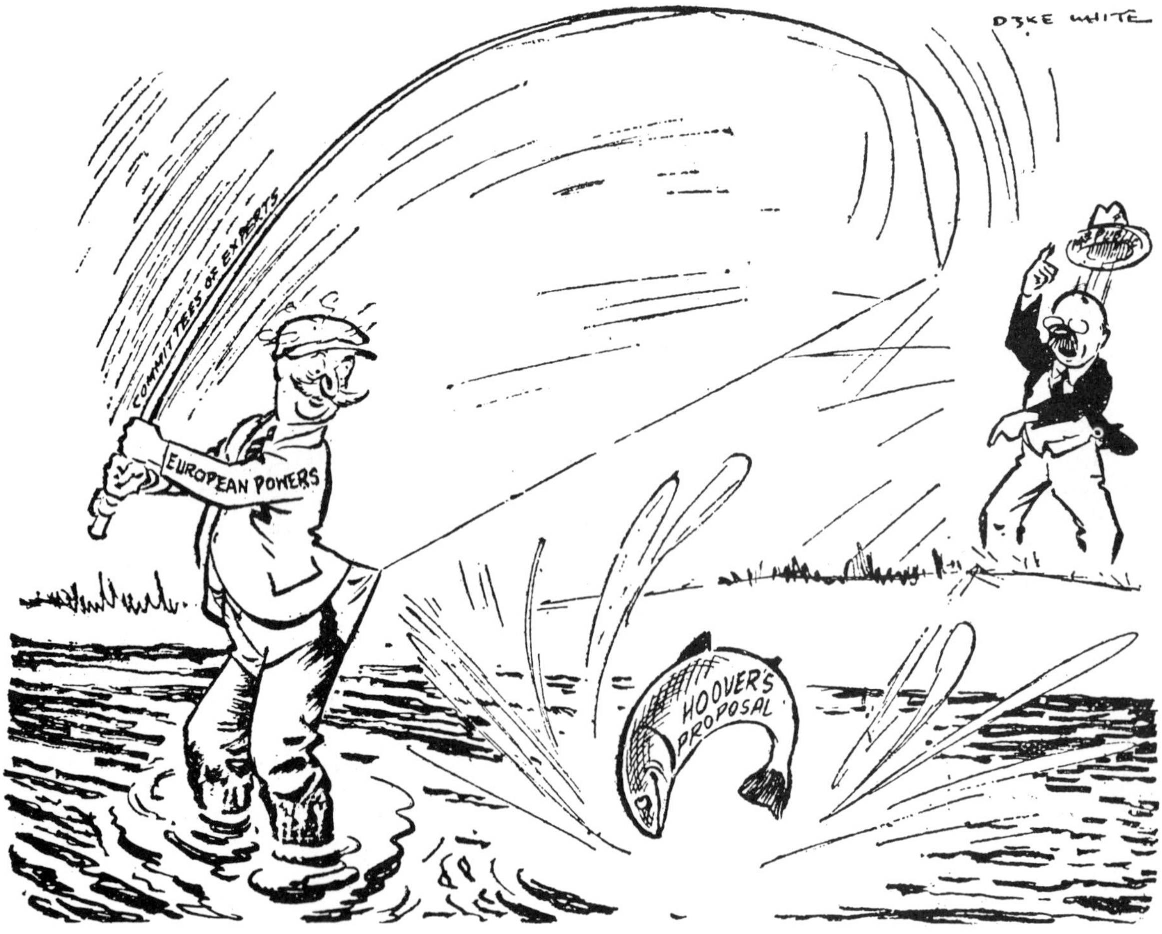
COMMITTEES OF EXPERTS
EUROPEAN POWERS
HOOVER'S
PROPOSAL

On His Own Hook.

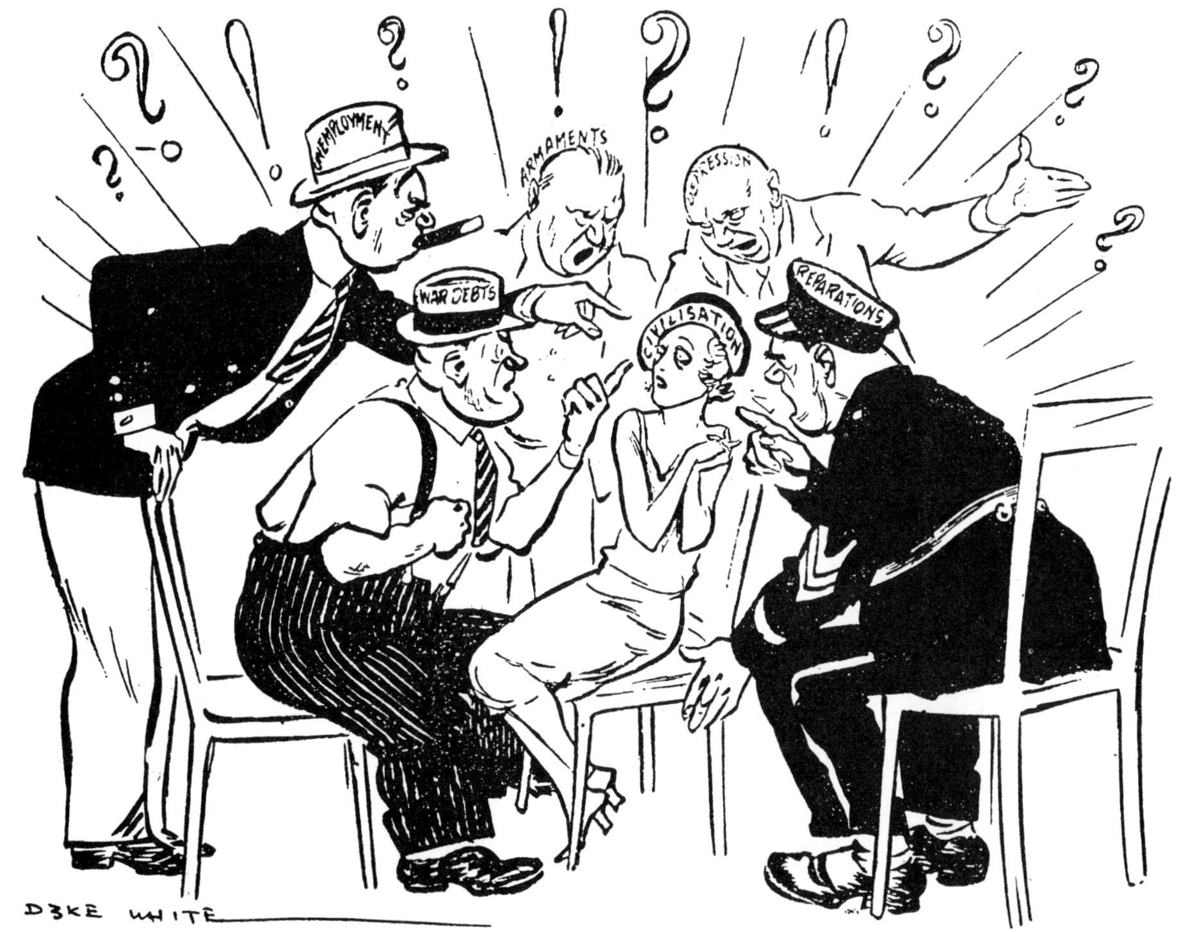
UNEMPLOYMENT
ARMAMENTS
WAR DEBTS
CIVILISATION
REPARATIONS

The Horrors of the "Third Degree."

His Masterpiece

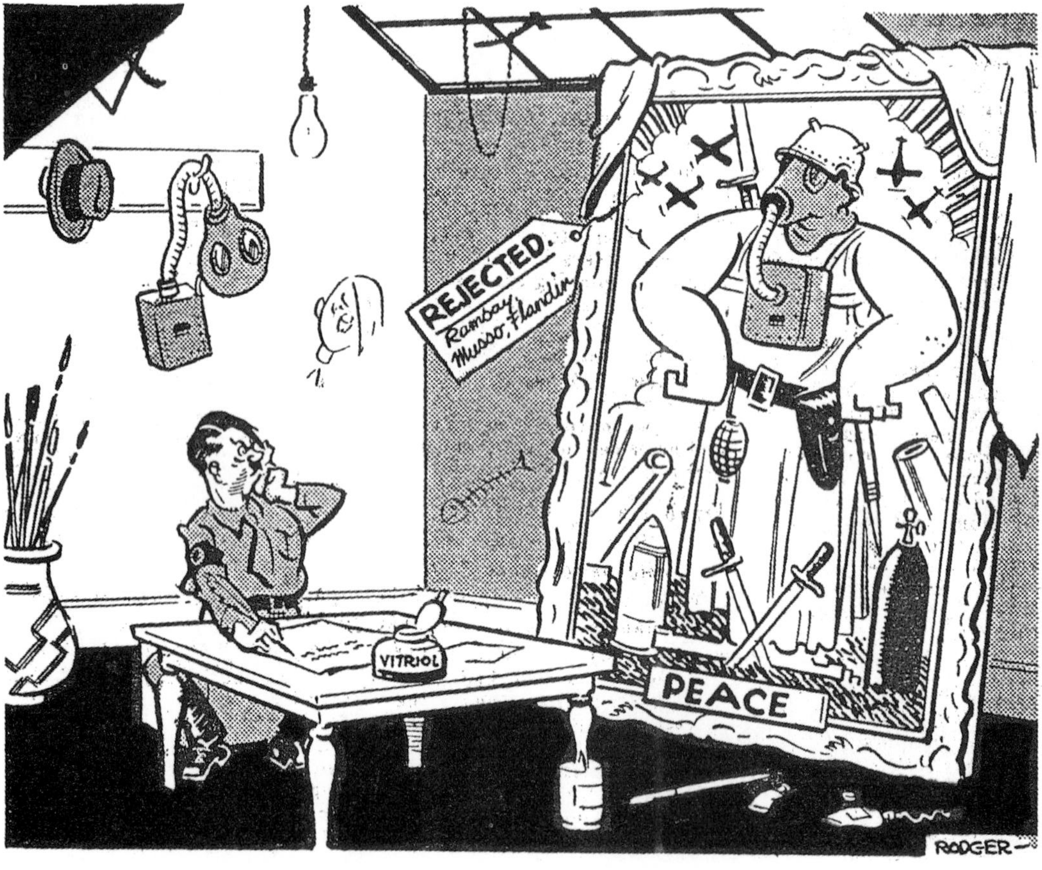
REJECTED.
Ramsay
Musso, Flandin
VITRIOL
PEACE
RODGER

Another Art Sensation In The Offing.

Making It Snappy

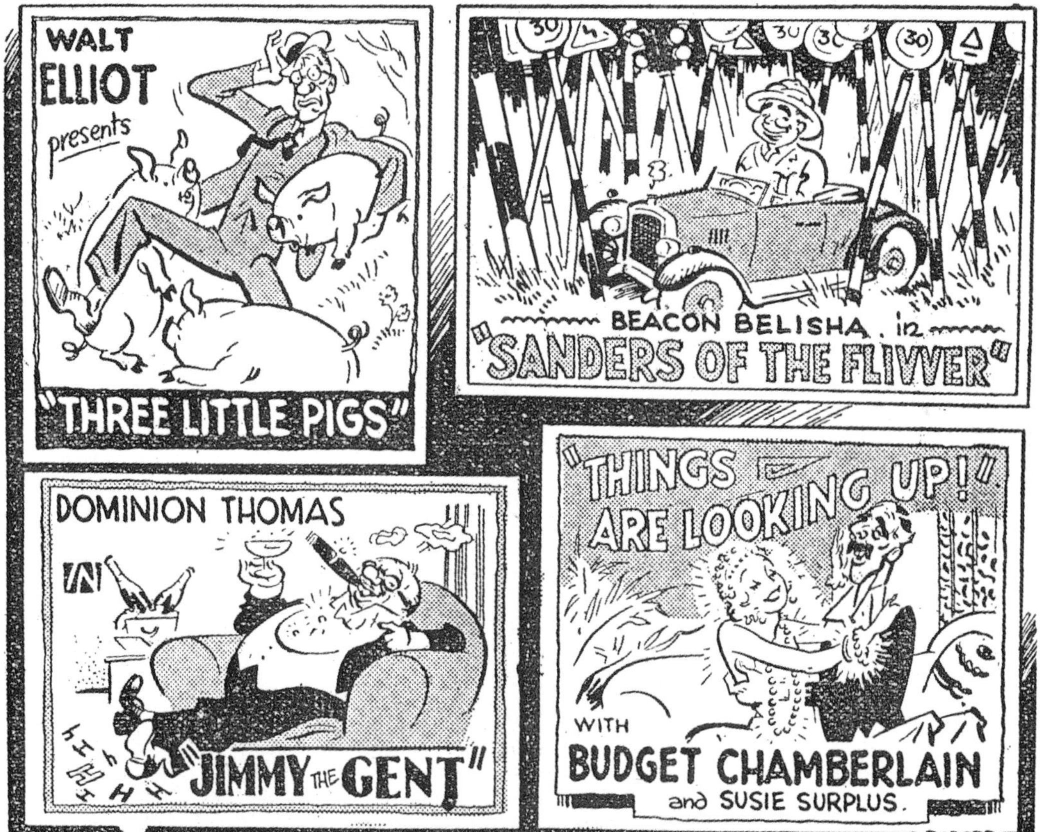
WALT ELLIOT presents
"THREE LITTLE PIGS"
BEACON BELISHA in
"SANDERS OF THE FLIVVER"
DOMINION THOMAS
"JIMMY THE GENT"
"THINGS ARE LOOKING UP!"
WITH
BUDGET CHAMBERLAIN
and SUSIE SURPLUS.
RODGER

National Government propaganda by mobile cinema begins to-day. Our cartoonist suggests a few special features.

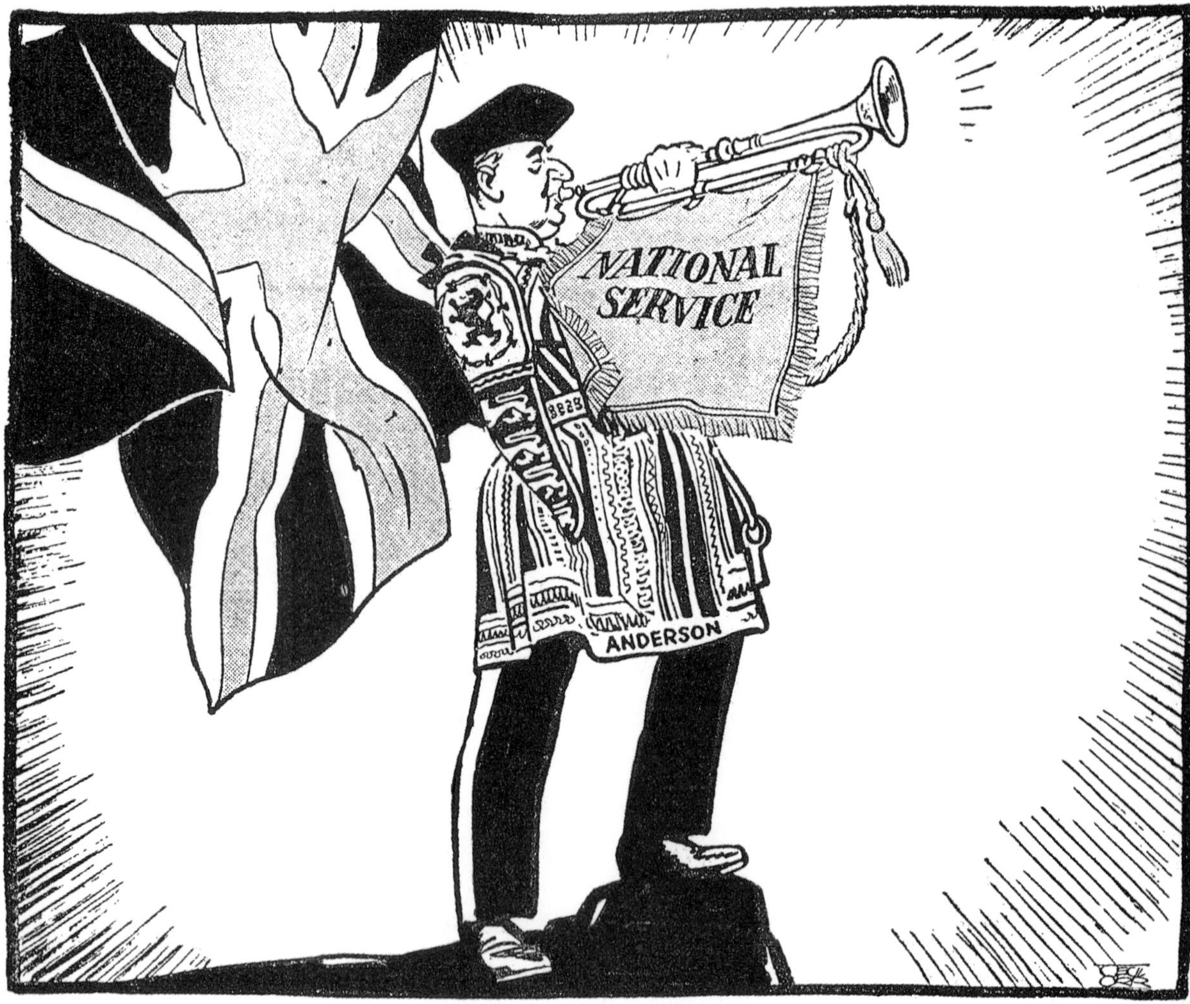
NATIONAL SERVICE
ANDERSON

Hope Springs Eternal

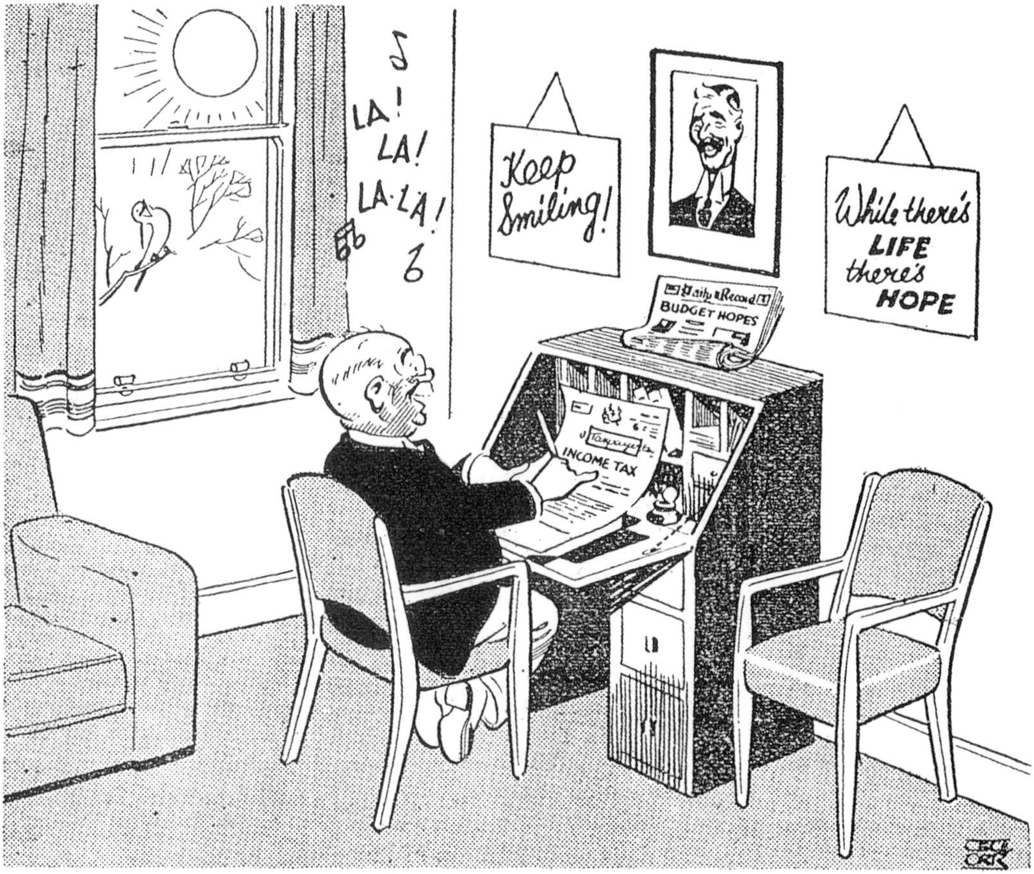
LA!
LA!
LA-LA!
Keep Smiling!
Daily Record
BUDGET HOPES
INCOME TAX
While there's LIFE there's HOPE
CECIL ORR

Income tax return forms are now being sent out.

Looking for sporting comments and illustrations at this time, the *Record* found someone on its own doorstep. Jack Lindsay worked in the print production department but was also a talented artist and cartoonist. Lindsay, his pen name, majored in football in the Monday morning slot. His speciality was humorous drawings and well observed comments on our national game. And even in those days, the

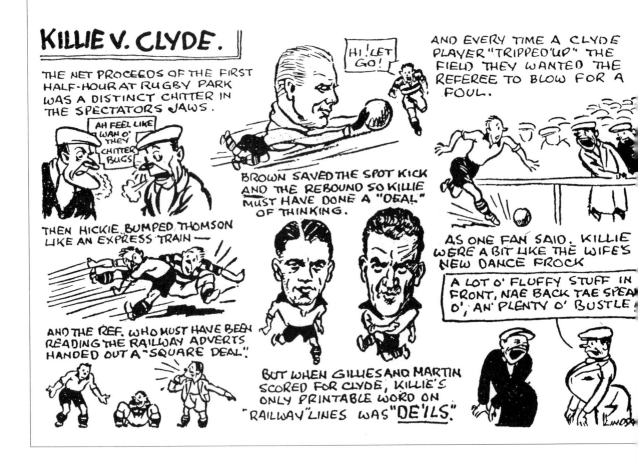

KILLIE V. CLYDE.

THE NET PROCEEDS OF THE FIRST HALF-HOUR AT RUGBY PARK WAS A DISTINCT CHITTER IN THE SPECTATORS JAWS.

AH FEEL LIKE WAN O' THEY CHITTER BUGS

THEN HICKIE BUMPED THOMSON LIKE AN EXPRESS TRAIN —

AND THE REF. WHO MUST HAVE BEEN READING THE RAILWAY ADVERTS HANDED OUT A "SQUARE DEAL."

HI! LET GO!

BROWN SAVED THE SPOT KICK AND THE REBOUND SO KILLIE MUST HAVE DONE A "DEAL" OF THINKING.

BUT WHEN GILLIES AND MARTIN SCORED FOR CLYDE, KILLIE'S ONLY PRINTABLE WORD ON "RAILWAY" LINES WAS "DE'ILS."

AND EVERY TIME A CLYDE PLAYER "TRIPPED UP" THE FIELD THEY WANTED THE REFEREE TO BLOW FOR A FOUL.

AS ONE FAN SAID, KILLIE WERE A BIT LIKE THE WIFE'S NEW DANCE FROCK

A LOT O' FLUFFY STUFF IN FRONT, NAE BACK TAE SPEAK O', AN' PLENTY O' BUSTLE.

exploits of those warriors who donned the battle dress of the Scottish strip were a rich source of material for artists who didn't lack a sense of humour. It's worth reflecting that if our national team had ever been in serious danger of winning a world cup, generations of cartoonists would have been out of business!

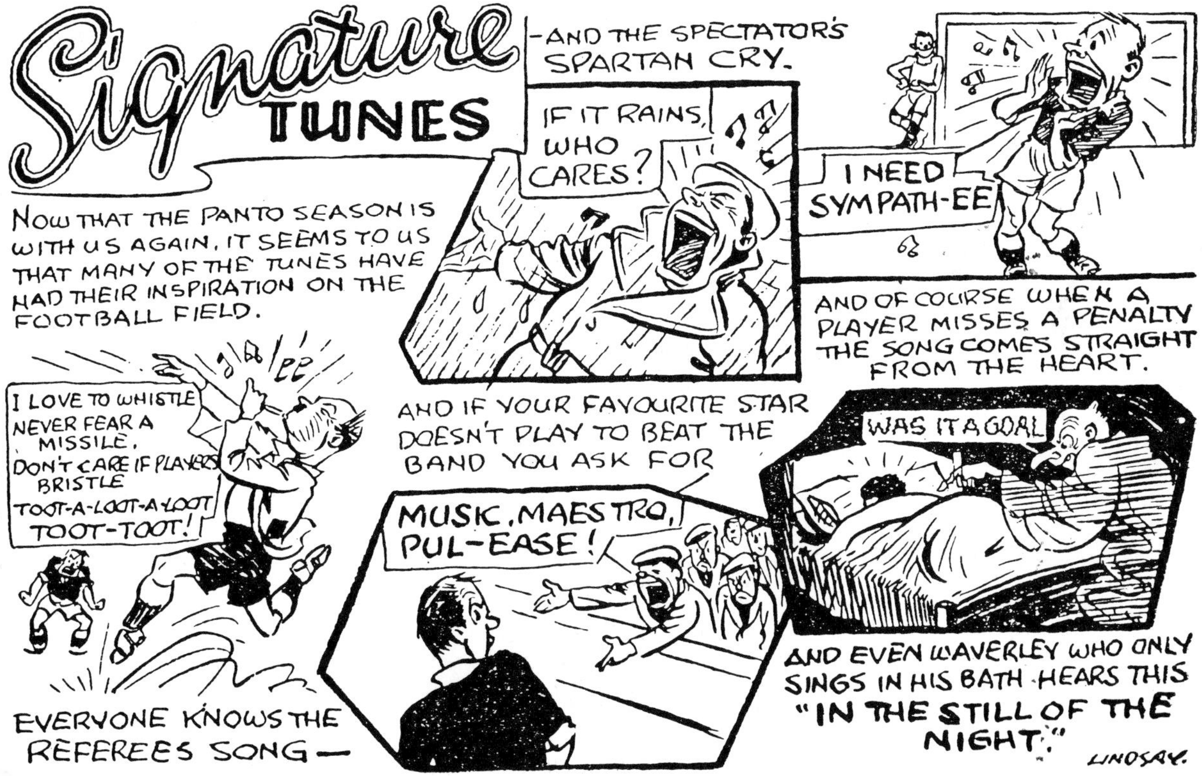
Signature TUNES
NOW THAT THE PANTO SEASON IS WITH US AGAIN, IT SEEMS TO US THAT MANY OF THE TUNES HAVE HAD THEIR INSPIRATION ON THE FOOTBALL FIELD.
I LOVE TO WHISTLE NEVER FEAR A MISSILE, DON'T CARE IF PLAYERS BRISTLE TOOT-A-LOOT-A-LOOT TOOT-TOOT!
EVERYONE KNOWS THE REFEREES SONG—
-AND THE SPECTATOR'S SPARTAN CRY.
IF IT RAINS, WHO CARES?
AND IF YOUR FAVOURITE STAR DOESN'T PLAY TO BEAT THE BAND YOU ASK FOR
MUSIC, MAESTRO, PUL-EASE!
I NEED SYMPATH-EE
AND OF COURSE WHEN A PLAYER MISSES A PENALTY THE SONG COMES STRAIGHT FROM THE HEART.
WAS IT A GOAL
AND EVEN WAVERLEY WHO ONLY SINGS IN HIS BATH HEARS THIS "IN THE STILL OF THE NIGHT."
LINDSAY.

Enter . . . Lauder, Willis and Gordon

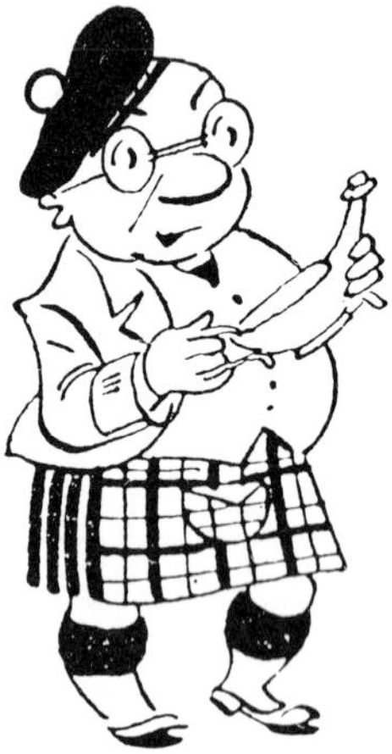

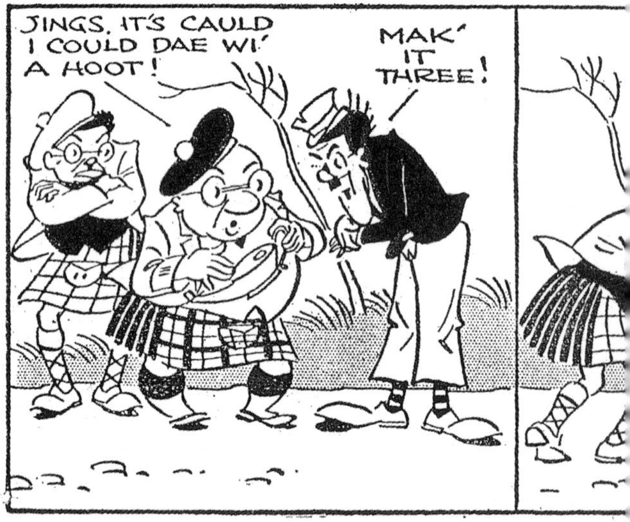
JINGS, IT'S CAULD I COULD DAE WI' A HOOT!
MAK' IT THREE!

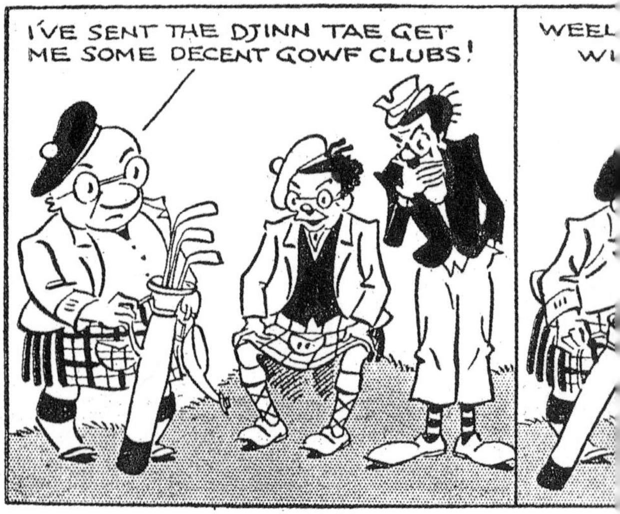
I'VE SENT THE DJINN TAE GET ME SOME DECENT GOWF CLUBS!

The *Record* was always looking for new ideas to enhance its pages and entertain it's readers. The 'Lauder, Willis and Gordon' cartoon strip certainly did that. What did the trick was the fact that it was very Scottish, featured Scots folk and mentioned well-known Scottish places.

This has long proved a selling point for those newspapers who have cultivated their core audience. It is no accident that the *Daily Record* adopted a slogan of being edited, printed and published in Scotland. Patriotism sells papers.

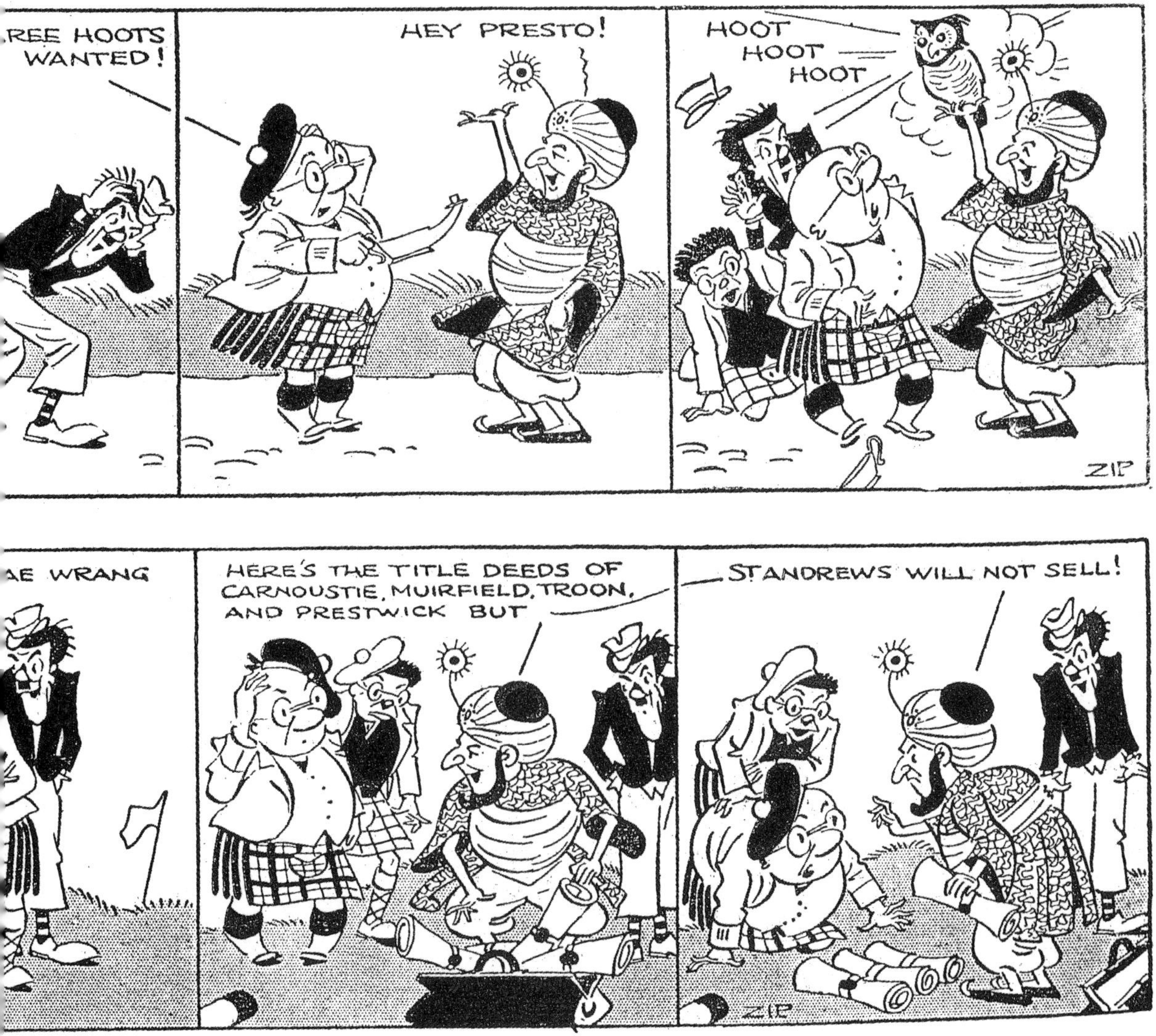
REE HOOTS WANTED!
HEY PRESTO!
HOOT HOOT HOOT
ZIP
AE WRANG
HERE'S THE TITLE DEEDS OF CARNOUSTIE, MUIRFIELD, TROON, AND PRESTWICK BUT
ST. ANDREWS WILL NOT SELL!
ZIP

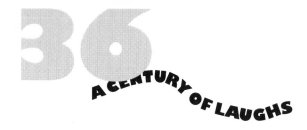

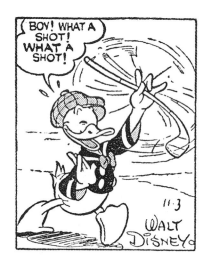

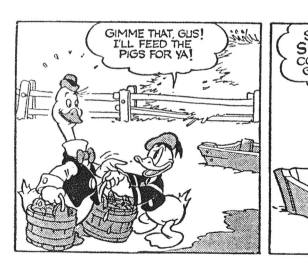

BOY! WHAT A SHOT! WHAT A SHOT!
11-3
WALT DISNEY
GIMME THAT, GUS! I'LL FEED THE PIGS FOR YA!

and Donald Duck

YOU BOYS HAVE ALL THOSE LEAVES RAKED UP WHEN I GET BACK!
TIME PASSES

Of course, intrinsically Scottish cartoon strips were few and far between. But as the entertainment content of the paper increased, so too did the efforts of the *Record* to showcase the best available. And they didn't come any bigger than straight from the pen of Walt Disney Studios. Which brings us to the acquisition of Donald Duck. Donald and friends were to feature in the paper throughout most of the thirties and forties.

And while we're speaking about the fabulous forties . . .

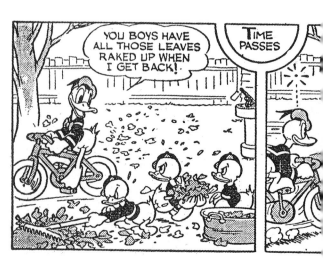

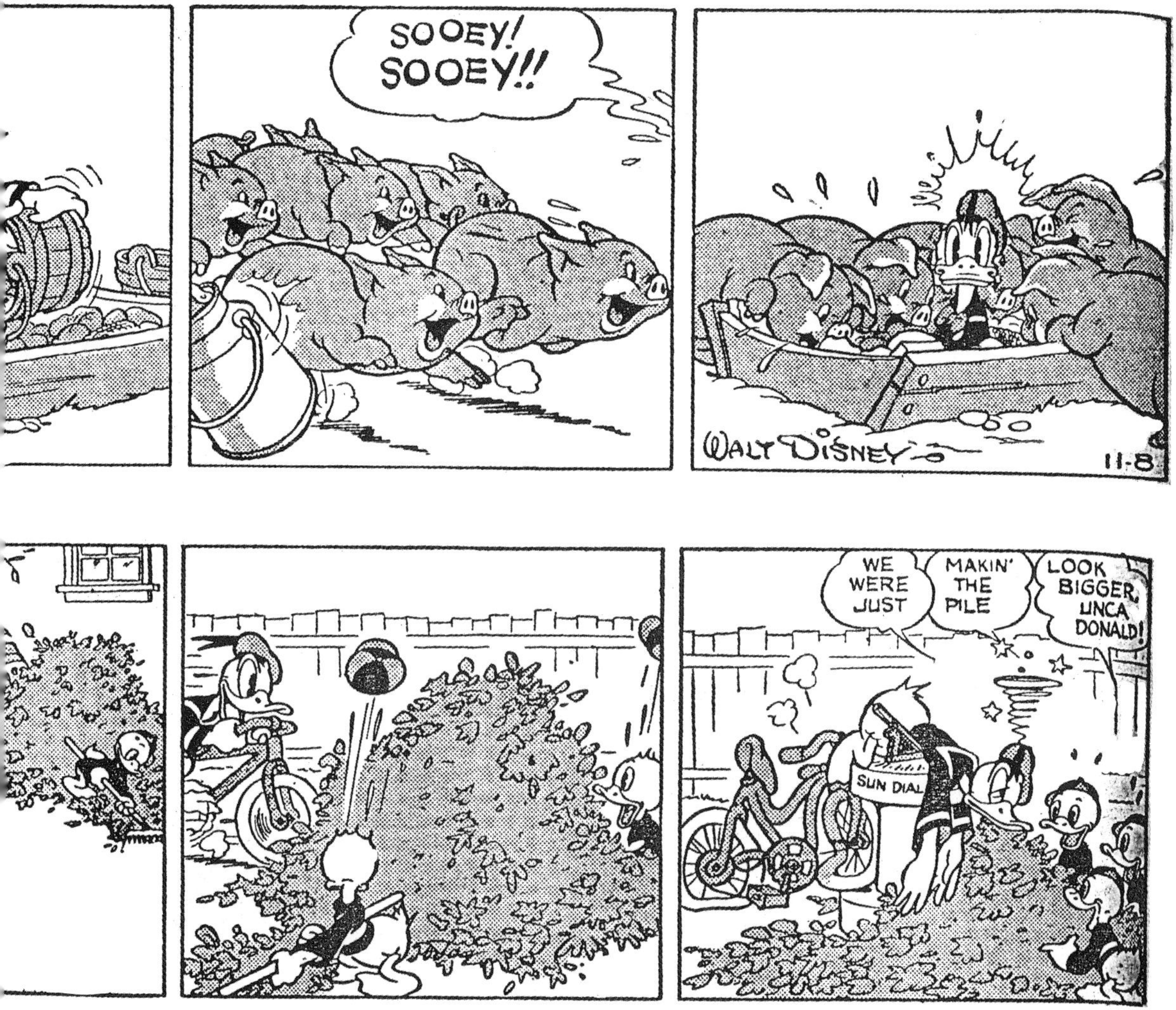
SOOEY! SOOEY!!
WALT DISNEY
11-8
WE WERE JUST
MAKIN' THE PILE
LOOK BIGGER, UNCA DONALD!
SUN DIAL

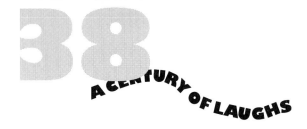

The Difficult Years

The war, which brought in its wake both immense courage and unimaginable horrors, tested to the full the comic talents of the illustrators and cartoonists of that era. There is nothing very amusing about conflict, yet there is arguably no more important moment in which to raise the spirits of a nation and remind it of the the power of humour to replenish the human soul.

Of necessity the *Daily Record* was reduced in size. There were fewer pages, fewer adverts, fewer pictures, fewer illustrations and, inevitably, fewer cartoons. But those available to draw for newspapers during this time did a

Daily Record

Silent Service Creates Chaos On Iron Ore Skulk Route

NAVY PUTS NAZIS IN A FUNK

WATCH ON THE COVERED WAY

WHEN WE WOULD FIGHT RUSSIA

R.A.F. Casualties

MAN WHO FLEW MILLION MILES

TURKS ATTACK GERMANY

New Onslaught On Hitler's Claims

AMERICA'S BEST PLANES FOR ALLIES

NAZI RUMANIA BID STIRS BULGARIA

JUST A MINUTE, YOU, TILL I TIGHTEN MY BELT!
ON HIS MAJESTY'S SERVICE
OFFICIAL PAID
RATION BOOK
J. Taxpayer
OPEN CAREFULLY
Serial Number of Book
E 131313

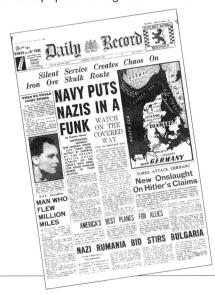

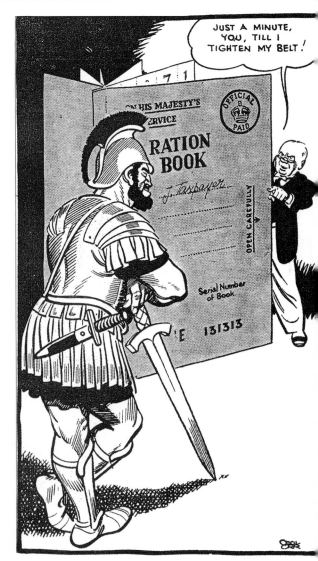

wonderful job in keeping the nation smiling. Their contribution to the national morale should not be underestimated. Often some of the jokes which circulated in the darker moments of the war years were cut out and sent to serving soldiers, sailors and airmen, and staple fare like Mac and Harry Smith became, in their way, an important part of Britain's war effort.

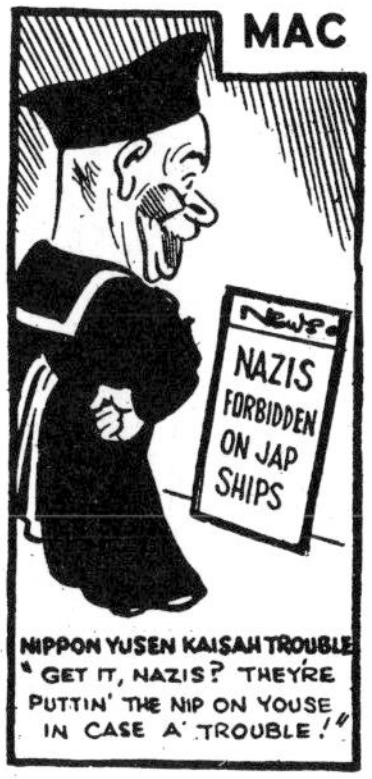
MAC
NEWS
NAZIS FORBIDDEN ON JAP SHIPS
NIPPON YUSEN KAISAH TROUBLE
"GET IT, NAZIS? THEY'RE PUTTIN' THE NIP ON YOUSE IN CASE A' TROUBLE!"

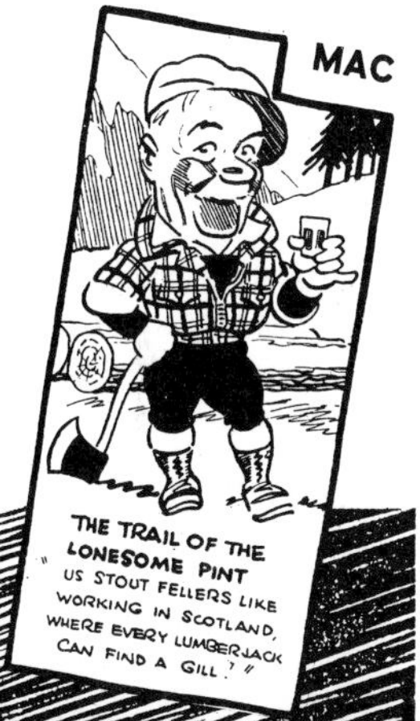
MAC
THE TRAIL OF THE LONESOME PINT
"US STOUT FELLERS LIKE WORKING IN SCOTLAND, WHERE EVERY LUMBERJACK CAN FIND A GILL?"

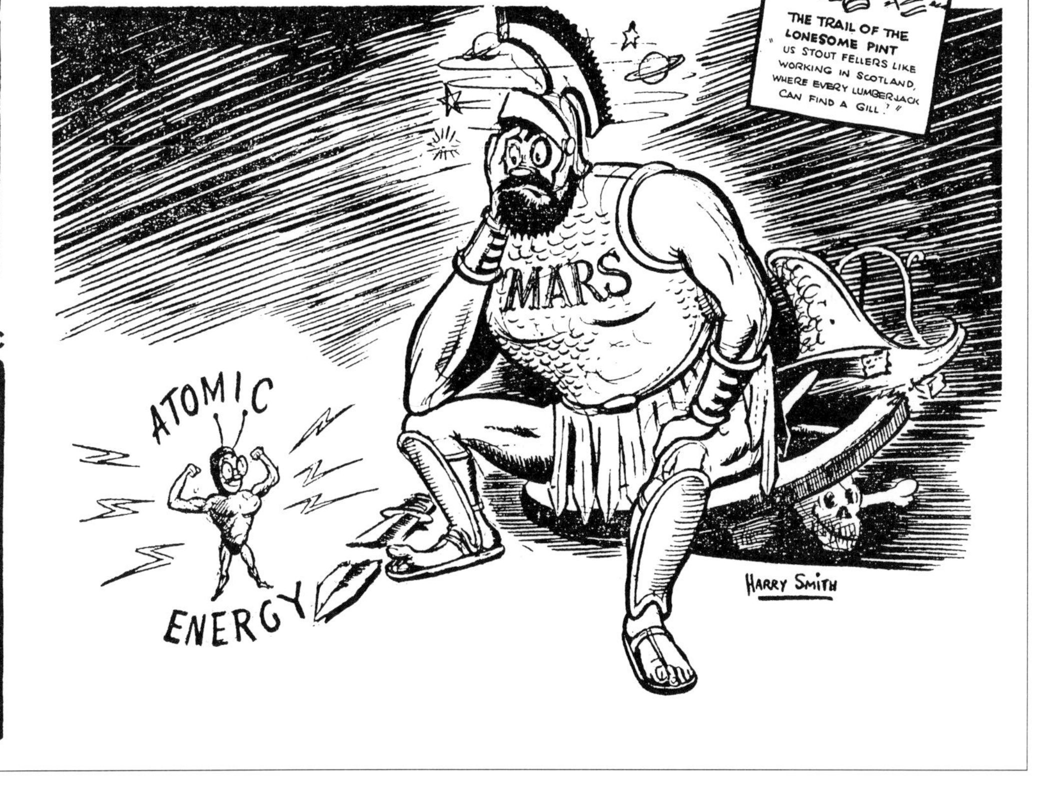
MARS
ATOMIC
ENERGY
HARRY SMITH

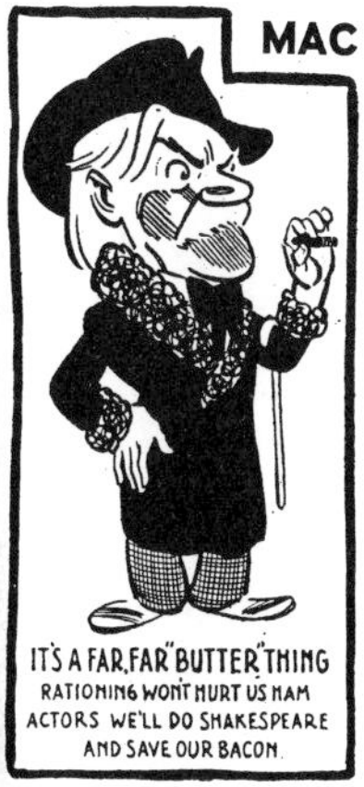
MAC
IT'S A FAR, FAR "BUTTER" THING
RATIONING WON'T HURT US HAM ACTORS WE'LL DO SHAKESPEARE AND SAVE OUR BACON.

Much the same could be said of the 'Breakfast Smile' which, unusually, was the product of several different pens. But despite a variety of authors the smiles could always be relied upon to capture the popular mood of the moment. This was a war being waged on several different fronts, and the cartoonists were an important component in stoking the home fires, whilst giving long distance support to the men and women serving at the sharp end. Laughter can't end conflict, but sometimes it makes it more bearable.

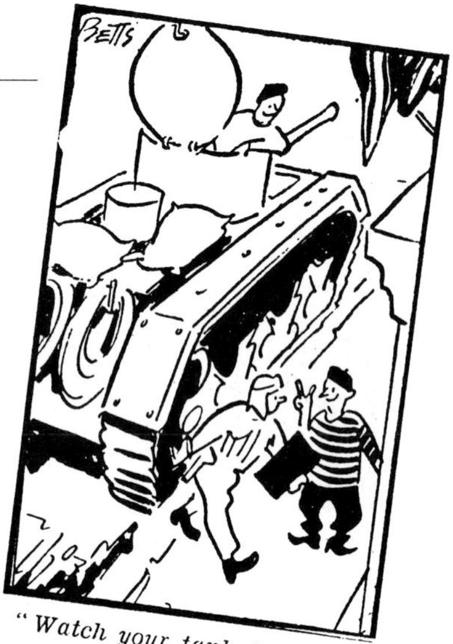

"Watch your tank, M'sieu?"

BREAKFAST SMILE

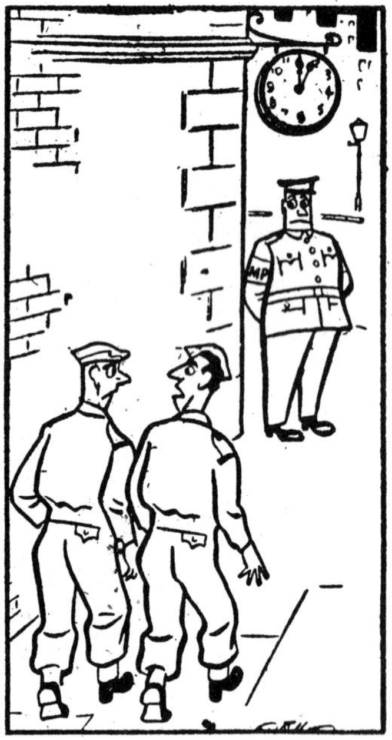

"Now we just saunter up and ask the time, it always averts suspicion."

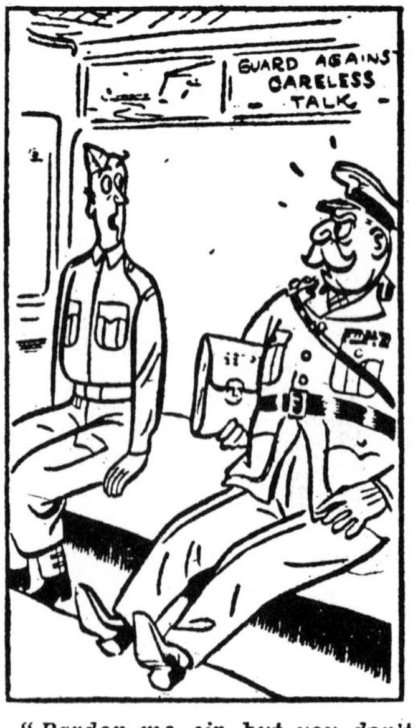
GUARD AGAINST CARELESS TALK

"Pardon me, sir, but you don't half spill the beans in your sleep, sir."

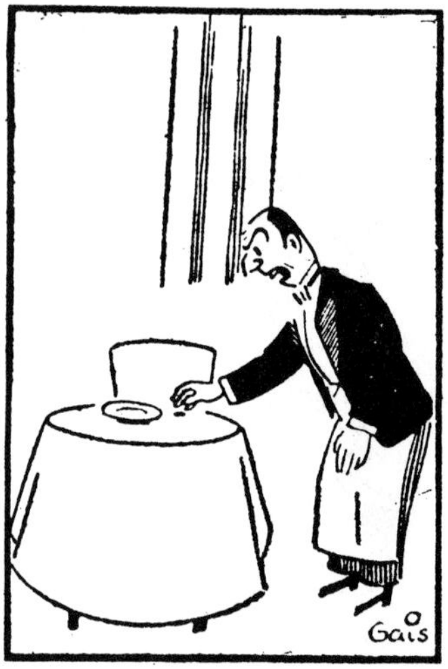

"A ha'penny! Another of those tip and run eaters!"

A CENTURY OF LAUGHS

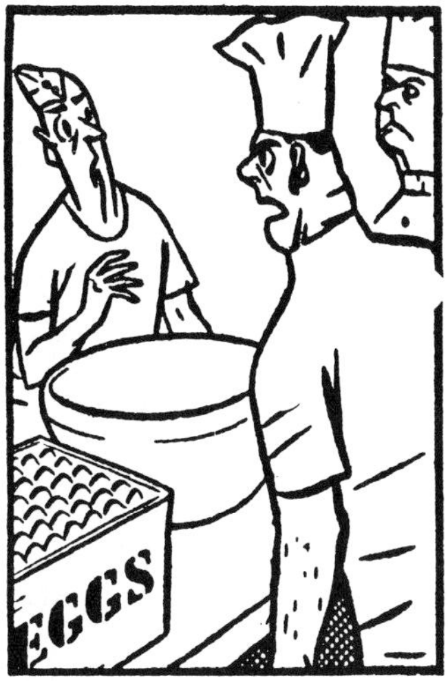
EGGS

"Omelette for four hundred— get cracking!"

Football too continued to play its part and Jack Lindsay returned to his regular Monday morning commentry on the weekend sport, as illustrated on the following pages.

It took some time after the war years for the paper to increase its pagination and some time also for old and new cartoonists to emerge. But emerge they did . . .

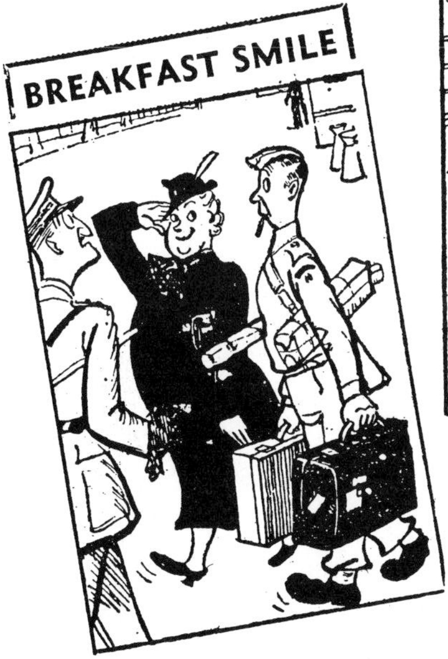
BREAKFAST SMILE

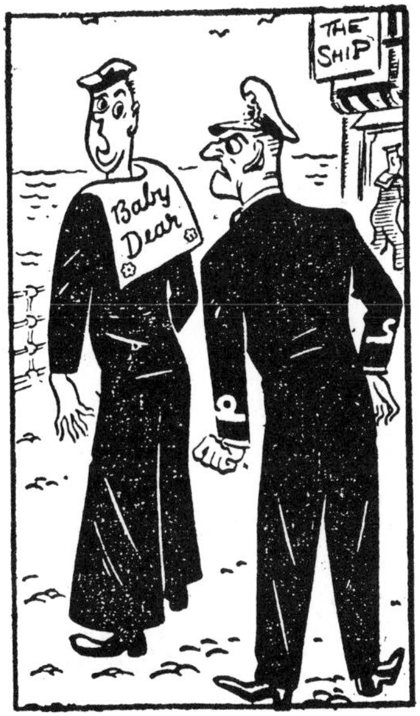
THE SHIP
Baby Dear

"I know sir — and I've reported it to the laundry, sir."

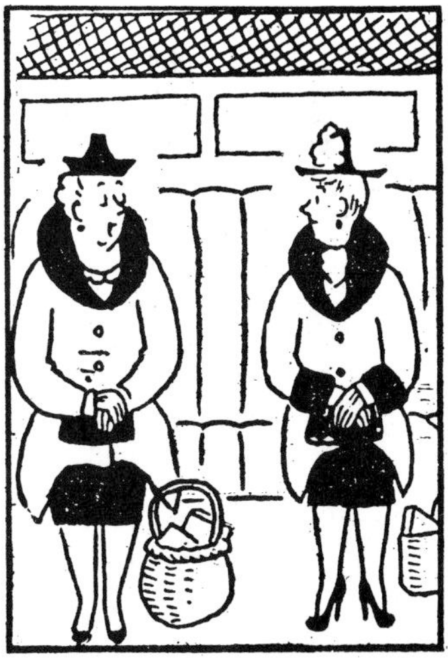

"That is the end of the news . . . here are the headlines again!"

HAVING BEEN TOLD IN OUR YOUTH THAT IT WAS ONLY "WEE COOPERS WHA LEEVED IN FIFE, NICKETTY, NACKETTY, BLAH, BLAH, BLAH!" —

NAE WEE COOPERS, ONY A BIG AITKEN PAIN!

RANGERS V. EAST FIFE

THE MINER'S DREAM OF HOME

WE WERE INTERESTED TO HEAR THAT EAST FIFE HAD QUITE A FEW MINERS IN THEIR TEAM, SO LEAVING "WAVERLEY" TO TELL YOU HOW THEY PLAY FOOTBALL WE WILL

CONCENTRATE ON TELLING YOU HOW THEY TRAIN FOR IT. REAL TOUGH BABIES THESE MINERS, THEY DON'T HACK OUT COAL WITH ANYTHING SO EFFEMINATE AS A PICK, THEY KICK IT TO BITS WITH THEIR FITBA' BOOTS.

WHICH PRODUCES GUYS LIKE SAMMY STEWART WHOSE TRAINING CONSISTS OF A LITTLE LIGHT MASSAGE WITH A SHOVEL AND WHO THINKS NOTHING OF A "STINT" THE SIZE OF WILLIE WADDELL.

THEN THERE'S JIMMY PHILP WHO HAD TO HAVE A HUGE PATCH ON HIS EYE. IF MR. PHILP'S HEAD HAD COME RIGHT OFF IN A TACKLE

BEND DOON TILL AH PLASTER YE!

AH'LL KEEP THE HEID, YOU DON'T NEED TAE!

HIS TRAINER WOULD HAVE STUCK PLASTER ON HIS NECK AND TOLD HIM NO' TAE BE A BIG SAFTIE.

DEFINITELY A HARD BUNCH, THESE FIFERS, RANGERS ARE VERY GLAD THERE ISN'T A WEST, NORTH OR SOUTH FIFE,

DUNCAN, A REAL HAZEL NUT.

WHIT'S IN A NAME, THEY'RE A' TOUGH!

JACK LINDSAY

AT WHICH HIBS GIVE A HOLLOW LAUGH AND MUTTER IN A-MAYES-MENT, "HAVEN'T YOU EVER HEARD OF DUNFERMLINE?

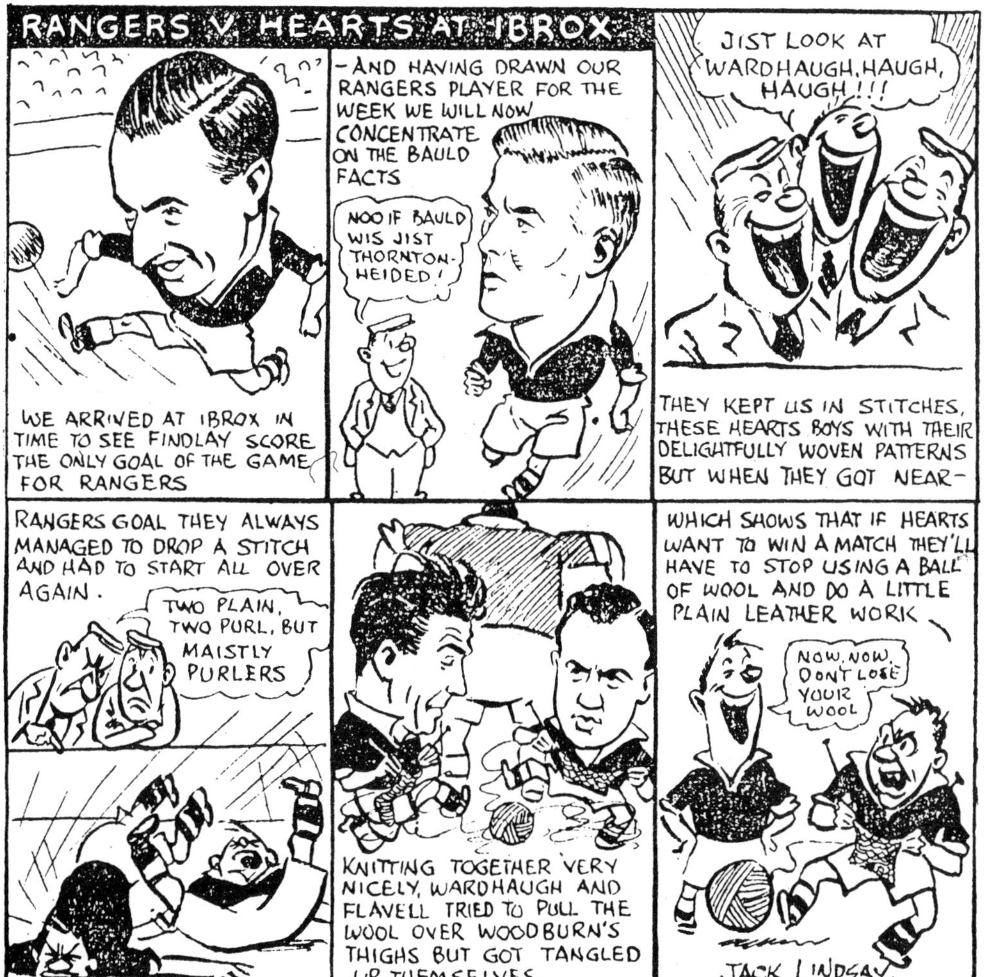
RANGERS V. HEARTS AT IBROX
WE ARRIVED AT IBROX IN TIME TO SEE FINDLAY SCORE THE ONLY GOAL OF THE GAME FOR RANGERS
-AND HAVING DRAWN OUR RANGERS PLAYER FOR THE WEEK WE WILL NOW CONCENTRATE ON THE BAULD FACTS
NOO IF BAULD WIS JIST THORNTON-HEIDED!
JIST LOOK AT WARDHAUGH, HAUGH, HAUGH!!!
THEY KEPT US IN STITCHES, THESE HEARTS BOYS WITH THEIR DELIGHTFULLY WOVEN PATTERNS BUT WHEN THEY GOT NEAR-
RANGERS GOAL THEY ALWAYS MANAGED TO DROP A STITCH AND HAD TO START ALL OVER AGAIN.
TWO PLAIN, TWO PURL, BUT MAISTLY PURLERS
KNITTING TOGETHER VERY NICELY, WARDHAUGH AND FLAVELL TRIED TO PULL THE WOOL OVER WOODBURN'S THIGHS BUT GOT TANGLED UP THEMSELVES.
WHICH SHOWS THAT IF HEARTS WANT TO WIN A MATCH THEY'LL HAVE TO STOP USING A BALL OF WOOL AND DO A LITTLE PLAIN LEATHER WORK
NOW, NOW, DON'T LOSE YOUR WOOL
JACK LINDSAY.

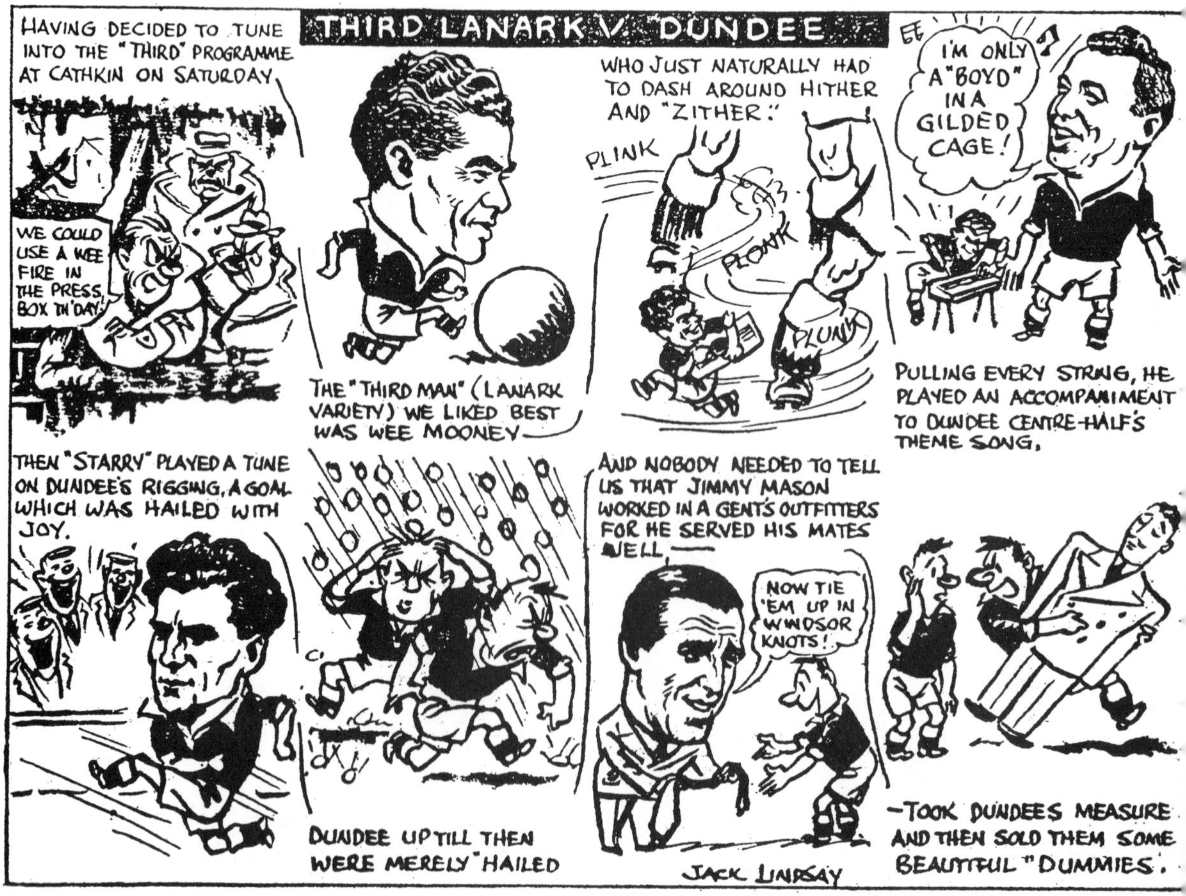
THIRD LANARK V. DUNDEE
HAVING DECIDED TO TUNE INTO THE "THIRD" PROGRAMME AT CATHKIN ON SATURDAY
WE COULD USE A WEE FIRE IN THE PRESS BOX TH'DAY!
THE "THIRD MAN" (LANARK VARIETY) WE LIKED BEST WAS WEE MOONEY
WHO JUST NATURALLY HAD TO DASH AROUND HITHER AND "ZITHER."
PLINK
PLONK
PLUNK
I'M ONLY A "BOYD" IN A GILDED CAGE!
PULLING EVERY STRING, HE PLAYED AN ACCOMPANIMENT TO DUNDEE CENTRE-HALF'S THEME SONG.
THEN "STARRY" PLAYED A TUNE ON DUNDEE'S RIGGING, A GOAL WHICH WAS HAILED WITH JOY.
DUNDEE UP TILL THEN WERE MERELY "HAILED
AND NOBODY NEEDED TO TELL US THAT JIMMY MASON WORKED IN A GENT'S OUTFITTERS FOR HE SERVED HIS MATES WELL
NOW TIE 'EM UP IN WINDSOR KNOTS!
JACK LINDSAY
-TOOK DUNDEES MEASURE AND THEN SOLD THEM SOME BEAUTIFUL "DUMMIES".

Without Words

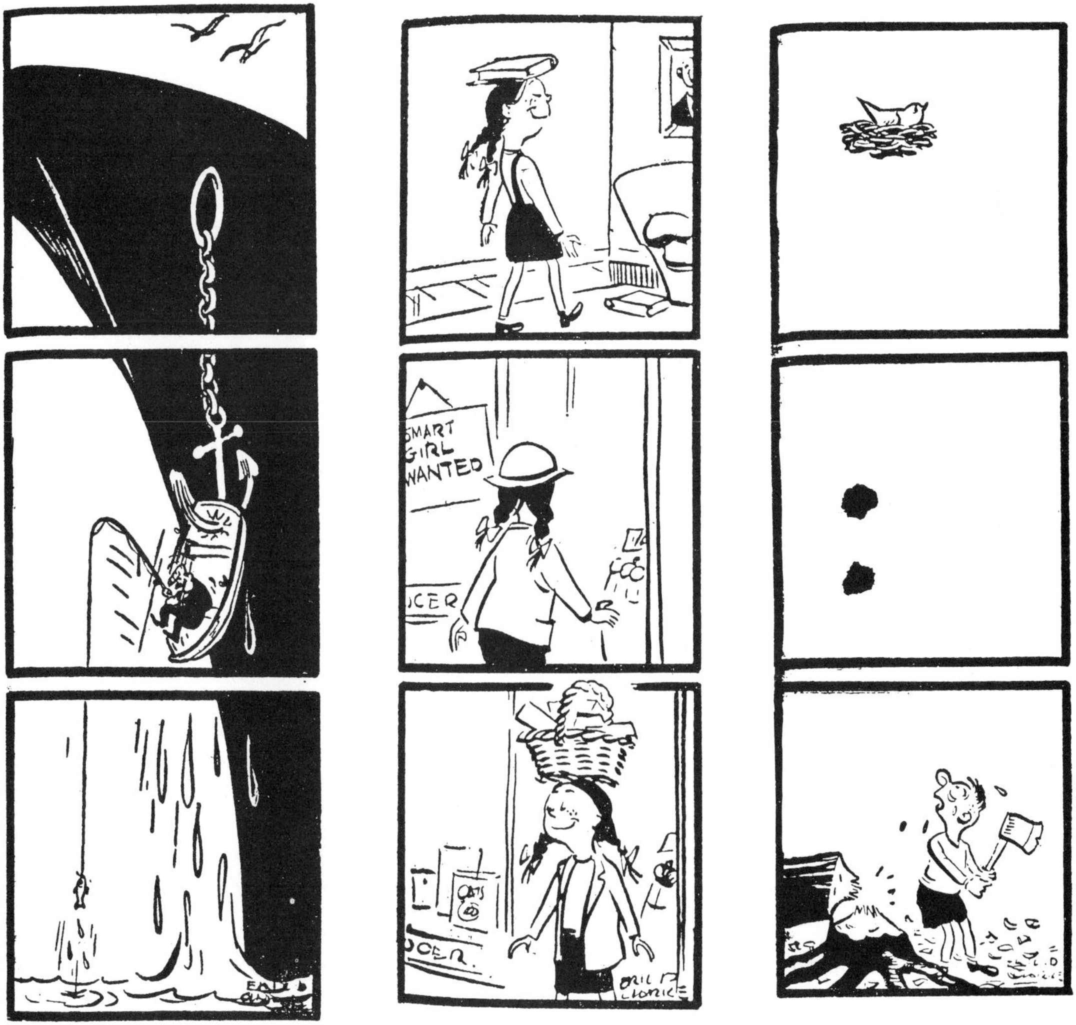
SMART
GIRL
WANTED
OATS

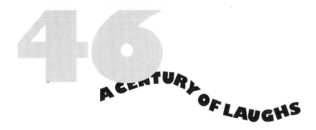

Into the Fifties . . . and there's nothing like an election to bring out the cartoonists

Whenever the cartoonist is sitting staring at that blank sheet of paper, scrabbling for inspiration, desperately searching for a new idea, the one event which saves his bacon is . . . another election. And the Fifties were kind enough to bring a whole batch of them.

Daily Record

Sport 4 Pages

George Younger's Alloa Ales

Labour's jubilee is "ideal opportunity"

ELECTION NEXT MONTH IS NOW LIKELY

Hurt man gasps: 'I fell from express'

'You are my sunshine'

Hungary told to pack up

Scots film man's yacht ablaze

No sign of trawler

'Mercy' doctor on murder charge

Harry netted backers nearly £5000

VOTE LABOUR
NOT TOO LITTLE —
VOTE LIBERAL
— NOT TOO MUCH —
VOTE CONSERVATIVE
— BUT JUST RIGHT !!

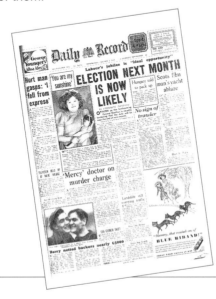

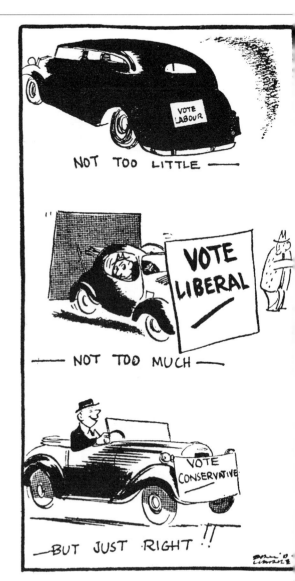

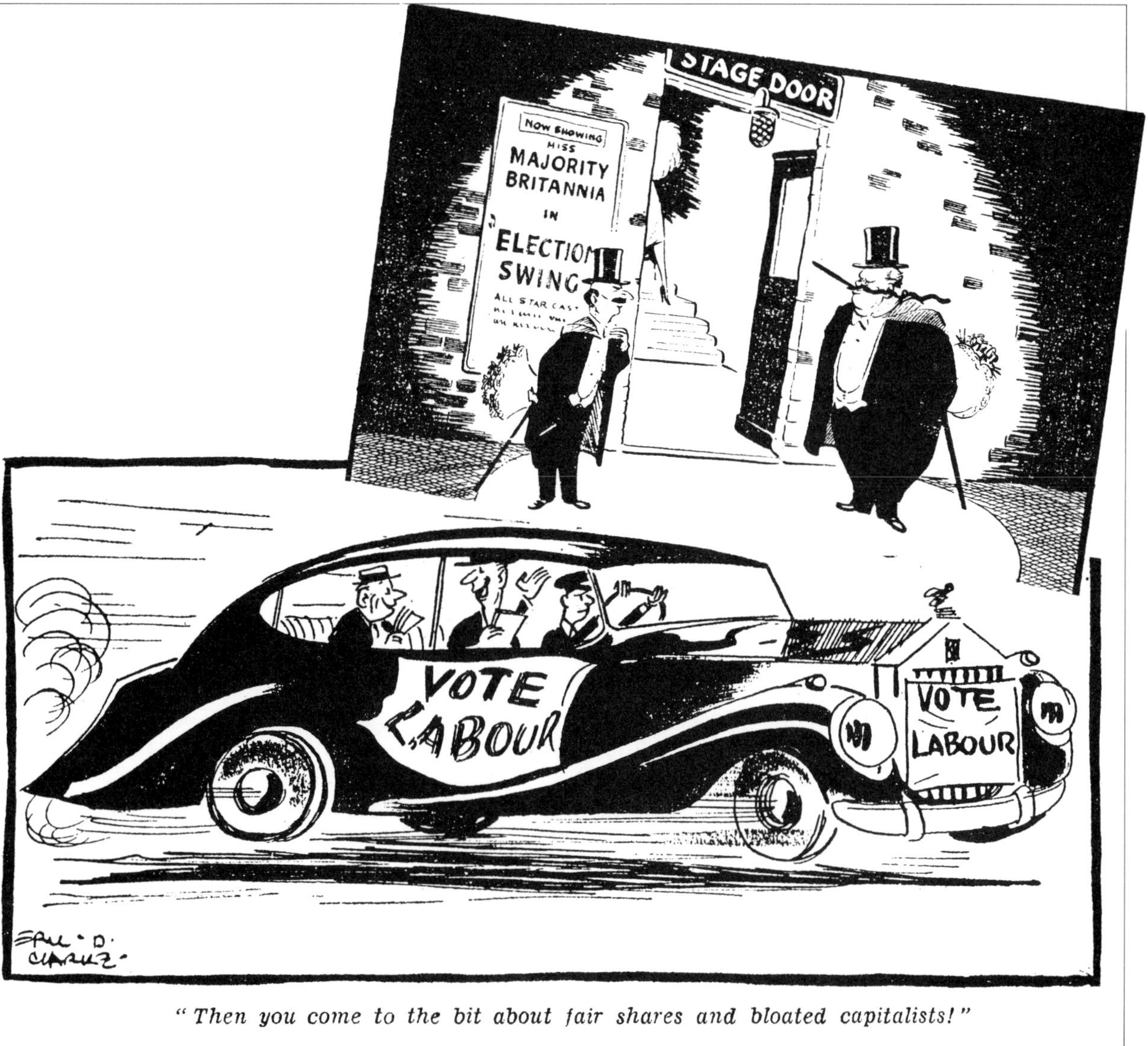
STAGE DOOR
NOW SHOWING
MISS
MAJORITY
BRITANNIA
IN
ELECTION
SWING
ALL STAR CAST
VOTE LABOUR
VOTE LABOUR

"Then you come to the bit about fair shares and bloated capitalists!"

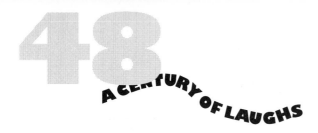

or a Budget

And no matter who gets in, the new government will assure the electorate that they are in a mess because the last lot couldn't count. In contrast they are now about to bring in a really sensible budget. And what they all forget is that voters hate taxes whoever thinks them up.

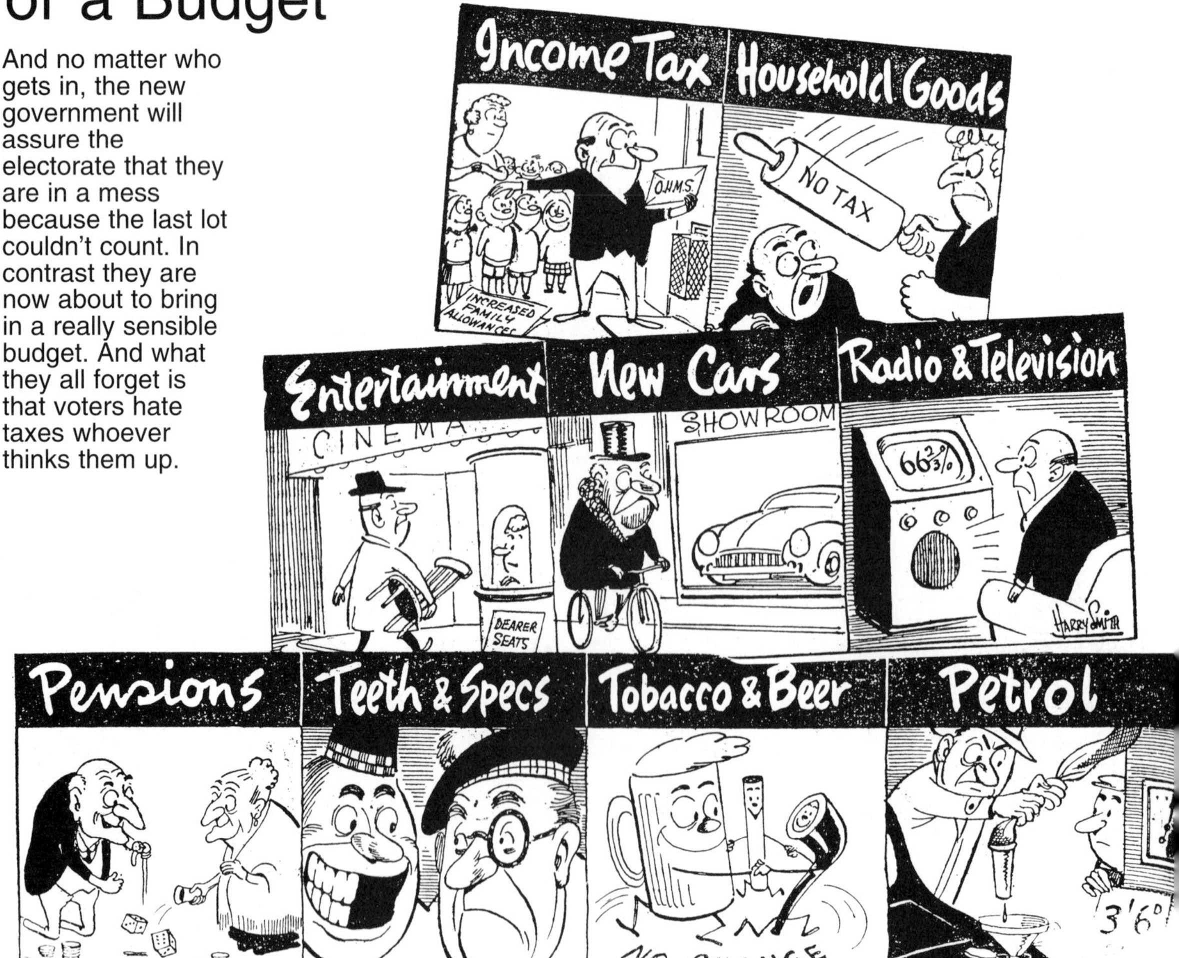
Income Tax
O.H.M.S.
INCREASED FAMILY ALLOWANCES
Household Goods
NO TAX
Entertainment
CINEMA
DEARER SEATS
New Cars
SHOWROOM
Radio & Television
66⅔%
HARRY SMITH
Pensions
Teeth & Specs
Tobacco & Beer
NO CHANGE
Petrol
3'6d

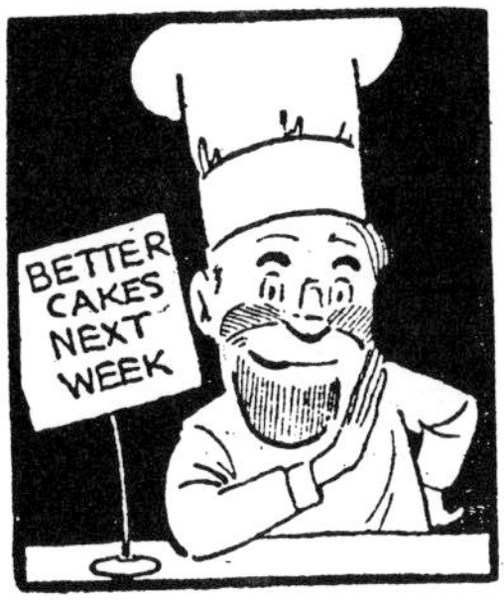
BETTER CAKES NEXT WEEK

MAC says: “ *We'll be making some nice election custard pies!*”

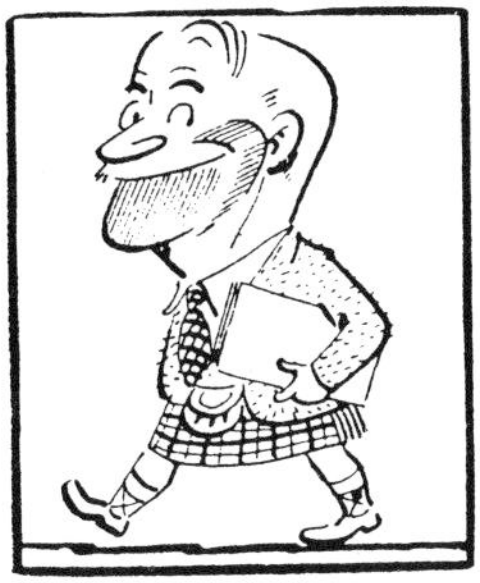

MAC says: “ *Wales is having a Covenant, too. It agrees that London can't govern*

The fifties also brought a fresh outbreak of tabloid wars . . . and an urgent need to deploy some fresh troops. The *Record* recruited a couple of crackers! On the home front the wit and wisdom of the incomparable Mac was deployed alongside the international nitwittery of Useless Eustace, whose popularity with women readers might well have had something to do with the fact that he confirmed all their suspicions about the brain power of the average man! But for whatever reason, Mac and Eustace became a dynamic duo who kept the *Record*'s reputation for spotting cartoon winners intact.

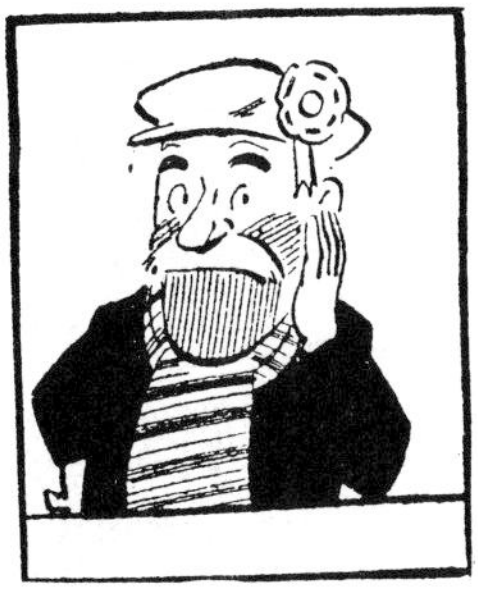

MAC says: “ *Ach, oor right wing's ower conservative, and oor left's labourin' a bit.*”

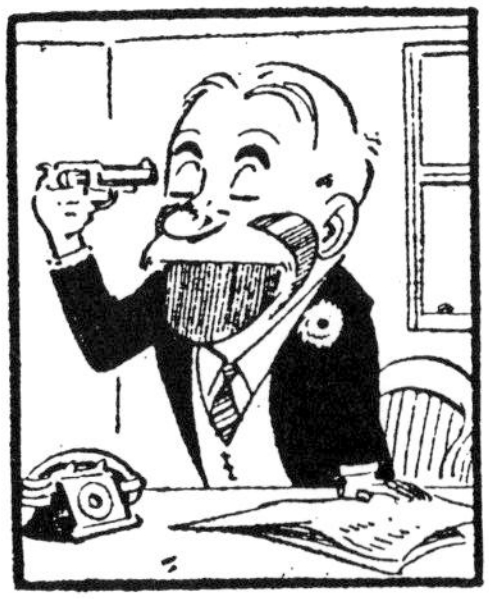

MAC says: “ *And here is a final report on the Budget—*”

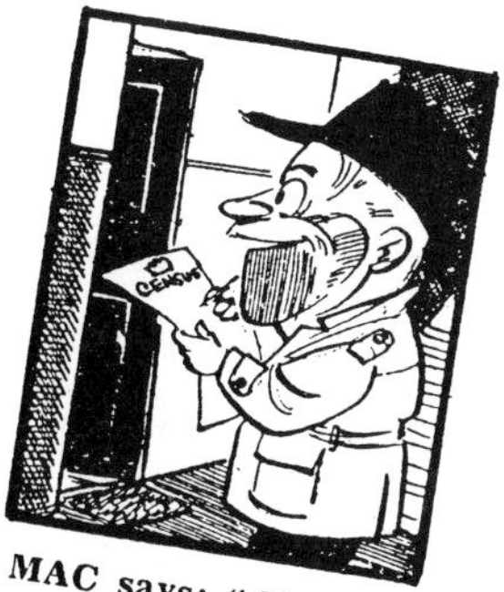
CENSUS

MAC says: “ *No, the census won't get you a house, but it'll put you in a nice pigeon-hole.*”

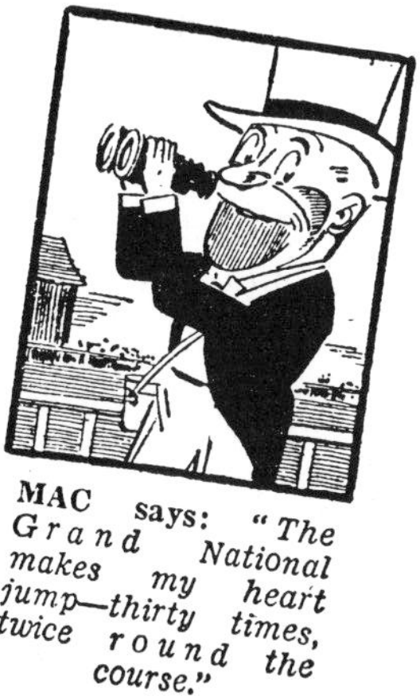

MAC says: “ *The Grand National makes my heart jump—thirty times, twice round the course.*”

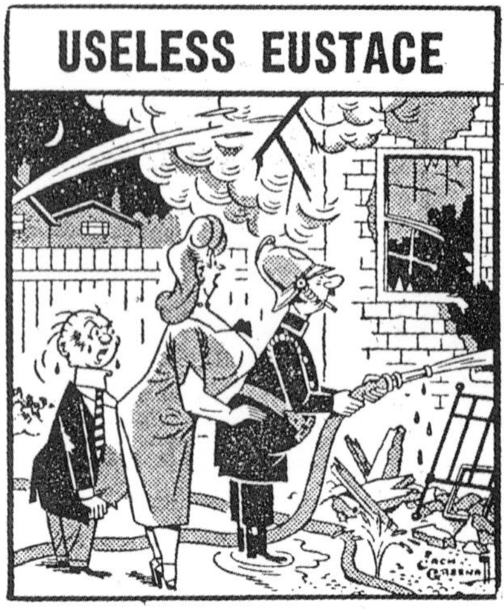
USELESS EUSTACE

" You and your darned candlelight dinners! "

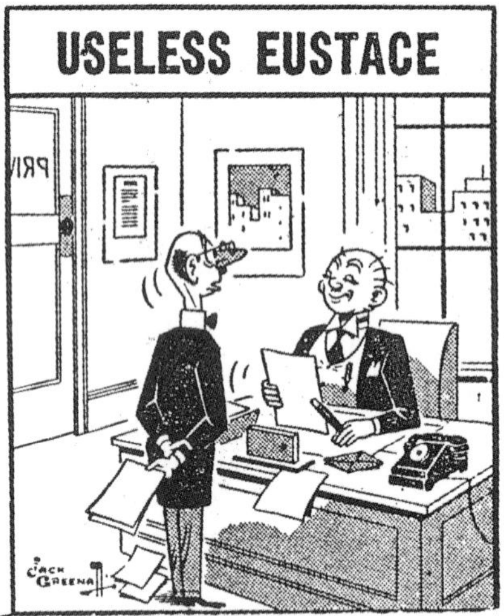
USELESS EUSTACE

" You'll find your pay packet a little heavier in future, Fishwick— We're using thicker envelopes!!"

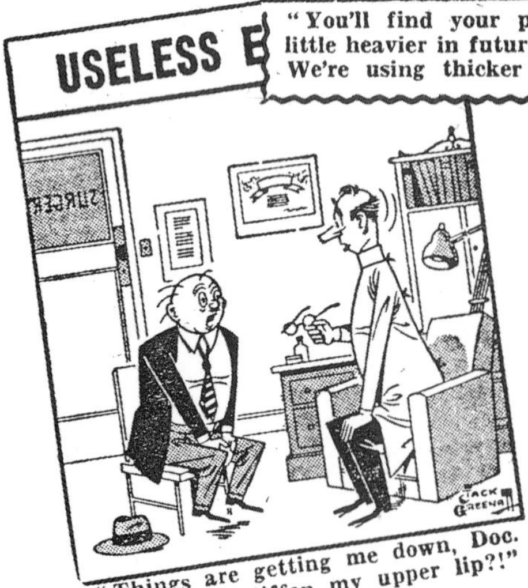
USELESS E

" Things are getting me down, Doc. — can you stiffen my upper lip?!"

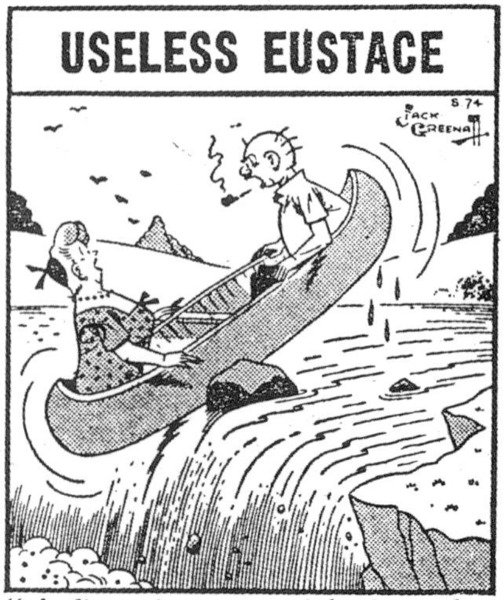
USELESS EUSTACE

" A fine time you picked to play see-saw, I must say ! "

Og, Capp and Neill . . . a hat-trick of goodies

If Mac and Eustace were a timely twosome, Angus Og, Andy Capp and Bud Neill were certainly a midfield trio to conjure with. Almost an embarrassment of riches for the editor of the day, but all different enough to command their own loyal army of fans. First to sign up was Bud Neill, an enigmatic figure in real life, but a legend to those who lapped up his wee Glesca wifies and the incomparable Lobey Dosser.

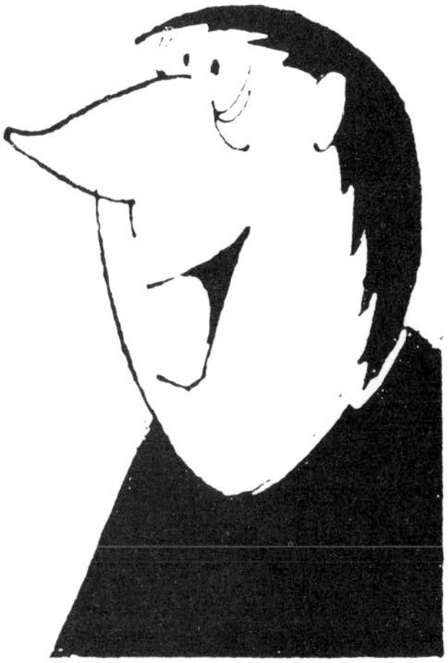

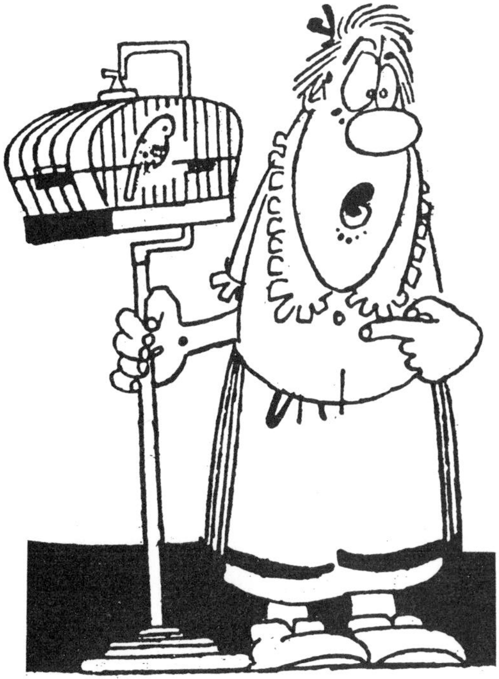

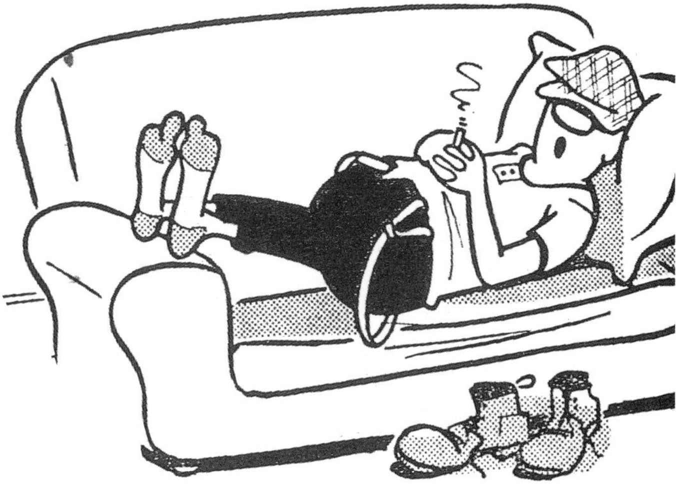

Bud's first cartoon in the Record

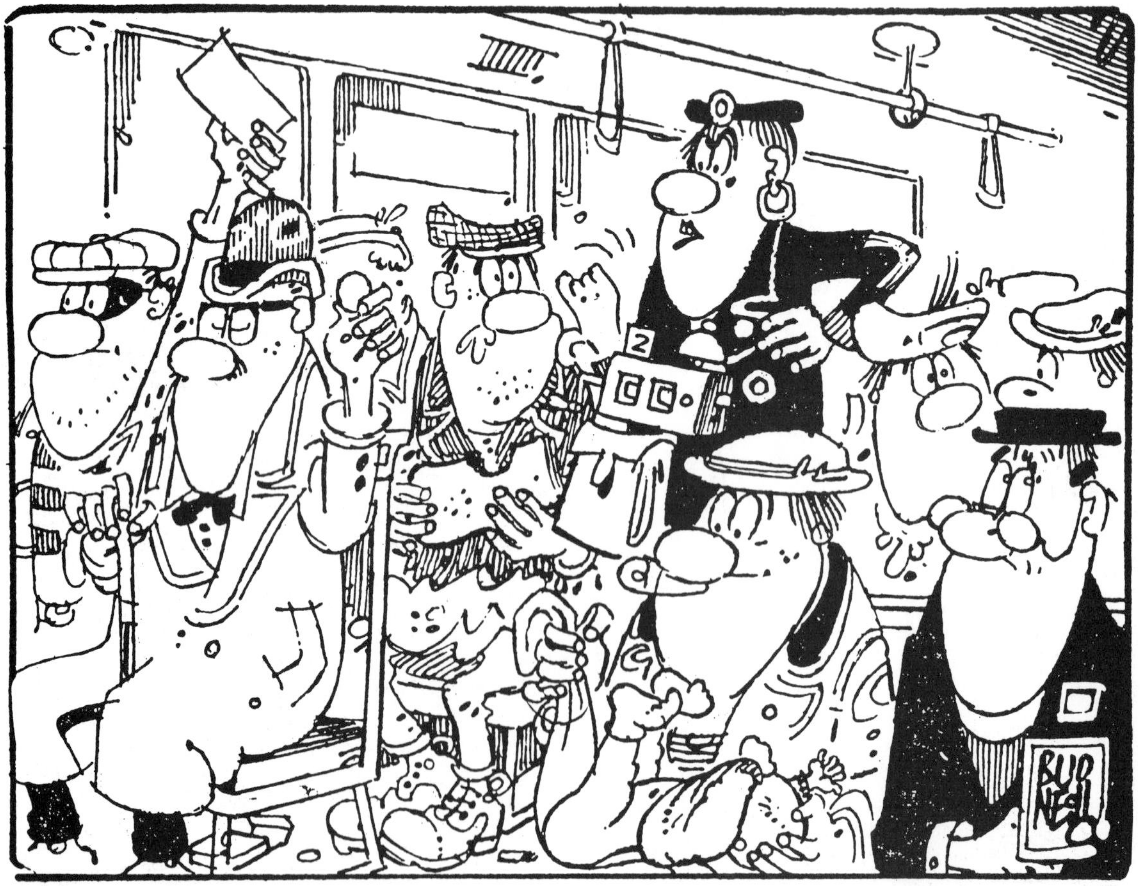
BUD NEILL

" Nae eatin' chits in the caur, you. Ye wantin' mice aboot the place ?"

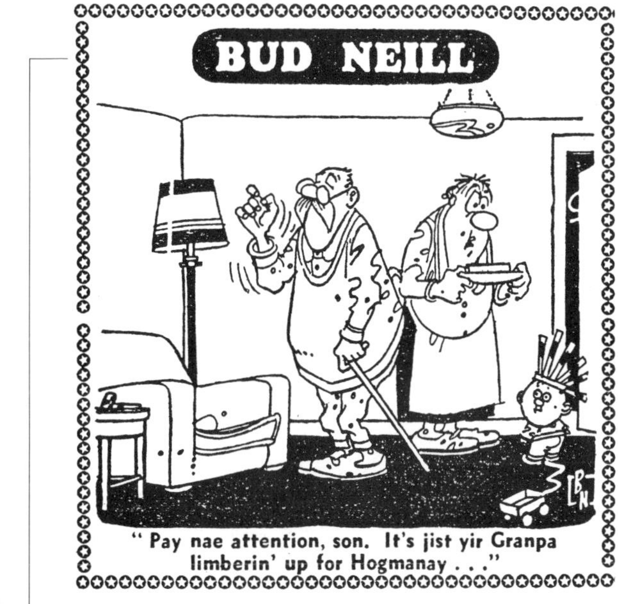
BUD NEILL

" Pay nae attention, son. It's jist yir Granpa limberin' up for Hogmanay . . ."

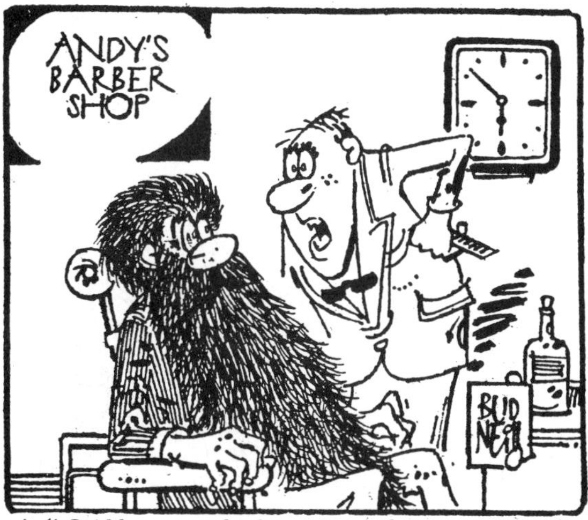
ANDY'S
BARBER
SHOP
BUD
NEILL

* " Could ye come back the morn aboot nine an' we'll make a day o' it?" *

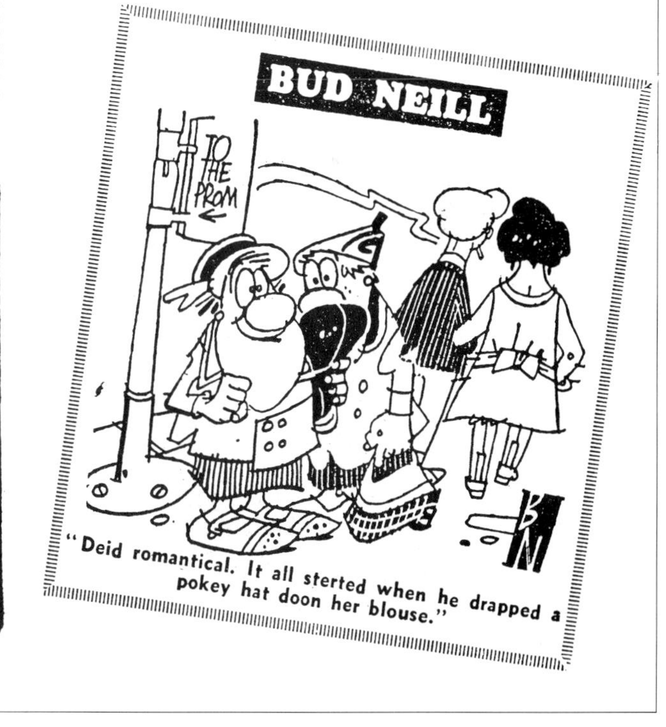
BUD NEILL
TO
THE
PROM

"Deid romantical. It all sterted when he drapped a pokey hat doon her blouse."

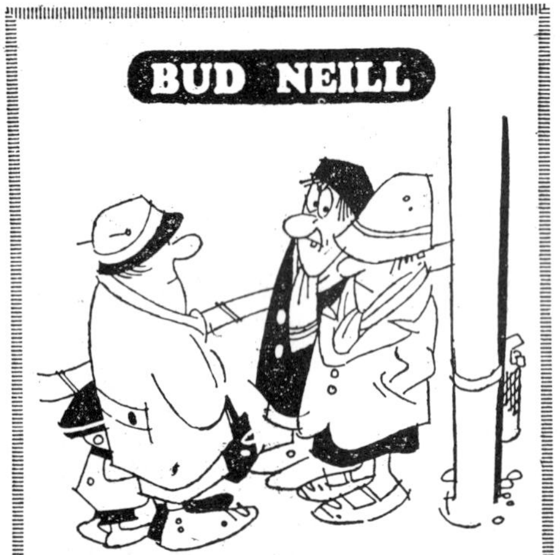
BUD NEILL

" Naebody's goin' tae spill Mrs. Thomson ower tae Wick, are they, Mrs. Thomson? "

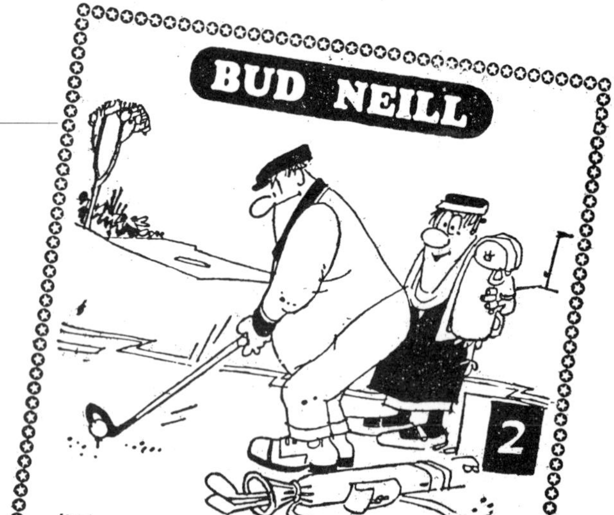
BUD NEILL

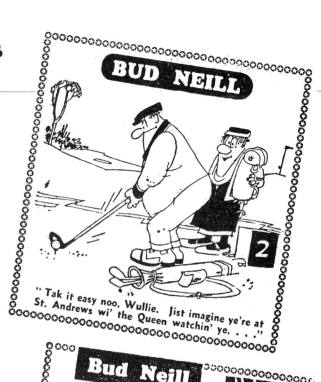

" Tak it easy noo, Wullie. Jist imagine ye're at St. Andrews wi' the Queen watchin' ye. . . ."

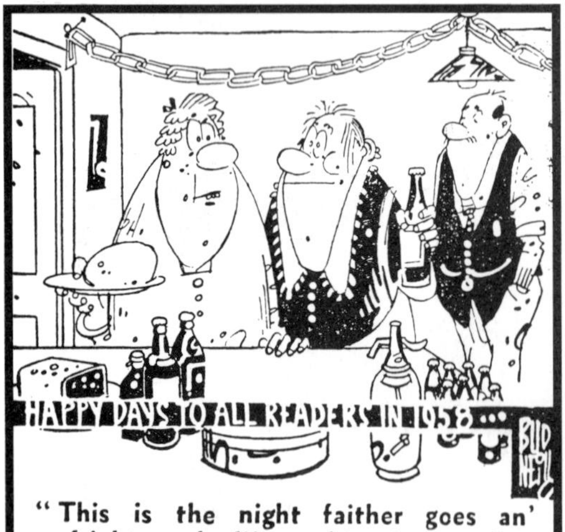
HAPPY DAYS TO ALL READERS IN 1958 ...
BUD NEILL

" This is the night faither goes an' frightens the life oot his ulcer. . . ."

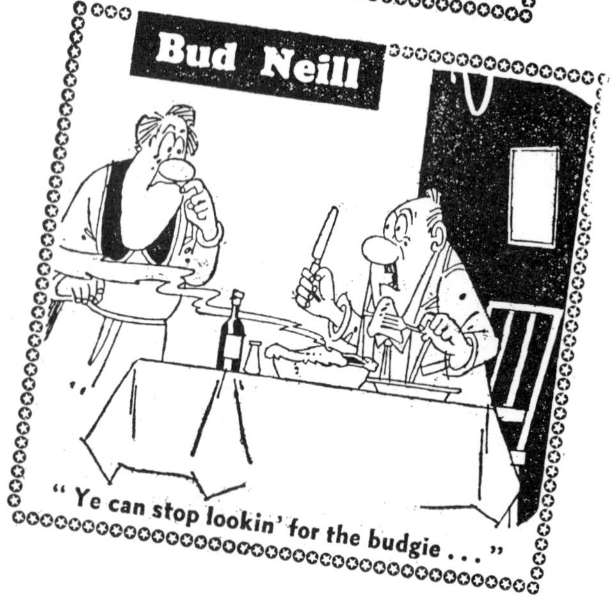
Bud Neill

" Ye can stop lookin' for the budgie . . . "

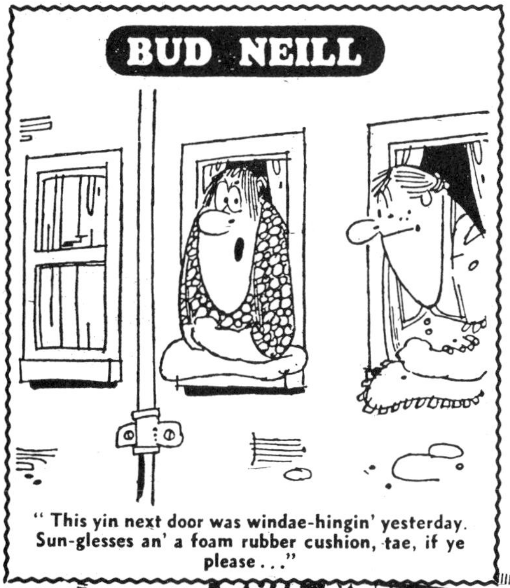
BUD NEILL

" This yin next door was windae-hingin' yesterday. Sun-glesses an' a foam rubber cushion, tae, if ye please . . ."

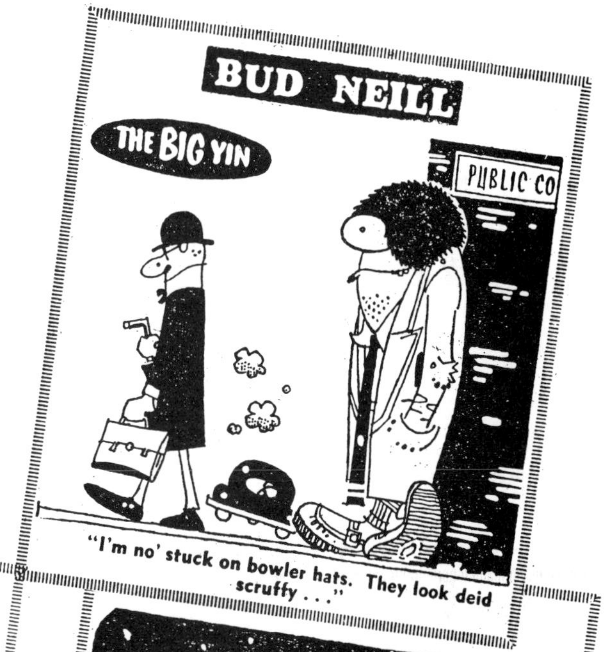
BUD NEILL
THE BIG YIN
PUBLIC CO

"I'm no' stuck on bowler hats. They look deid scruffy . . ."

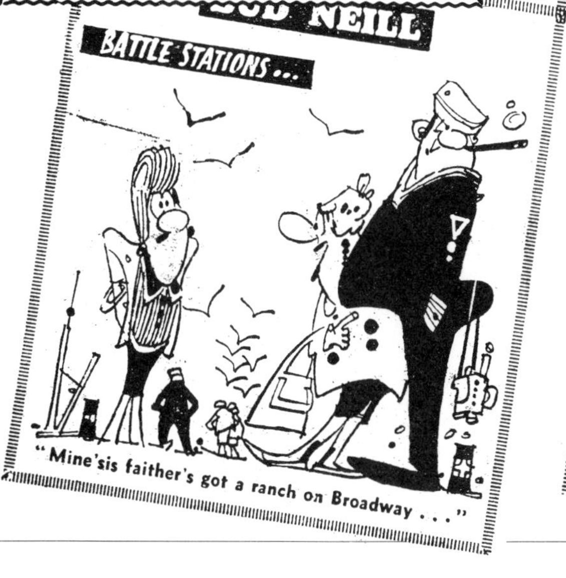
BATTLE STATIONS ...

" Mine'sis faither's got a ranch on Broadway . . ."

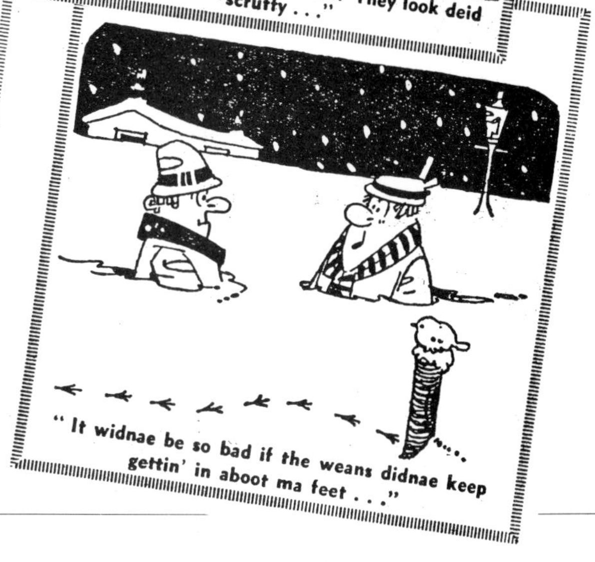

" It widnae be so bad if the weans didnae keep gettin' in aboot ma feet . . ."

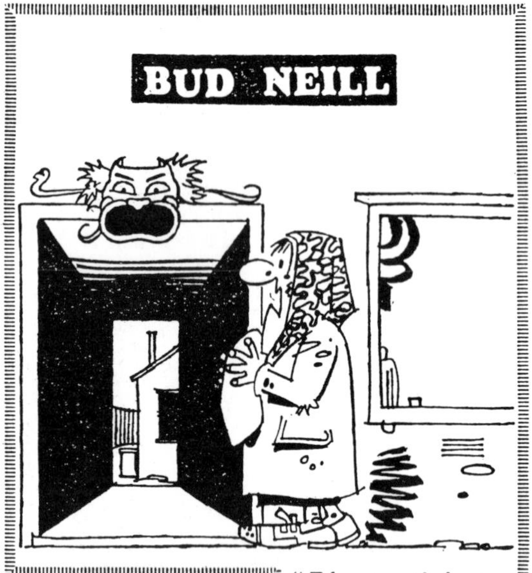
BUD NEILL

"That reminds me, I've nothin' for me man's tea . . ."

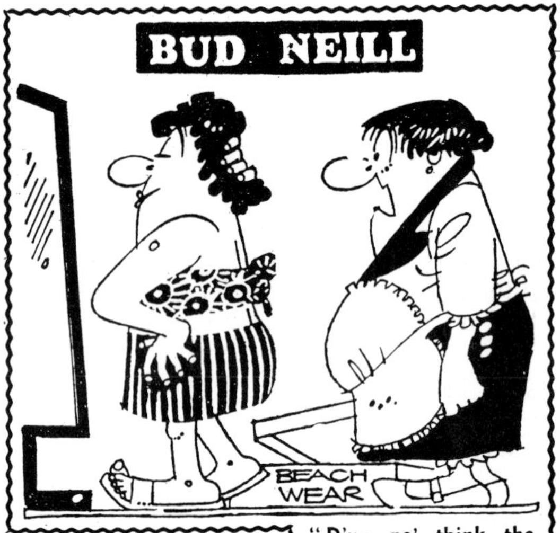
BUD NEILL
BEACH WEAR

"D'ye no' think the Saltcoats polis'll be busy enough in July?"

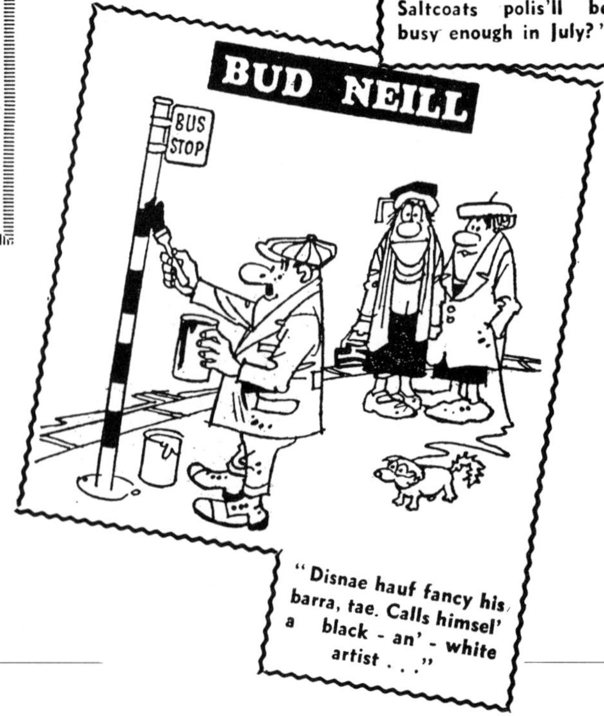
BUD NEILL
BUS STOP

"Disnae hauf fancy his barra, tae. Calls himsel' a black - an' - white artist . . ."

And, in addition to these household characters, the strips pages were adding to their cast list with more syndicated offerings like The Flutters. Albert and Bert might seem a pretty inept breed of wide-boys to today's audience, but in their time they were the likely lads that everyone turned to. If Arthur Daley had begun his career in dodgy deals in newspapers, he'd probably have made his debut in this slot.

But as would be con men, this pair couldn't hold a candle to the man who provided the original design format for Britain's best-known male chauvinist pig. Reg Smythe couldn't have known that he'd given birth to a legend when he created Andy Capp.

THE FLUTTERS
Albert and Bert
THIS'LL DO. NOW, TRY TO LOOK LESS LIKE A TAPE-WORM WHAT'S HAD BAD NEWS AND MORE LIKE A BUSINESS GENTLEMAN IN SEARCH OF HIS MID-MORNIN' APERITIF!
'MORNING, MY MAN. TWO EYE BATHS OF YOUR NOURISHIN' SHERRY WINE, IF YOU PLEASE
CERTAINLY, SAIR. DRY, SAIR?
WE'LL HAVE IT WET, THANKS... HOW MUCH? FOUR POUND TEN?... TA... CATCH HOLD, ALBERT!
WE'D QUITE LIKELY OVERHEAR A HANDY STOCK MARKET TIP IN A PLACE LIKE THIS...
SSHLOOP
THAT'S IF YOU'D STOP MAKIN' A NOISE LIKE A CART-LOAD OF GRAVEL BEIN' UNTIPPED!

THE FLUTTERS
Albert and Bert
WOULD YOU FLIPPIN' WELL BELIEVE IT? AGNES NICKS MY LOLLY THEN HAS THE BLOOMIN' NERVE TO CASH IN ON A WINNER WINKLED OUT BY YOUR PERISHIN' GENIUS!
SHE MUST HAVE ABOUT FIFTY QUID SALTED AWAY SOMEWHERE! BLIMEY, I'M GOIN' TO HAVE A SHOWDOWN ABOUT THIS!
HALF A JIFF!
YOU WANT TO GIVE THIS A BIT OF THOUGHT, TARZAN, BEFORE YOU GO SWINGIN' THROUGH THE JUNGLE TO CROWN YOUR MATE...
C'MON! WE'VE GOT TO GO THROUGH THAT PERISHIN' HOUSE WITH A MINE DETECTOR. WE WON'T GET NOTHIN' BY ARGUIN' THE TOSS WITH HER!

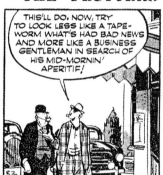

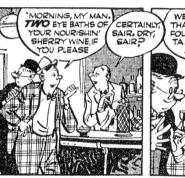

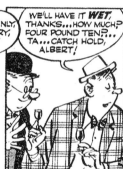

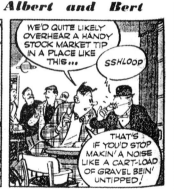

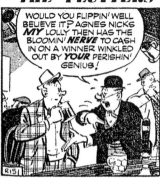

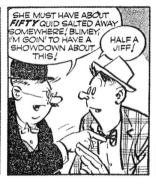

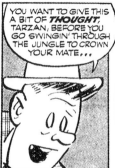

Reg had actually been drawing for the *Record*'s sister paper, the *Mirror*, for some time before Andy and all his works were unleashed on the Scottish public. And he certainly revised their opinion of how the average English gent might behave. Andy's missus, the long suffering Florrie, did of course

Smythe

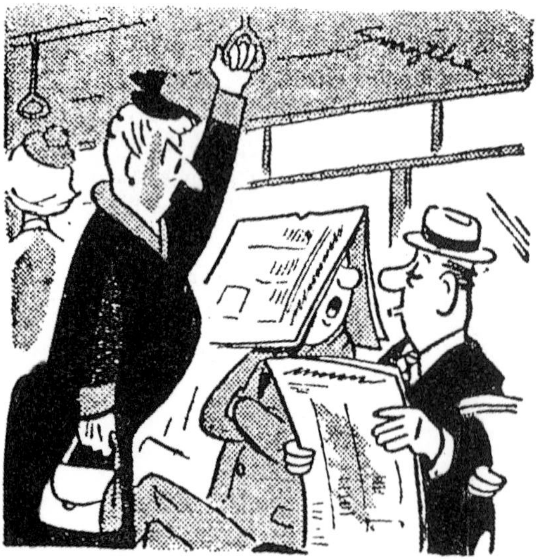

' I can't bear to see a woman standing "

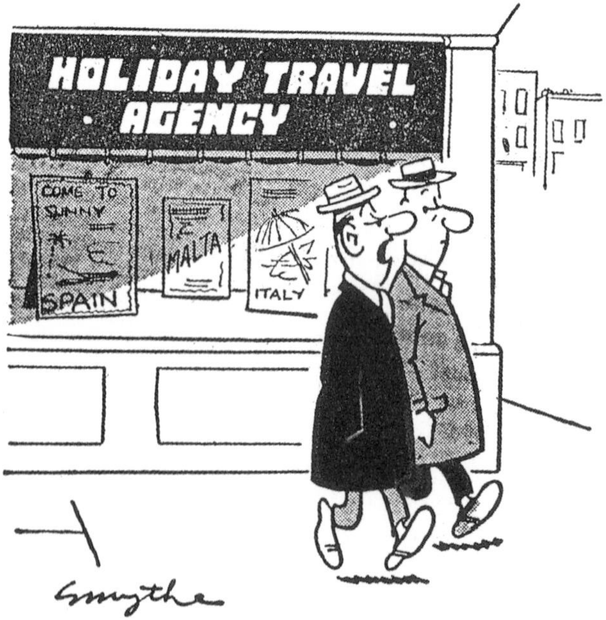
HOLIDAY TRAVEL AGENCY
COME TO SUNNY
SPAIN
MALTA
ITALY

" Don't make the holiday arrangements myself—my wife tells me where, my boss tells me when, and my bank manager tells me how long."

have Andy's number. But that didn't always keep her ahead on points as the husband who gave boorishness a bad name continued his rake's progress around the clubs, pubs and snooker halls of the north of England. Scottish wives weren't exactly unfamiliar with the breed. They just didn't fancy Andy giving their spouses more bad ideas.

"If it comes to that, YOU don't look so pretty in the morning either!"

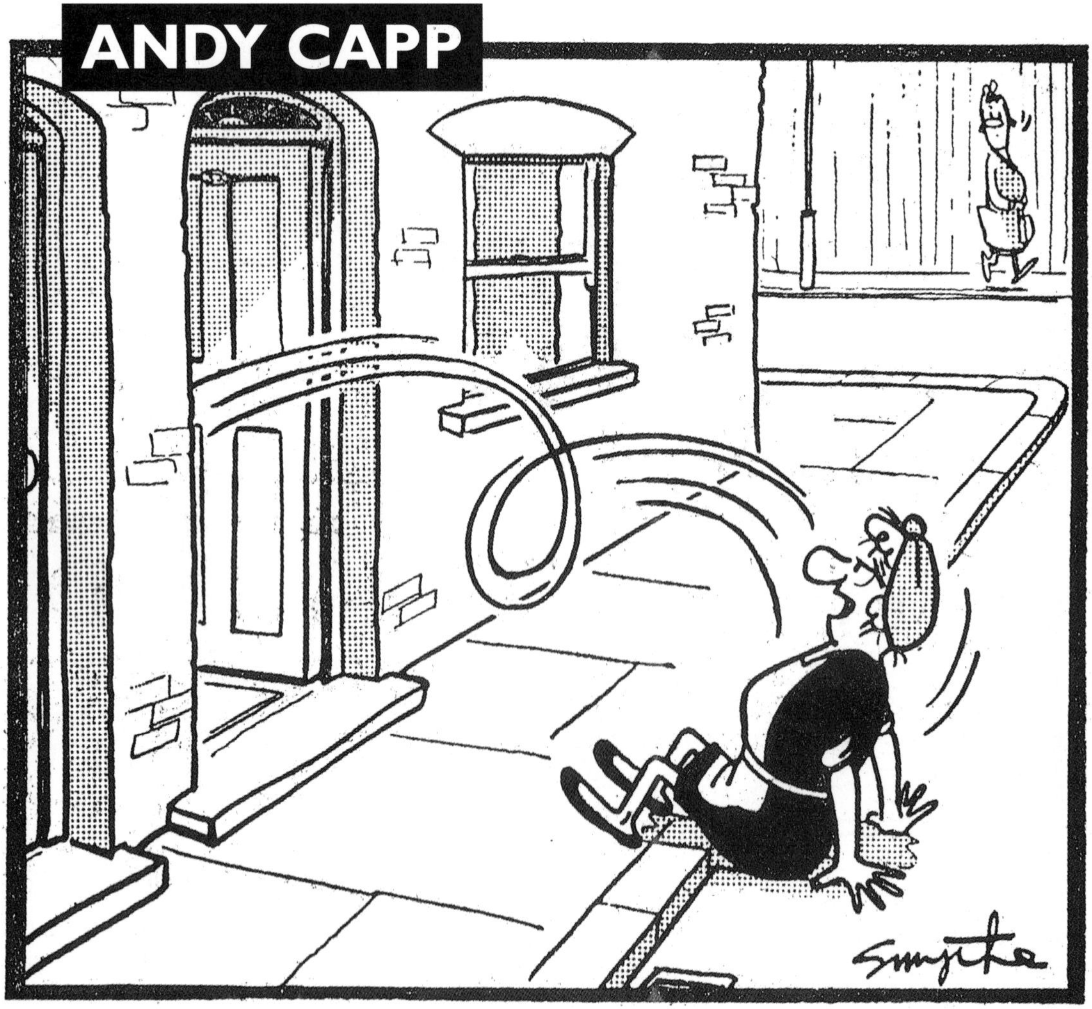
ANDY CAPP

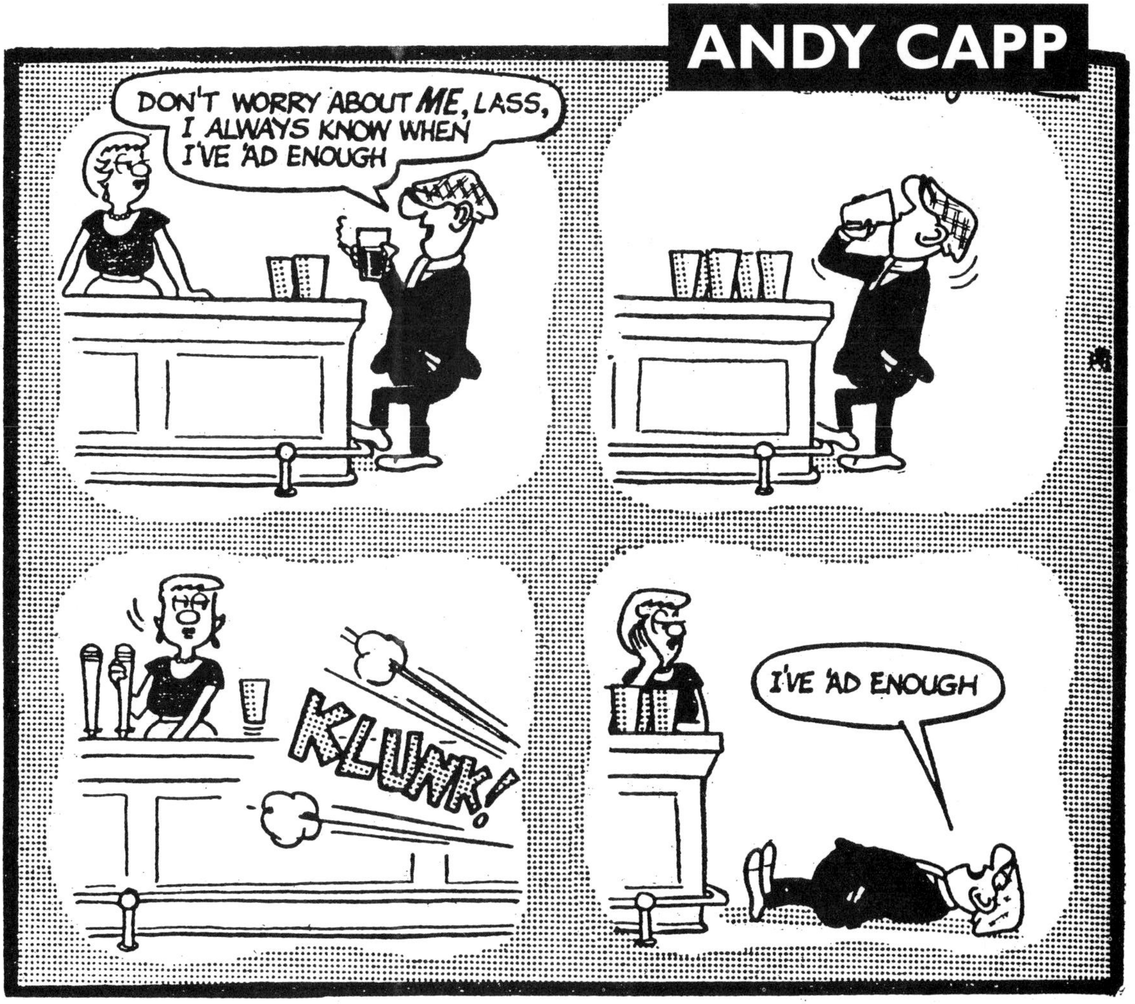
ANDY CAPP
DON'T WORRY ABOUT *ME*, LASS, I ALWAYS KNOW WHEN I'VE 'AD ENOUGH
KLUNK!
I'VE 'AD ENOUGH

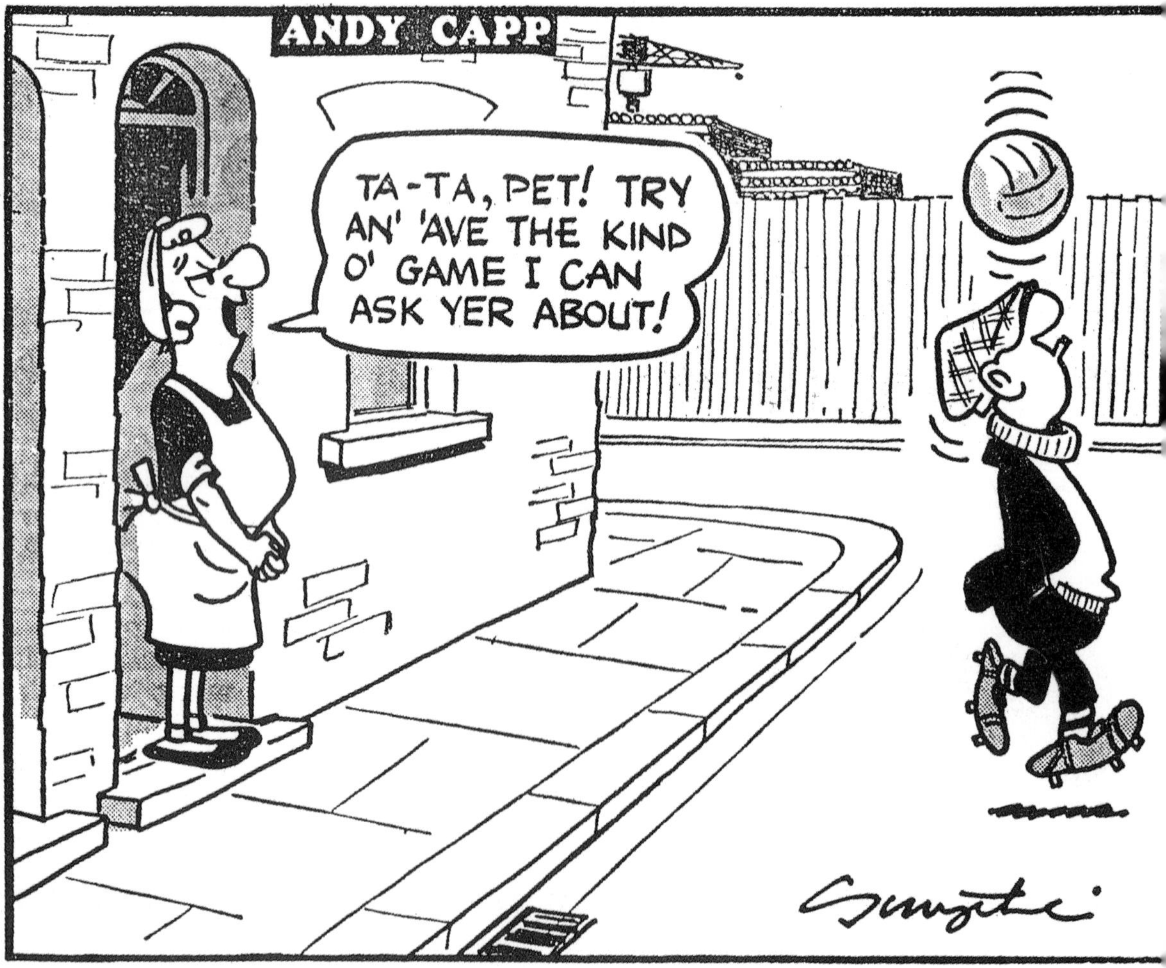
ANDY CAPP
TA-TA, PET! TRY AN' 'AVE THE KIND O' GAME I CAN ASK YER ABOUT!

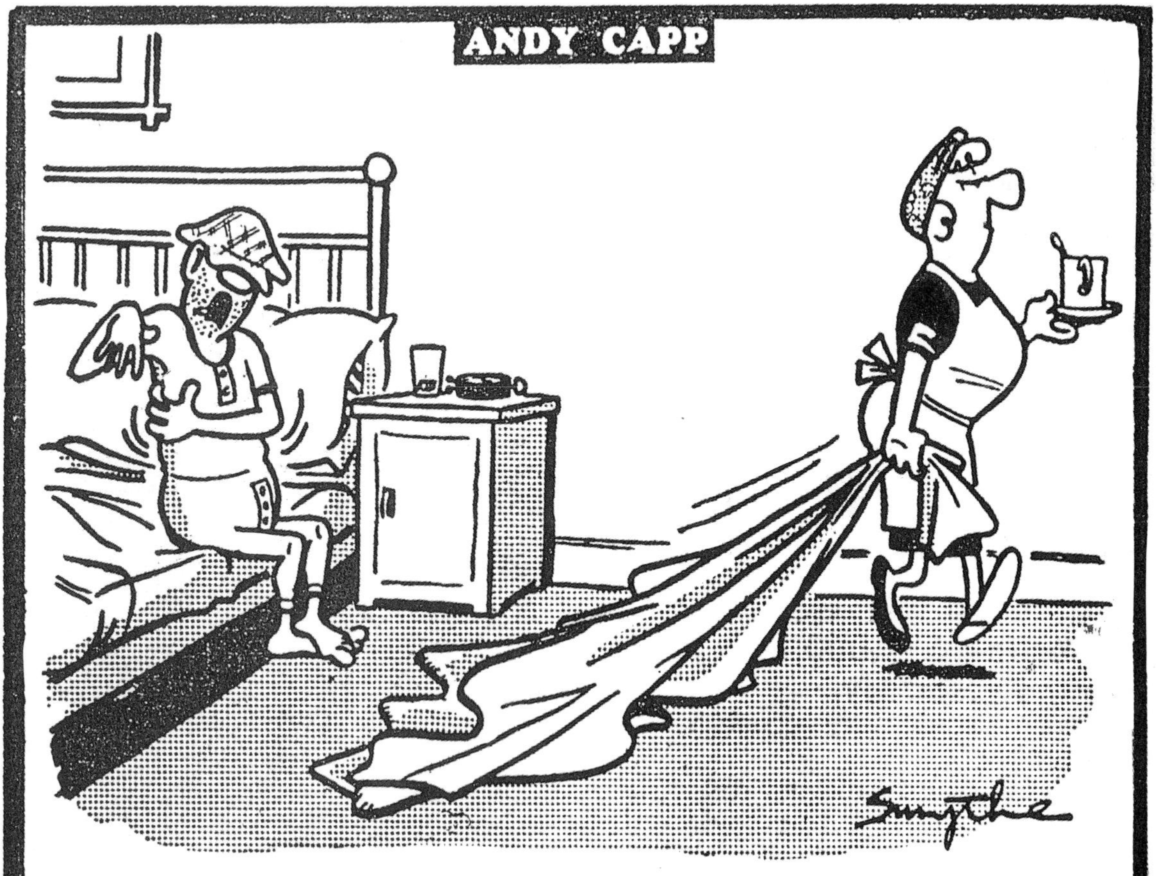
ANDY CAPP
Smythe

"If there's one thing gets me down it's gettin' up!"

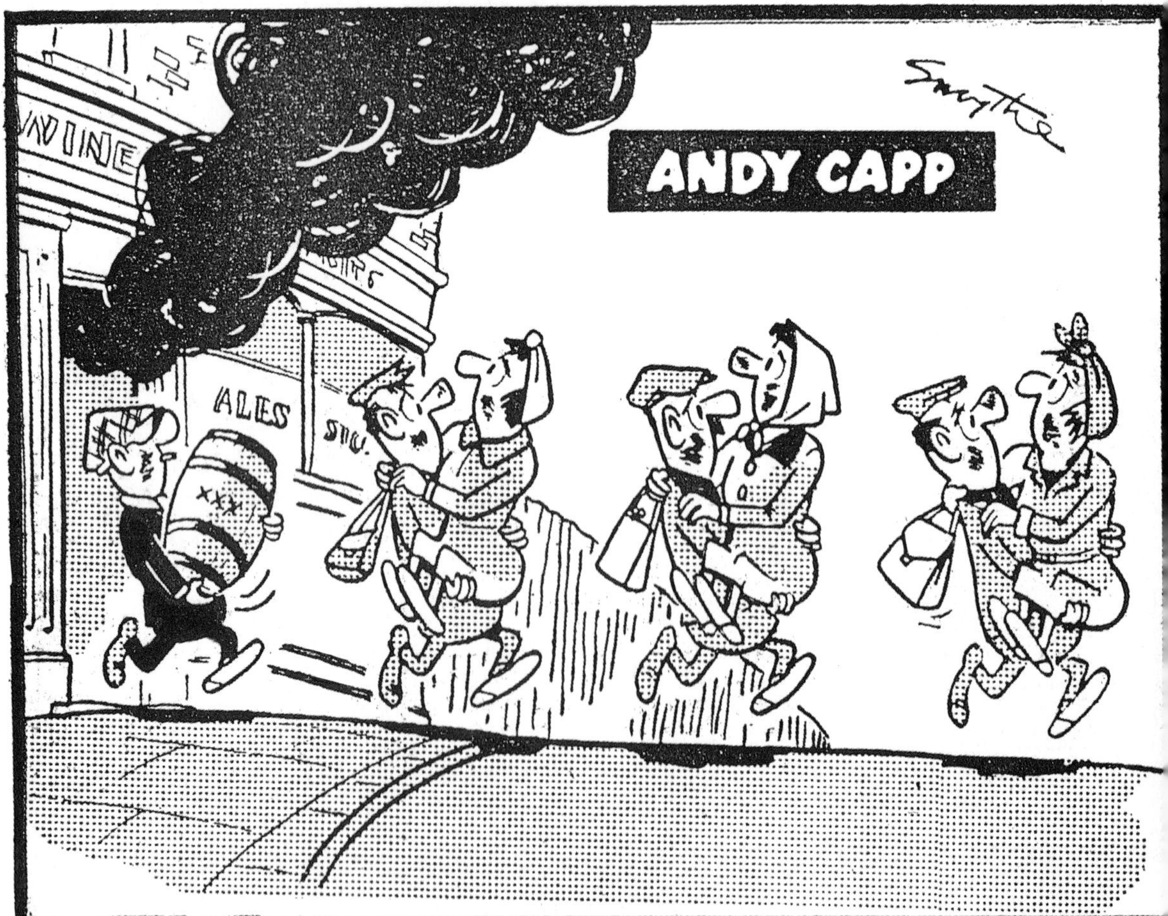
ANDY CAPP
Smythe
WINE
ALES

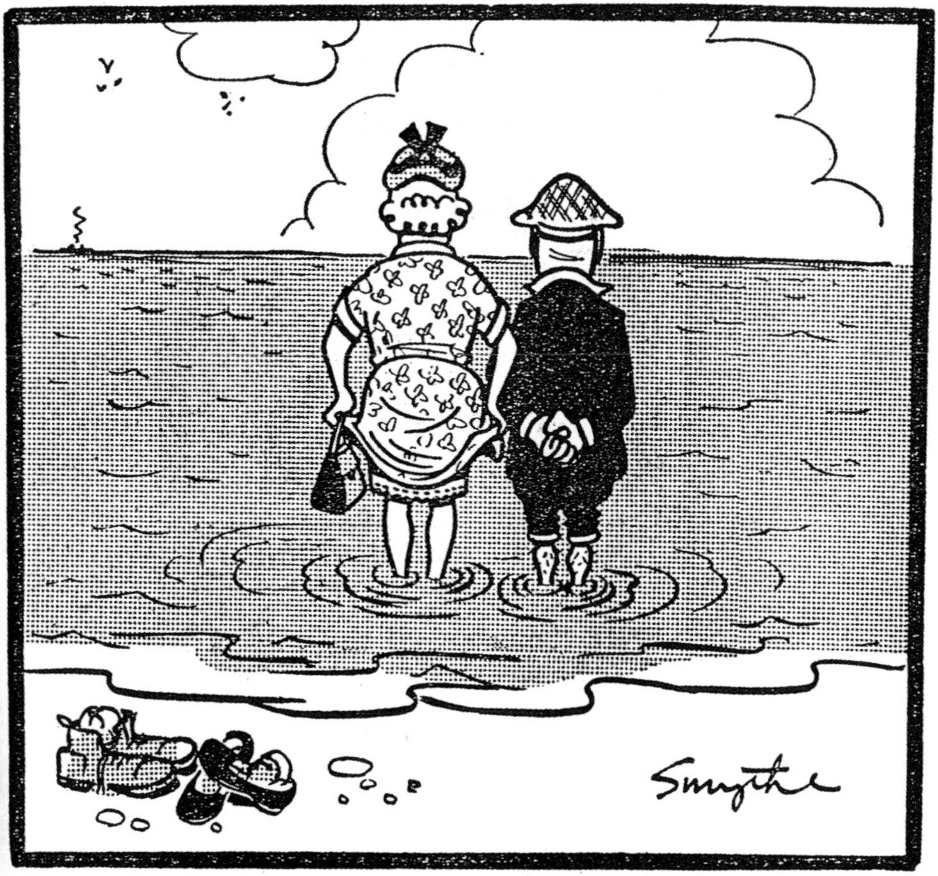
Smythe

" I think I'll make me way back to the chara, Florrie—the sight of all this water makes me feel sick! "

Laugh!

"... and now, ladies and gentlemen —Marvo, and his blasted performing dogs!"

"Reelot Underfloor Heating?—I wish to make a complaint."

By the time the sixties came along the Laugh! page was also in full swing. This was the spot which showcased the pocket cartoon, offering scope to all kinds of new talent who flooded the *Record* office with their ideas. But what made them different from the modern breed was the fact that they went for a timeless gag rather than gearing their humour to the hot topic of the day. Alongside the Laugh! page in pocket form ran Calamity Gulch, a Wild Western belle who gave as good as she got! Top names like Keith Waite, the *Daily Mirror* political cartoonist also featured around the time.

Calamity Gulch

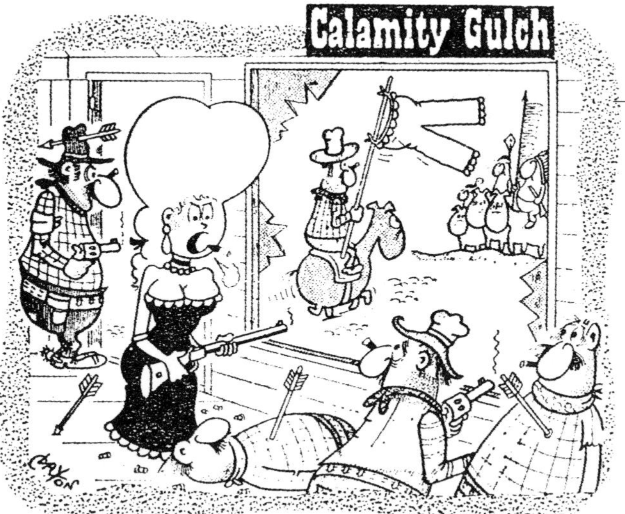
Calamity Gulch

"This is the very LAST time Ah help you guys out wi' a flag o' truce!"

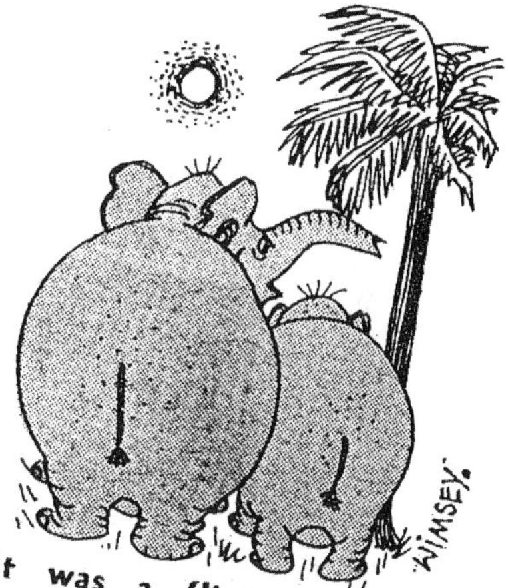
WIMSEY

"It was a flight of three hundred storks that brought you—now shut up!"

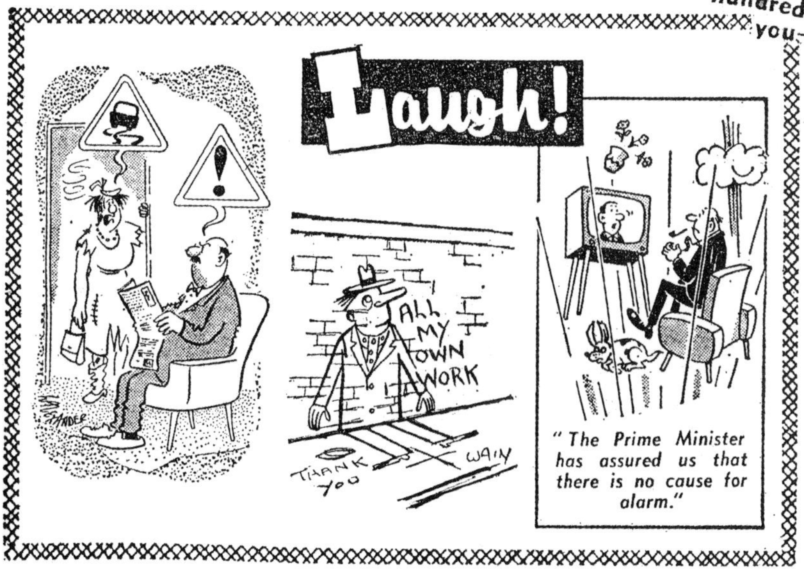
Laugh!
ALL MY OWN WORK
THANK YOU
WAIN

"The Prime Minister has assured us that there is no cause for alarm."

" I'd keep out of his Majesty's way this morning—there's been another big oil strike in the North Sea."

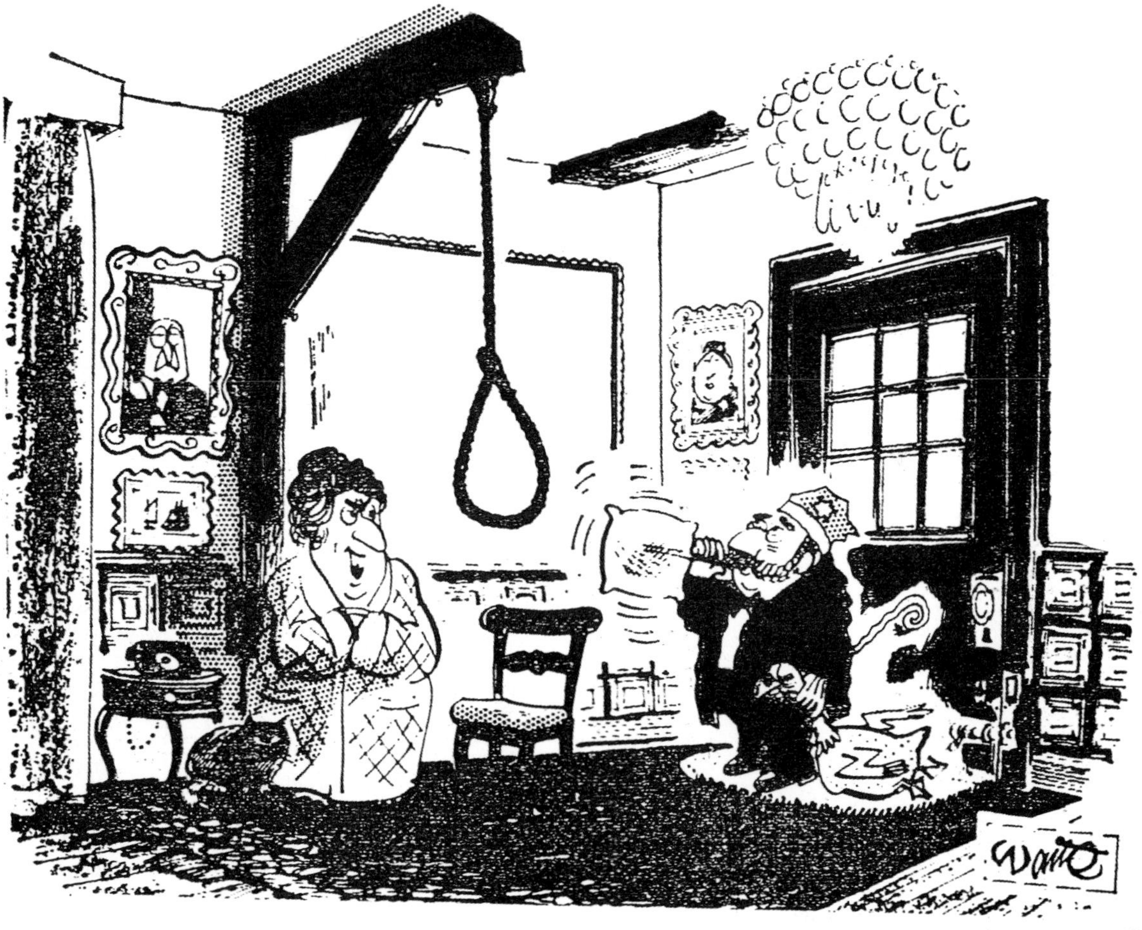
Waite

"Well, it's not necessarily going to be abolished in THIS house."

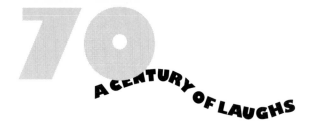

Into the Sixties with the Adventures of Angus Og

Angus Og had a close shave with destiny before he found his true home in the *Record*. He'd been born in *The Bulletin*, a mainly picture paper which was about to fall victim to the market forces of the day. But on the 1st of July 1960 the *Record* threw him a lifeline and he 'chust neffer' looked back.

Drawn by art teacher Ewen Bain the wily Angus, native Utter Hebridean, roamed the parish of Drambeg with his soul mate Lachie Mohr, intent on doing as little work as possible and, at all costs, avoiding the lovelorn Mairleen.

From the sea
chust like an
island

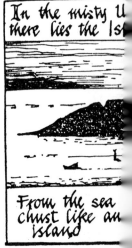

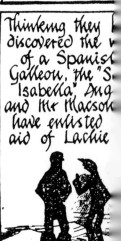

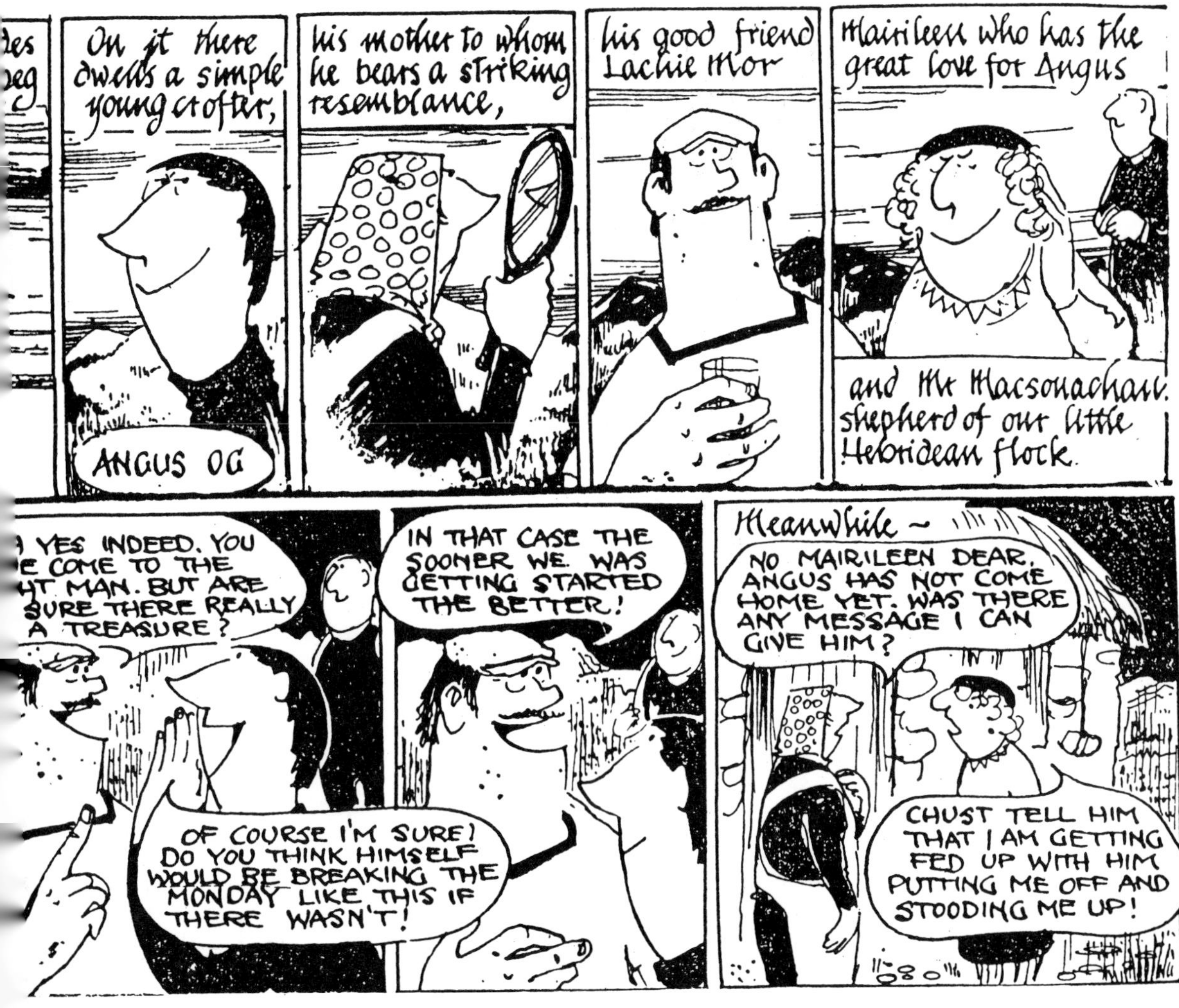
On it there dwells a simple young crofter,
ANGUS OG
his mother to whom he bears a striking resemblance,
his good friend Lachie Mor
Mairileen who has the great love for Angus
and Mr Macsonachan shepherd of our little Hebridean flock.
YES INDEED. YOU COME TO THE MAN. BUT ARE SURE THERE REALLY A TREASURE?
OF COURSE I'M SURE! DO YOU THINK HIMSELF WOULD BE BREAKING THE MONDAY LIKE THIS IF THERE WASN'T!
IN THAT CASE THE SOONER WE WAS GETTING STARTED THE BETTER!
Meanwhile ~
NO MAIRILEEN DEAR. ANGUS HAS NOT COME HOME YET. WAS THERE ANY MESSAGE I CAN GIVE HIM?
CHUST TELL HIM THAT I AM GETTING FED UP WITH HIM PUTTING ME OFF AND STOODING ME UP!

ANGUS OG

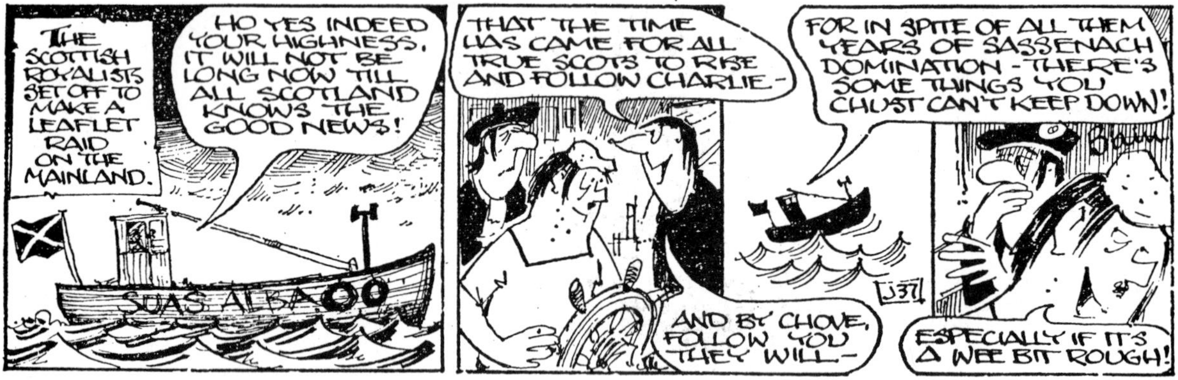
THE SCOTTISH ROYALISTS SET OFF TO MAKE A LEAFLET RAID ON THE MAINLAND.
HO YES INDEED YOUR HIGHNESS. IT WILL NOT BE LONG NOW TILL ALL SCOTLAND KNOWS THE GOOD NEWS!
SUAS ALBA
THAT THE TIME HAS CAME FOR ALL TRUE SCOTS TO RISE AND FOLLOW CHARLIE-
AND BY CHOVE, FOLLOW YOU THEY WILL-
J37
FOR IN SPITE OF ALL THEM YEARS OF SASSENACH DOMINATION - THERE'S SOME THINGS YOU CHUST CAN'T KEEP DOWN!
ESPECIALLY IF IT'S A WEE BIT ROUGH!

ANGUS OG

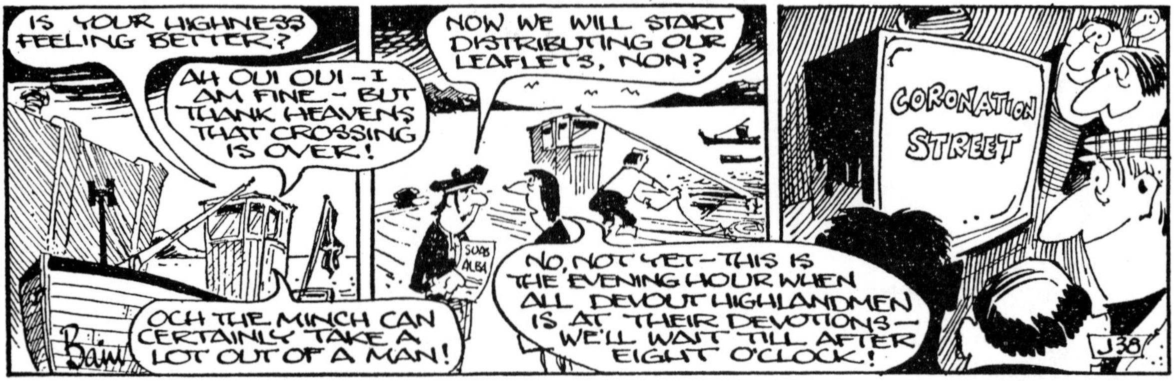
IS YOUR HIGHNESS FEELING BETTER?
AH OUI OUI - I AM FINE - BUT THANK HEAVENS THAT CROSSING IS OVER!
OCH THE MINCH CAN CERTAINLY TAKE A LOT OUT OF A MAN!
Bain
NOW WE WILL START DISTRIBUTING OUR LEAFLETS, NON?
SUAS ALBA
NO, NOT YET - THIS IS THE EVENING HOUR WHEN ALL DEVOUT HIGHLANDMEN IS AT THEIR DEVOTIONS - WE'LL WAIT TILL AFTER EIGHT O'CLOCK!
CORONATION STREET
J38

more Angus Og later... and in colour

ANGUS OG

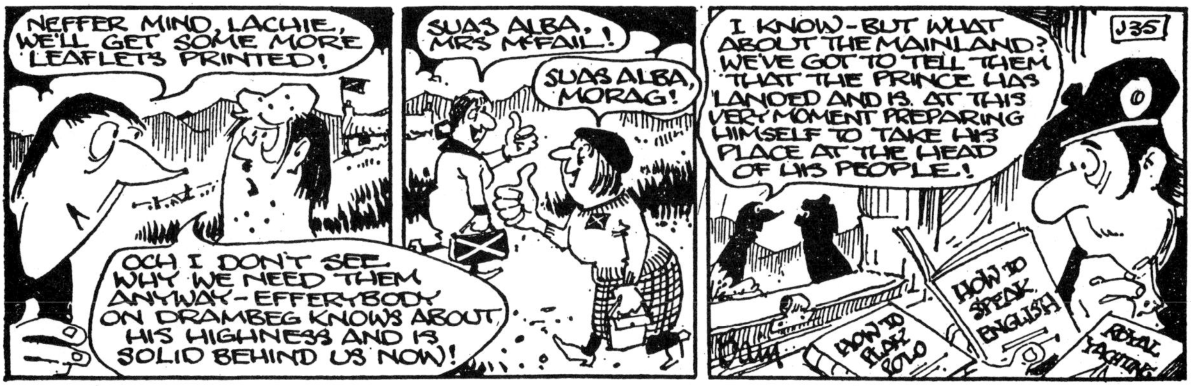
NEFFER MIND, LACHIE, WE'LL GET SOME MORE LEAFLETS PRINTED!
OCH I DON'T SEE WHY WE NEED THEM ANYWAY - EFFERYBODY ON DRAMBEG KNOWS ABOUT HIS HIGHNESS AND IS SOLID BEHIND US NOW!
SUAS ALBA, MRS McFAIL!
SUAS ALBA, MORAG!
J35
I KNOW - BUT WHAT ABOUT THE MAINLAND? WE'VE GOT TO TELL THEM THAT THE PRINCE HAS LANDED AND IS AT THIS VERY MOMENT PREPARING HIMSELF TO TAKE HIS PLACE AT THE HEAD OF HIS PEOPLE!
HOW TO PLAY SOLO
HOW TO SPEAK ENGLISH
ROYAL YACHTING

ANGUS OG

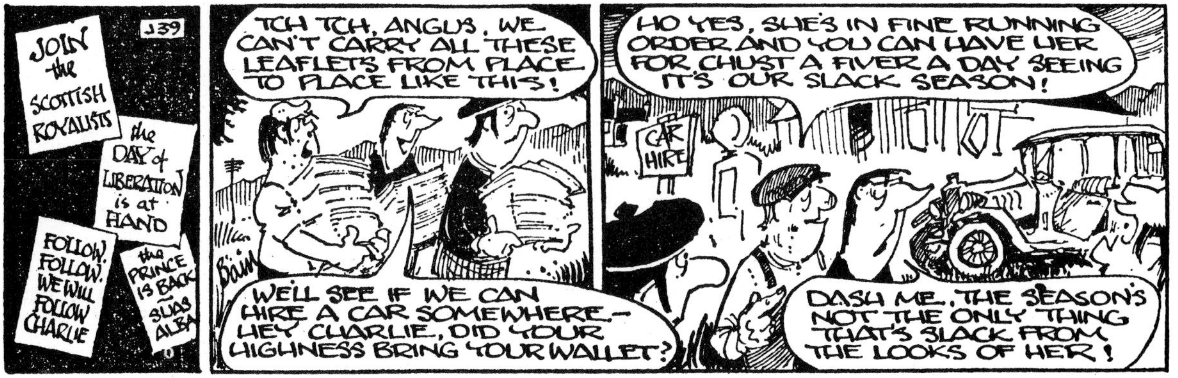
J39
JOIN the SCOTTISH ROYALISTS
the DAY of LIBERATION is at HAND
FOLLOW, FOLLOW, WE WILL FOLLOW CHARLIE
the PRINCE IS BACK - SUAS ALBA
TCH TCH, ANGUS, WE CAN'T CARRY ALL THESE LEAFLETS FROM PLACE TO PLACE LIKE THIS!
WE'LL SEE IF WE CAN HIRE A CAR SOMEWHERE - HEY CHARLIE, DID YOUR HIGHNESS BRING YOUR WALLET?
CAR HIRE
HO YES, SHE'S IN FINE RUNNING ORDER AND YOU CAN HAVE HER FOR CHUST A FIVER A DAY SEEING IT'S OUR SLACK SEASON!
DASH ME, THE SEASON'S NOT THE ONLY THING THAT'S SLACK FROM THE LOOKS OF HER!

Through the Sixties and into the Seventies

This was to prove a golden period for the *Record* as it began to overhaul, and finally overtake, the sales totals of all its rivals. And, again, part of the winning package was a cartoon element which soon became a page. Angus retained his pole position at the top, but plumbed into the mix, widening the appeal, came more sure-fire winners from syndicated stables including the ever popular Perishers. In some ways this resembled a UK version of Peanuts in as much as it starred some quarrelsome kids orchestrated by a female mini-mobster, all ultimately outgunned by a lovable, daffy dog.

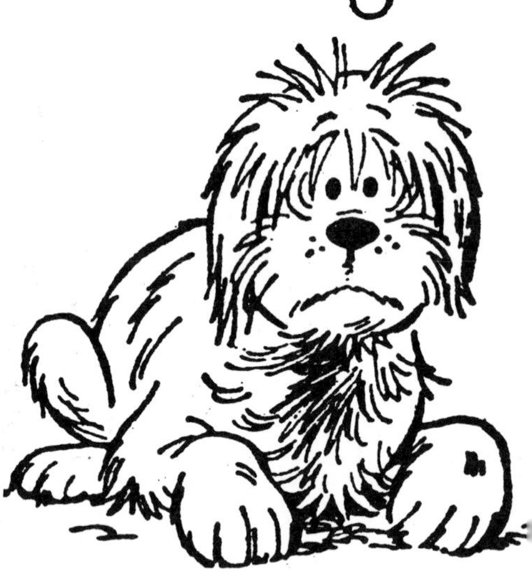

THE PERISHERS

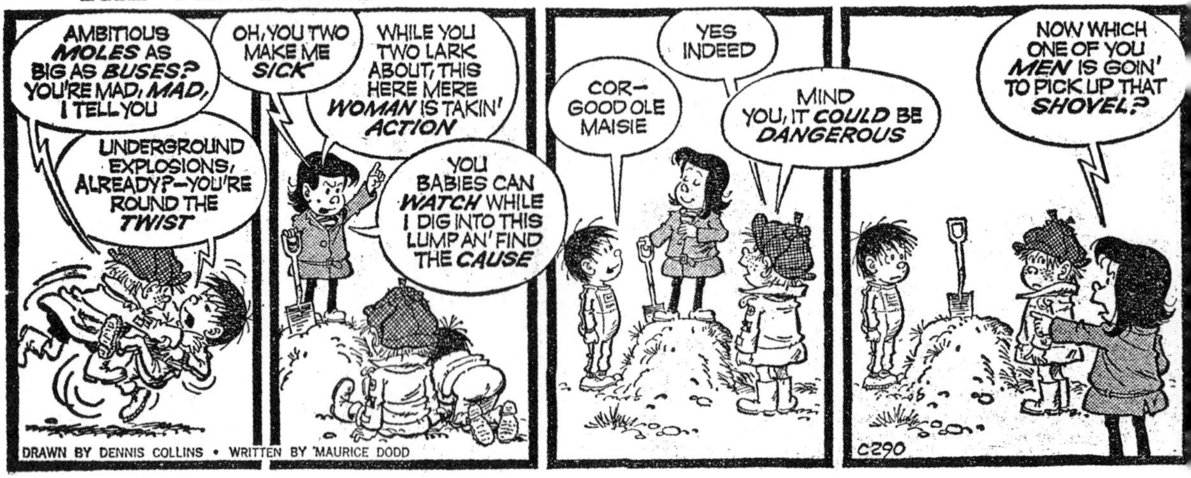
AMBITIOUS MOLES AS BIG AS BUSES? YOU'RE MAD, MAD, I TELL YOU
UNDERGROUND EXPLOSIONS, ALREADY?—YOU'RE ROUND THE TWIST
OH, YOU TWO MAKE ME SICK
WHILE YOU TWO LARK ABOUT, THIS HERE MERE WOMAN IS TAKIN' ACTION
YOU BABIES CAN WATCH WHILE I DIG INTO THIS LUMP AN' FIND THE CAUSE
COR—GOOD OLE MAISIE
YES INDEED
MIND YOU, IT COULD BE DANGEROUS
NOW WHICH ONE OF YOU MEN IS GOIN' TO PICK UP THAT SHOVEL?
DRAWN BY DENNIS COLLINS • WRITTEN BY MAURICE DODD
C290

THE PERISHERS

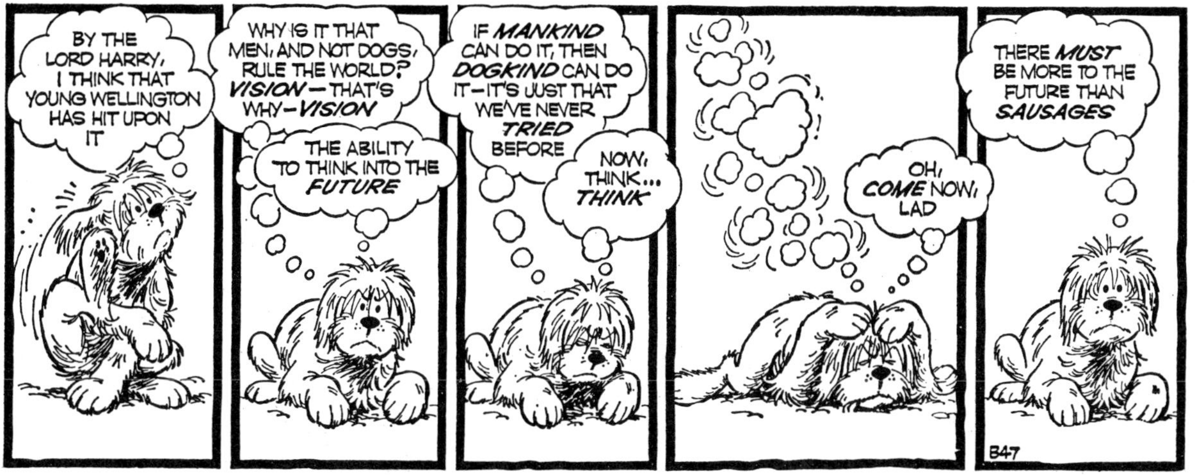
BY THE LORD HARRY, I THINK THAT YOUNG WELLINGTON HAS HIT UPON IT
WHY IS IT THAT MEN, AND NOT DOGS, RULE THE WORLD? VISION — THAT'S WHY — VISION
THE ABILITY TO THINK INTO THE FUTURE
IF MANKIND CAN DO IT, THEN DOGKIND CAN DO IT — IT'S JUST THAT WE'VE NEVER TRIED BEFORE
NOW, THINK... THINK
OH, COME NOW, LAD
THERE MUST BE MORE TO THE FUTURE THAN SAUSAGES
847

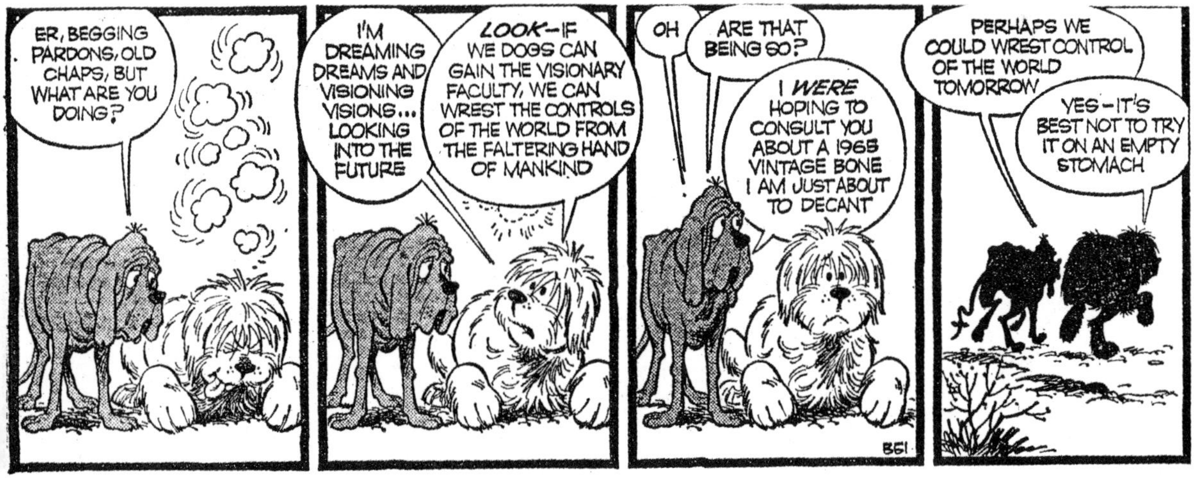
ER, BEGGING PARDONS, OLD CHAPS, BUT WHAT ARE YOU DOING?
I'M DREAMING DREAMS AND VISIONING VISIONS... LOOKING INTO THE FUTURE
LOOK — IF WE DOGS CAN GAIN THE VISIONARY FACULTY, WE CAN WREST THE CONTROLS OF THE WORLD FROM THE FALTERING HAND OF MANKIND
OH
ARE THAT BEING SO?
I WERE HOPING TO CONSULT YOU ABOUT A 1965 VINTAGE BONE I AM JUST ABOUT TO DECANT
PERHAPS WE COULD WREST CONTROL OF THE WORLD TOMORROW
YES — IT'S BEST NOT TO TRY IT ON AN EMPTY STOMACH
851

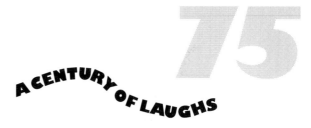

This was the era in which the *Record* pioneered daily colour which made the next move, colour cartoons, inevitable. Many of these were imported from the other side of the Atlantic. Vivienne Green brought us both 'Kisses' and 'Love Is'. That in turn spawned 'Agony Is' . . . and subsequently 'Aphrodite' and 'Virginia' by the artist Leon. They became fashionable around the hey day of the Page Three girls and left about the same time. They might have been funny, but we were moving into rather more politically correct times.

Kisses
By VIVIAN GREENE
WELL-L-L
IT LOOKS LIKE HIGH TIDE'S COMIN'.

ARE YOU GOING TO CHURCH ON CHRISTMAS, CLEVELAND?
OH YES! MY DAD TAKES ME TO CHURCH EVERY CHRISTMAS AND EASTER.
WHAT ABOUT THE REST OF THE YEAR?
HE HAS TO GO TO CHRISTMAS CLUB, TO WORSHIP WHAT HE WORSHIPS MOST... MONEY!

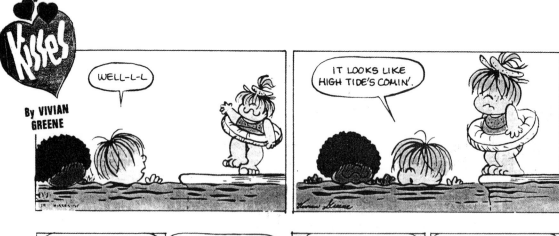

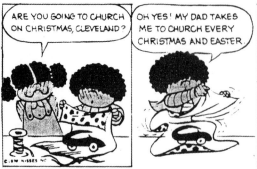

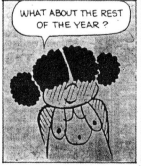

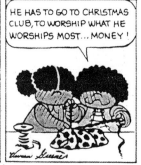

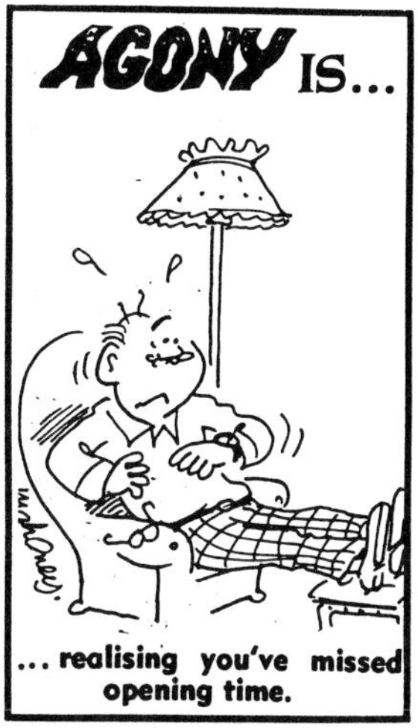
AGONY IS...
... realising you've missed opening time.

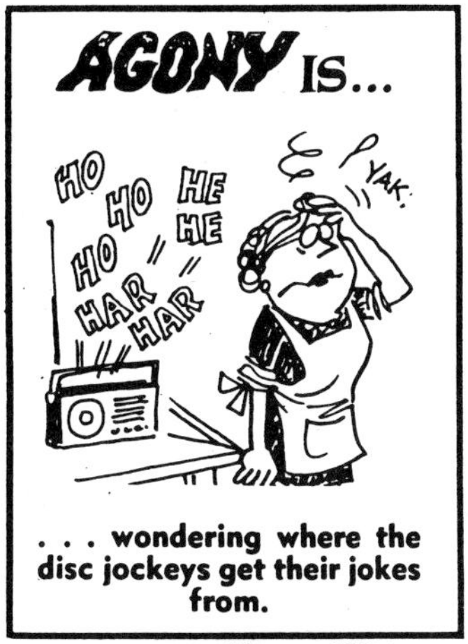
AGONY IS...
HO HO HE HE HO HAR HAR
YAK
. . . wondering where the disc jockeys get their jokes from.

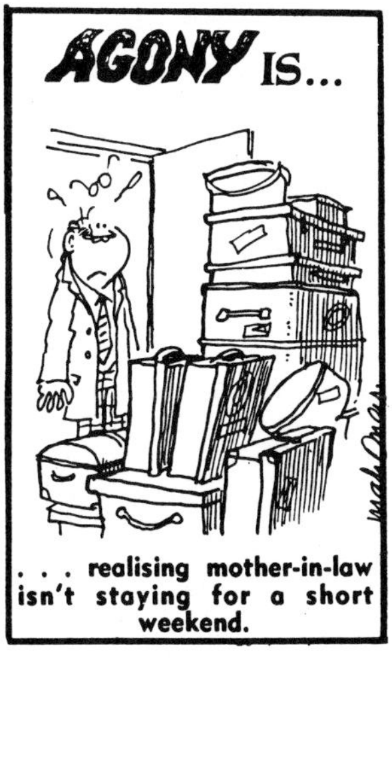
AGONY IS...
. . . realising mother-in-law isn't staying for a short weekend.

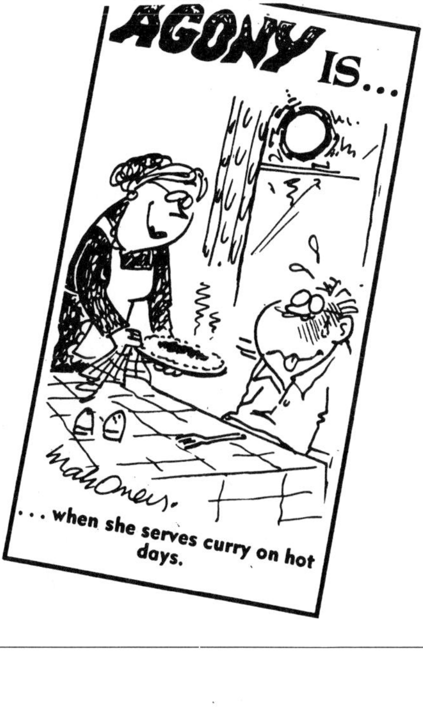
AGONY IS...
. . . when she serves curry on hot days.

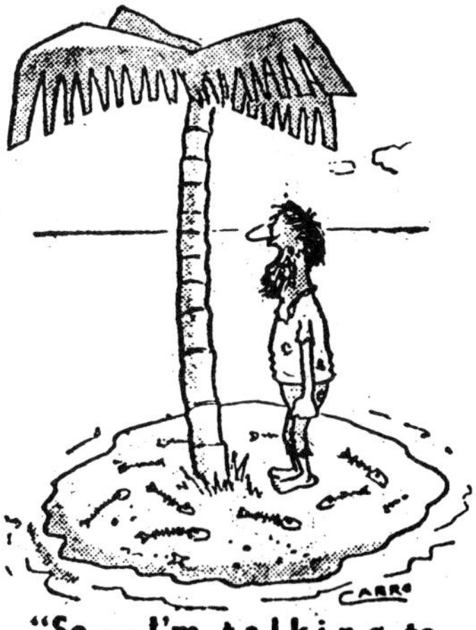
"So — I'm talking to myself. So what?"

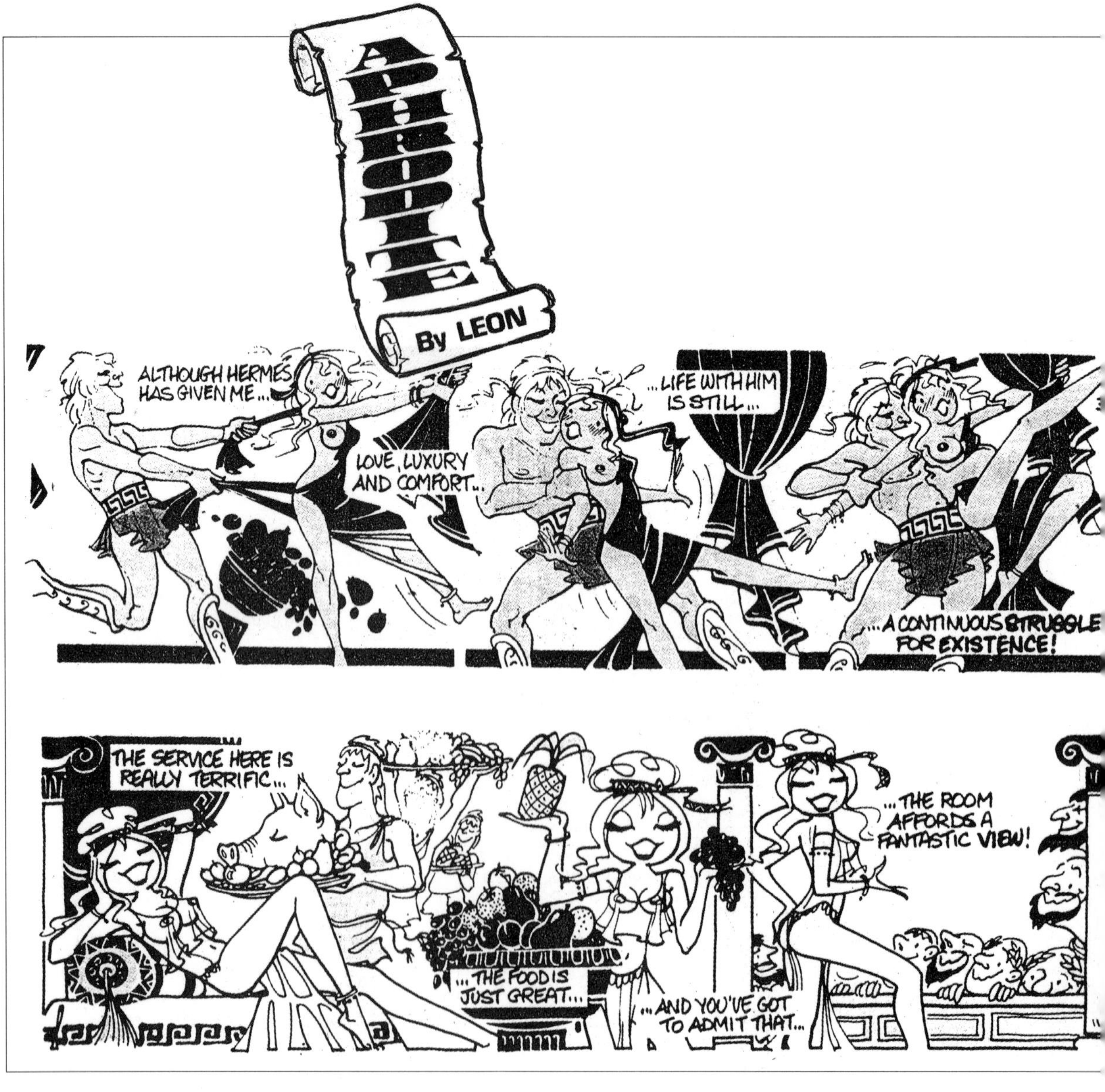
APHRODITE
By LEON
ALTHOUGH HERMES HAS GIVEN ME...
LOVE, LUXURY AND COMFORT...
...LIFE WITH HIM IS STILL...
...A CONTINUOUS STRUGGLE FOR EXISTENCE!
THE SERVICE HERE IS REALLY TERRIFIC...
...THE FOOD IS JUST GREAT...
...AND YOU'VE GOT TO ADMIT THAT...
...THE ROOM AFFORDS A FANTASTIC VIEW!

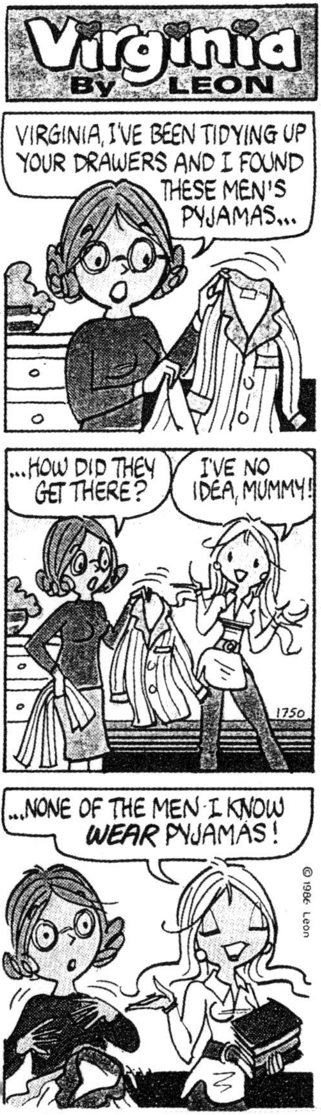
Virginia
By LEON
VIRGINIA, I'VE BEEN TIDYING UP YOUR DRAWERS AND I FOUND THESE MEN'S PYJAMAS...
...HOW DID THEY GET THERE?
I'VE NO IDEA, MUMMY!
1750
...NONE OF THE MEN I KNOW **WEAR** PYJAMAS!
© 1986 Leon

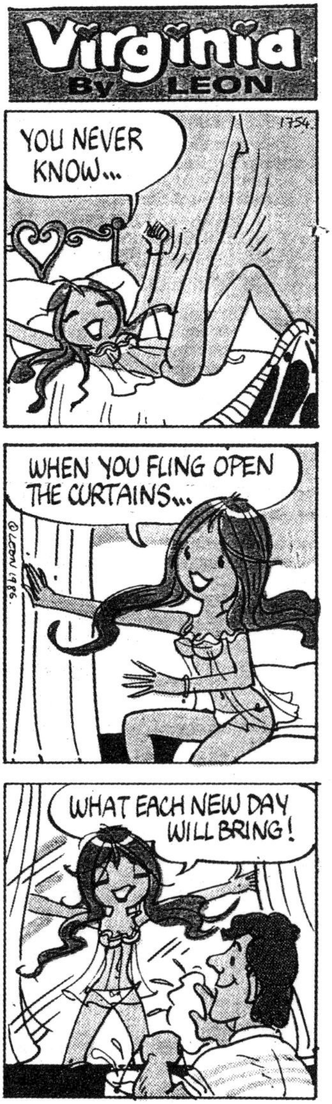
Virginia
By LEON
1754.
YOU NEVER KNOW...
WHEN YOU FLING OPEN THE CURTAINS...
© LEON 1986.
WHAT EACH NEW DAY WILL BRING!

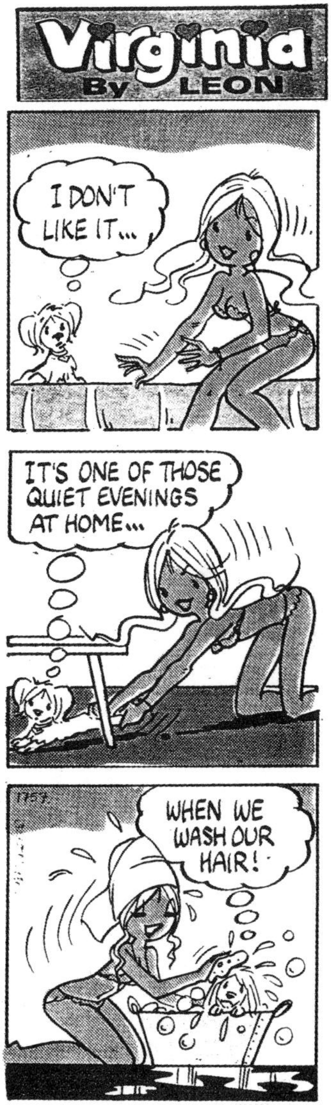
Virginia
By LEON
I DON'T LIKE IT...
IT'S ONE OF THOSE QUIET EVENINGS AT HOME...
1757.
WHEN WE WASH OUR HAIR!

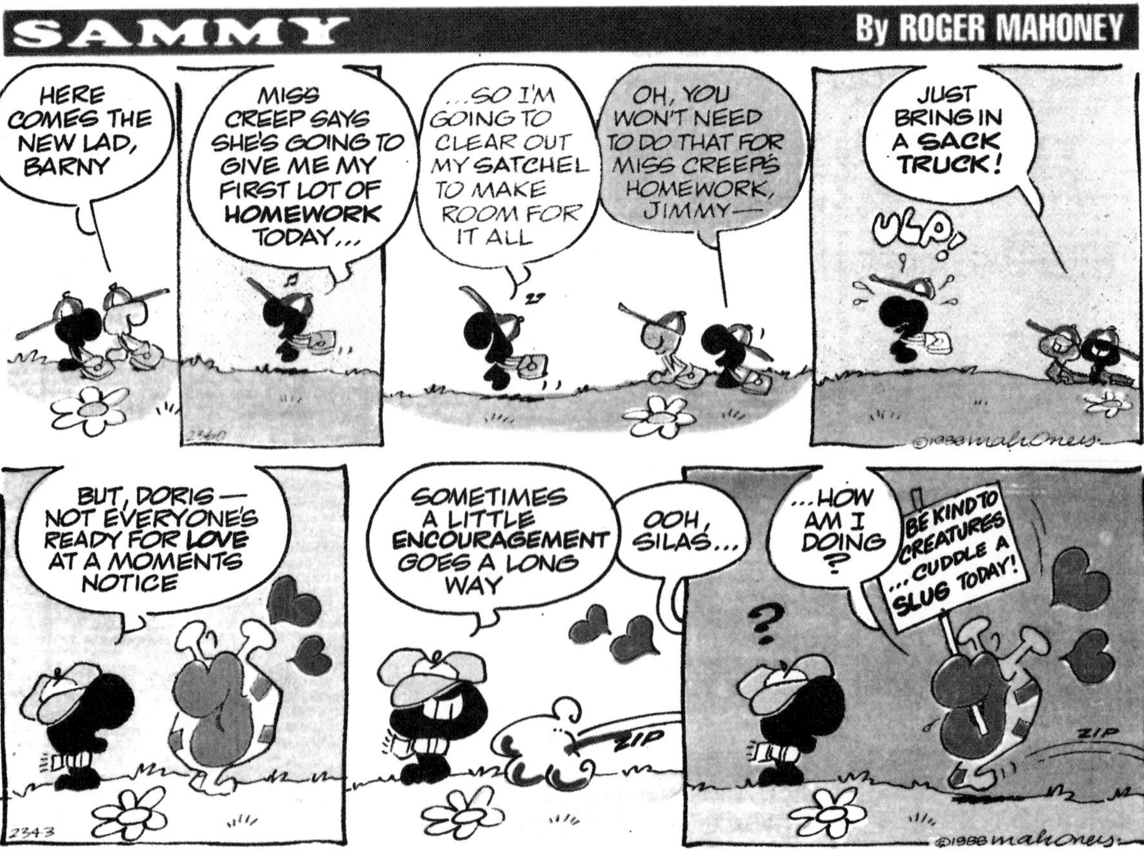
SAMMY
By ROGER MAHONEY
HERE COMES THE NEW LAD, BARNY
MISS CREEP SAYS SHE'S GOING TO GIVE ME MY FIRST LOT OF HOMEWORK TODAY...
...SO I'M GOING TO CLEAR OUT MY SATCHEL TO MAKE ROOM FOR IT ALL
OH, YOU WON'T NEED TO DO THAT FOR MISS CREEP'S HOMEWORK, JIMMY—
JUST BRING IN A SACK TRUCK!
ULP!
BUT, DORIS— NOT EVERYONE'S READY FOR LOVE AT A MOMENTS NOTICE
SOMETIMES A LITTLE ENCOURAGEMENT GOES A LONG WAY
OOH, SILAS...
ZIP
...HOW AM I DOING?
BE KIND TO CREATURES ...CUDDLE A SLUG TODAY!
ZIP

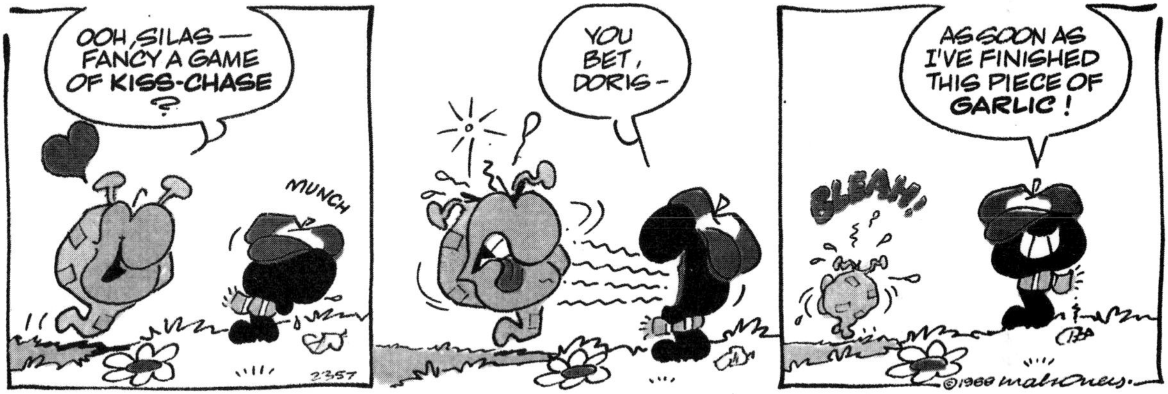
OOH, SILAS— FANCY A GAME OF KISS-CHASE ?
MUNCH
YOU BET, DORIS-
BLEAH!
AS SOON AS I'VE FINISHED THIS PIECE OF GARLIC !
©1988 mahoney

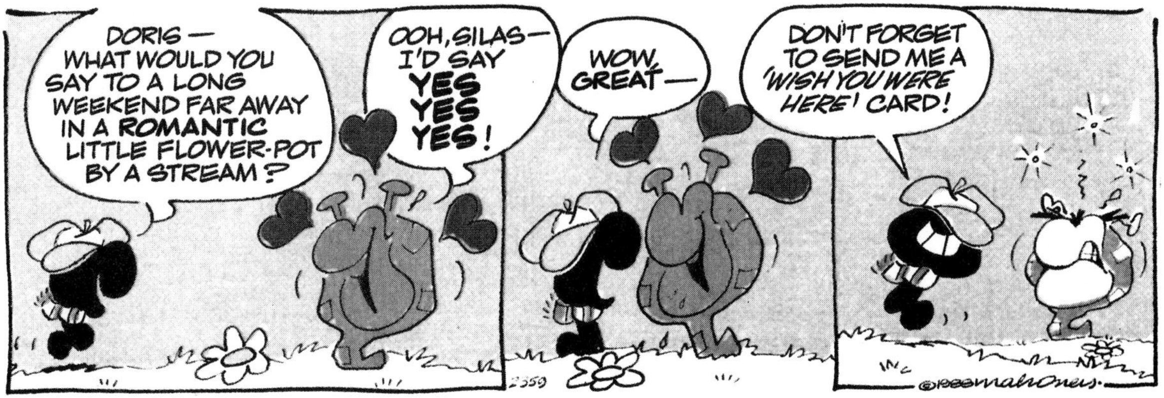
DORIS— WHAT WOULD YOU SAY TO A LONG WEEKEND FAR AWAY IN A ROMANTIC LITTLE FLOWER-POT BY A STREAM ?
OOH, SILAS— I'D SAY YES YES YES !
WOW, GREAT—
DON'T FORGET TO SEND ME A 'WISH YOU WERE HERE' CARD !
©1988 mahoney

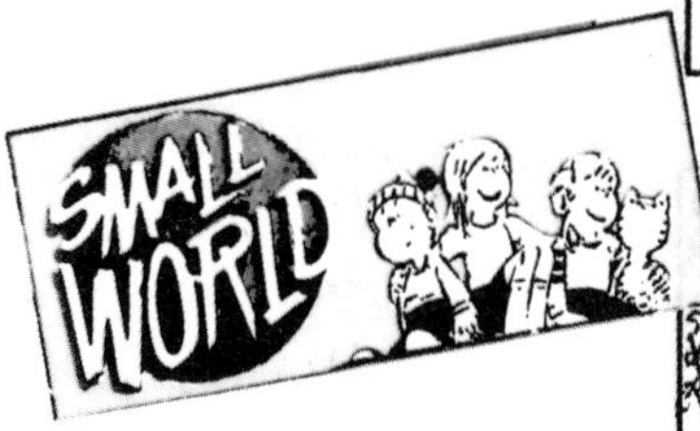
SMALL WORLD

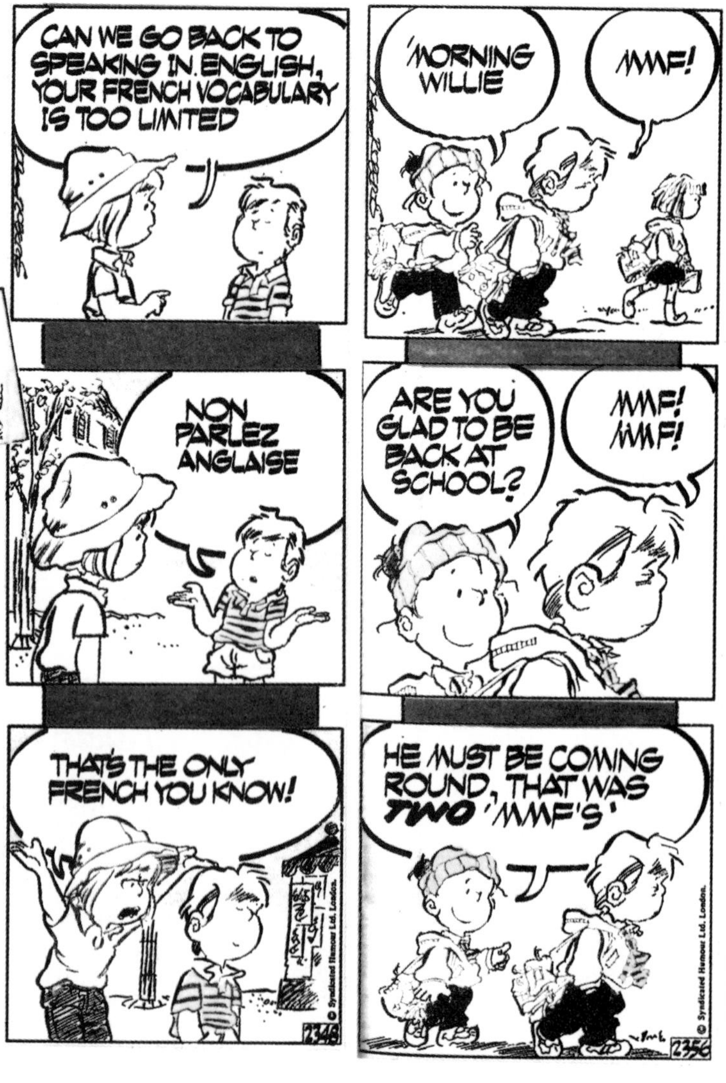
CAN WE GO BACK TO SPEAKING IN ENGLISH, YOUR FRENCH VOCABULARY IS TOO LIMITED
NON PARLEZ ANGLAISE
THAT'S THE ONLY FRENCH YOU KNOW!
'MORNING WILLIE
MMF!
ARE YOU GLAD TO BE BACK AT SCHOOL?
MMF! MMF!
HE MUST BE COMING ROUND, THAT WAS TWO 'MMF'S'

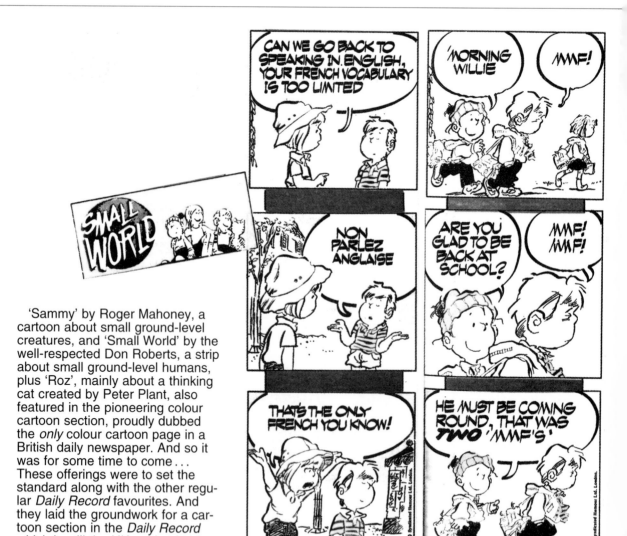

'Sammy' by Roger Mahoney, a cartoon about small ground-level creatures, and 'Small World' by the well-respected Don Roberts, a strip about small ground-level humans, plus 'Roz', mainly about a thinking cat created by Peter Plant, also featured in the pioneering colour cartoon section, proudly dubbed the *only* colour cartoon page in a British daily newspaper. And so it was for some time to come . . . These offerings were to set the standard along with the other regular *Daily Record* favourites. And they laid the groundwork for a cartoon section in the *Daily Record* which is still the UK market leader.

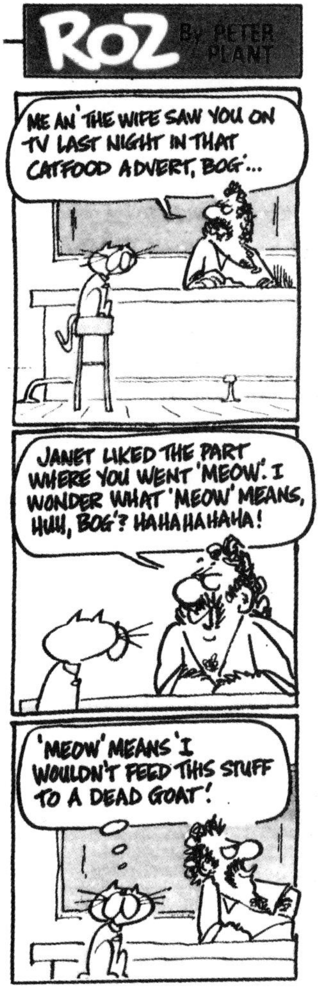
ROZ By PETER PLANT
ME AN' THE WIFE SAW YOU ON TV LAST NIGHT IN THAT CATFOOD ADVERT, BOG'...
JANET LIKED THE PART WHERE YOU WENT 'MEOW'. I WONDER WHAT 'MEOW' MEANS, HUH, BOG'? HAHAHAHAHA!
'MEOW' MEANS 'I WOULDN'T FEED THIS STUFF TO A DEAD GOAT'!

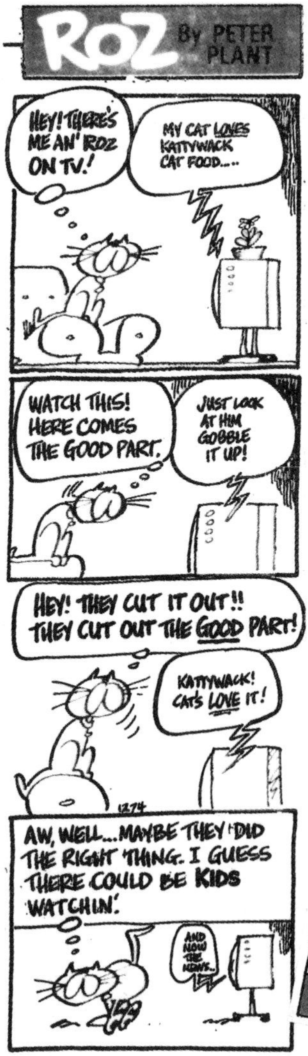
ROZ By PETER PLANT
HEY! THERE'S ME AN' ROZ ON TV!
MY CAT LOVES KATTYWACK CAT FOOD....
WATCH THIS! HERE COMES THE GOOD PART.
JUST LOOK AT HIM GOBBLE IT UP!
HEY! THEY CUT IT OUT!! THEY CUT OUT THE GOOD PART!
KATTYWACK! CAT'S LOVE IT!
AW, WELL...MAYBE THEY 'DID THE RIGHT 'THING. I GUESS THERE COULD BE KIDS WATCHIN'.
AND NOW THE NEWS...

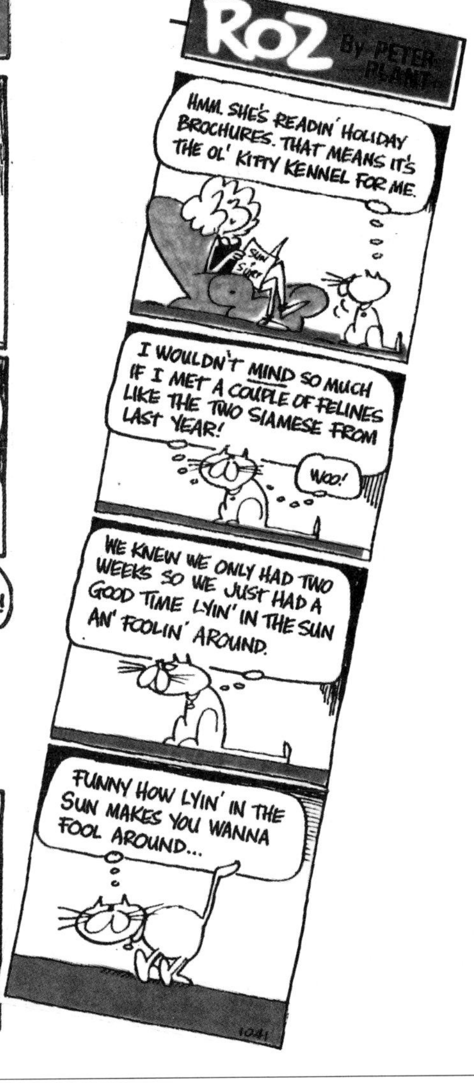
ROZ By PETER PLANT
HMM. SHE'S READIN' HOLIDAY BROCHURES. THAT MEANS IT'S THE OL' KITTY KENNEL FOR ME.
I WOULDN'T MIND SO MUCH IF I MET A COUPLE OF FELINES LIKE THE TWO SIAMESE FROM LAST YEAR!
WOO!
WE KNEW WE ONLY HAD TWO WEEKS SO WE JUST HAD A GOOD TIME LYIN' IN THE SUN AN' FOOLIN' AROUND.
FUNNY HOW LYIN' IN THE SUN MAKES YOU WANNA FOOL AROUND...

The LAUGH PARADE

"Congratulations, Capitan, you've been mentioned in dispatches— you're to be shot!"

"My slippers are facing the wrong way."

"Oh, Wallace lives his life, and I live mine."

POLICE BALL

"Aren't you from traffic control?"

"Don't be silly— we're not important enough to have a motor-cycle escort!"

From the Seventies through to the Nineties

While the Laughs! continued in colour and black and white another name joined the paper...

Rod a cartoonist of the pocket sized variety, hailed from the orient – arriving via the *West Lothian Courier* and the *Edinburgh Evening News*.

Surviving the initial culture shock, Rod launched into the daily adventure of trying to keep up with the sporting ongoings of the SFA, Rangers, the SFA, Celtic, the SFA, Hearts and Hibs, the SFA, the SRU, the SLTA, the SFL, the... well, all other sports organisations starting with 's'.

Rod, still stubbornly in black and white, now also contributes a topical news cartoon, thus proving that sports fans can do joined-up thinking as well. And when you think about it, politicians, soccer managers, civil servants, tennis stars, princesses, captains of industry and fly halfs all have much the same capacity to make a mess of their chosen trade. And there's just nothing more useful to the jobbing daily cartoonist than folks managing to get things spectacularly wrong.

" one shepherd's pie -- and hurry ! "

Rod on news

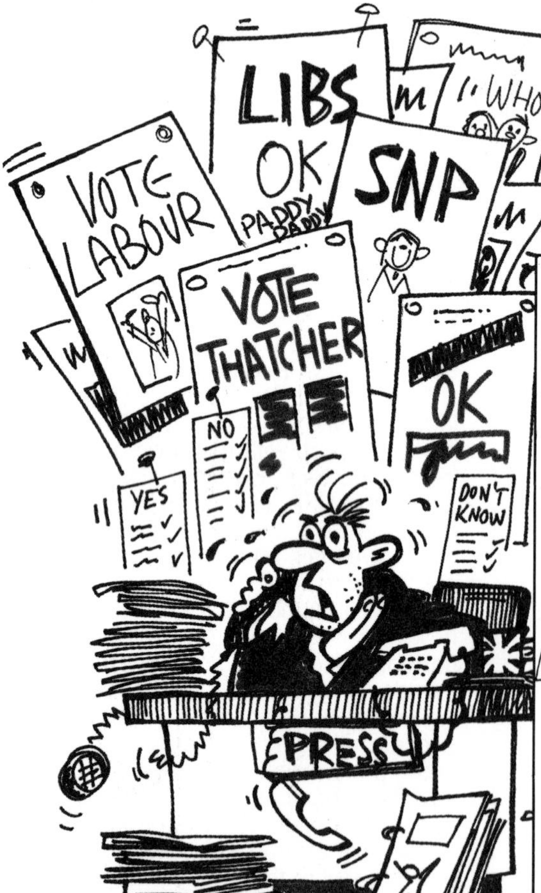
LIBS OK
PADDY
WHO
VOTE LABOUR
SNP
LOONIE PARTY
VOTE THATCHER
OK
NO
YES
DON'T KNOW
PRESS

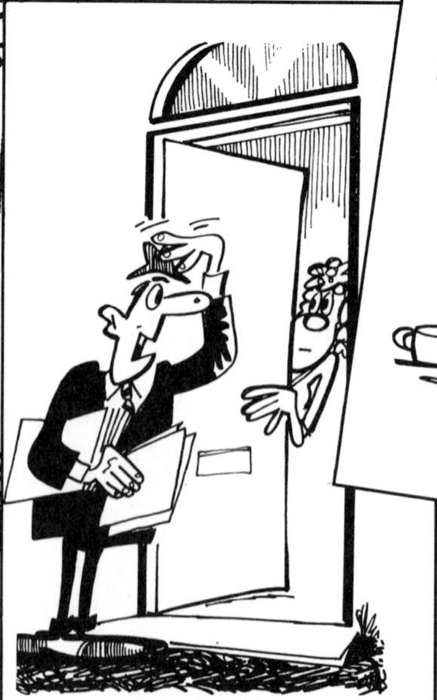

' you won't know me--
I'm your EURO MP

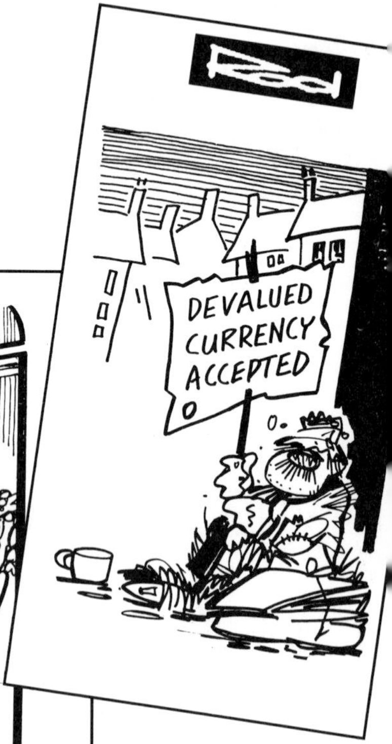
DEVALUED
CURRENCY
ACCEPTED

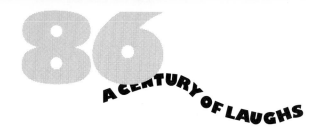

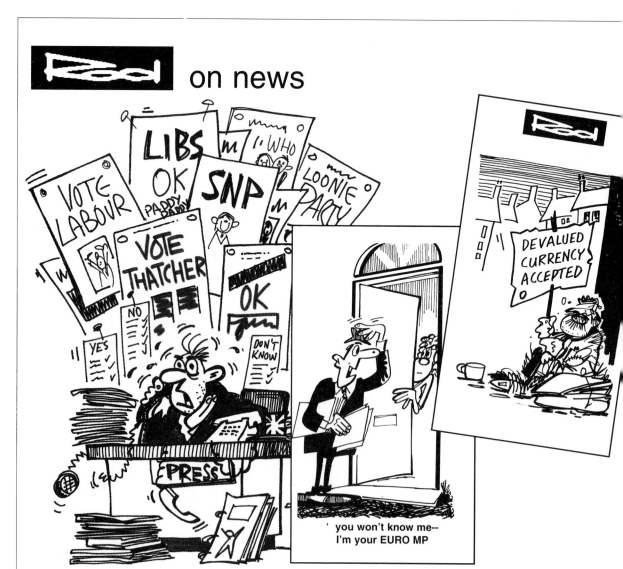

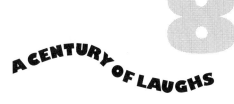

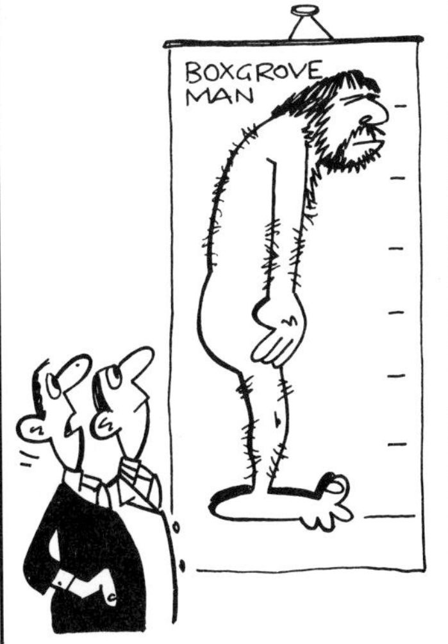
BOXGROVE MAN

' IS HE A LLOYDS NAME... '

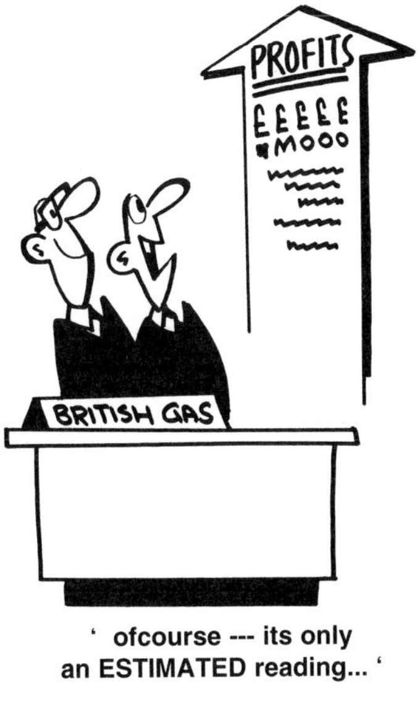
PROFITS
£££££
BRITISH GAS

' ofcourse --- its only an ESTIMATED reading... '

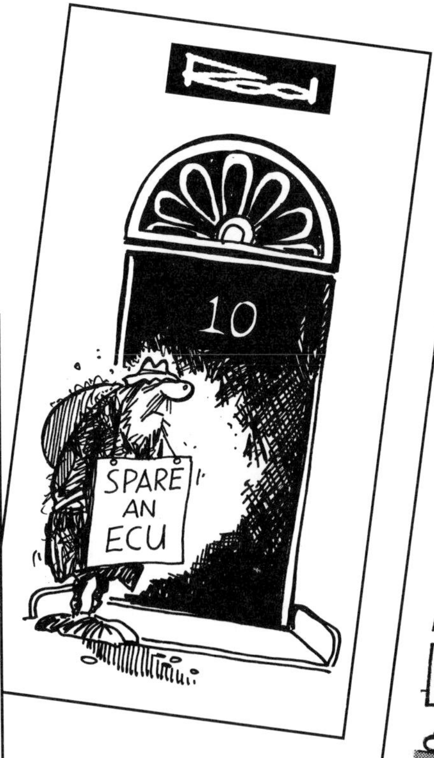
10
SPARE AN ECU

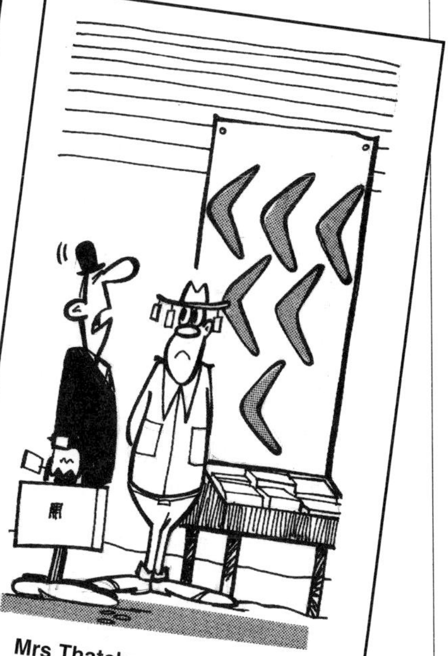

' Mrs Thatcher won't like them... they only do U TURNS...'

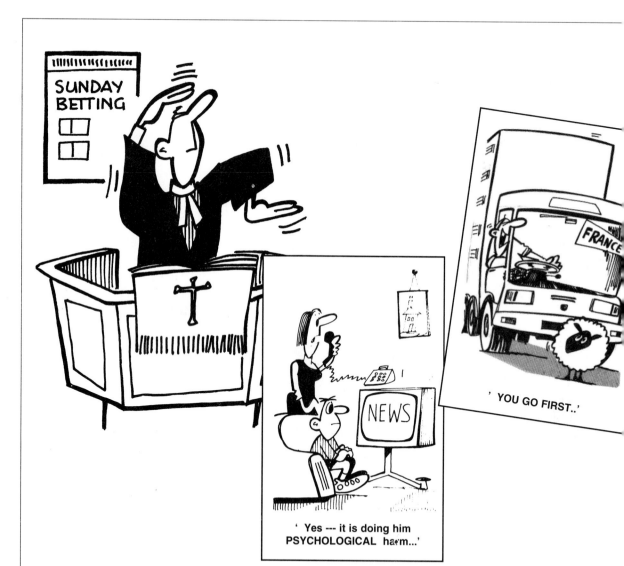

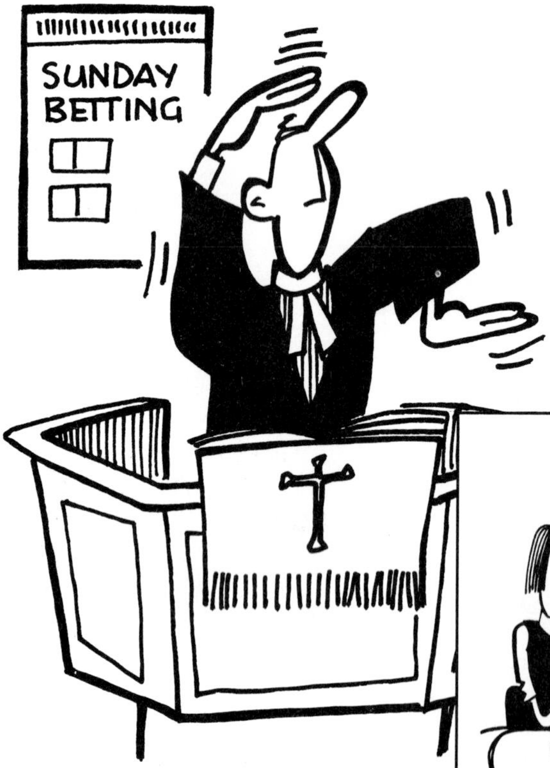
SUNDAY
BETTING

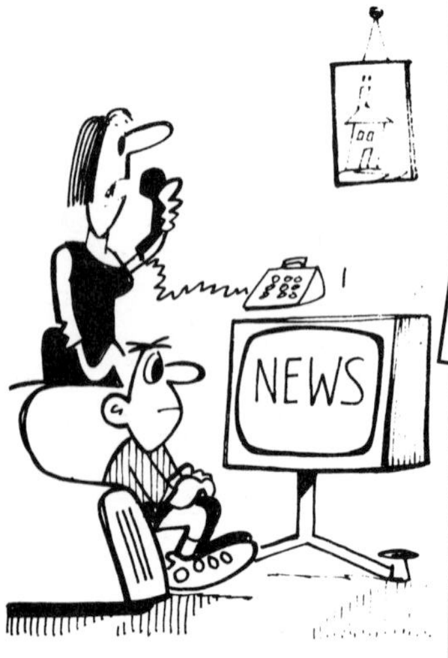
NEWS

' Yes --- it is doing him
PSYCHOLOGICAL harm...'

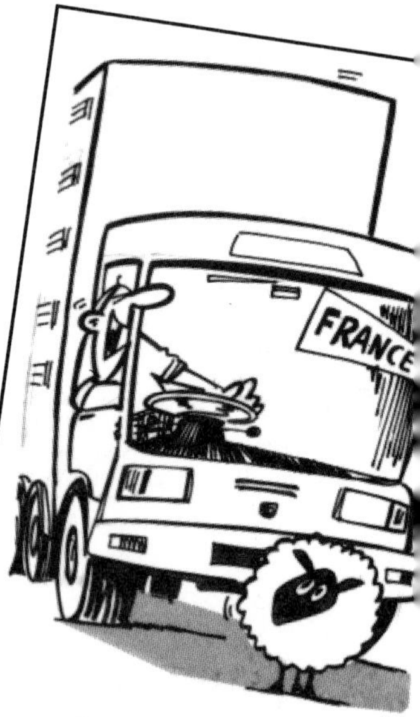
FRANCE

' YOU GO FIRST..'

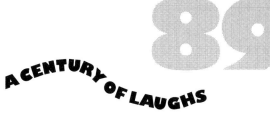

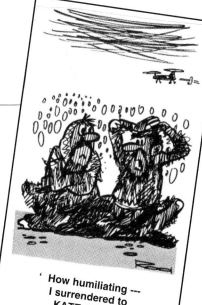

' How humiliating ---
I surrendered to
KATE ADIE...'

HOSPITAL

' AM I IN THE
RIGHT PLACE...'

IRAQ

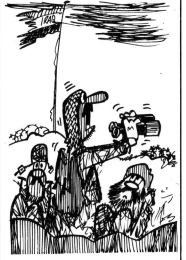

' Here they come...CBS, ABC,
NBC, BBC, SKY, ITN, ZDF.
DSF and CNN ... '

FAMILY DOCTOR

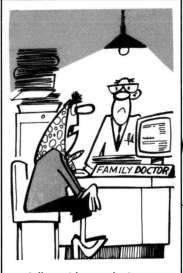

' I'm not happy doctor ---
I may take my illness
elsewhare... '

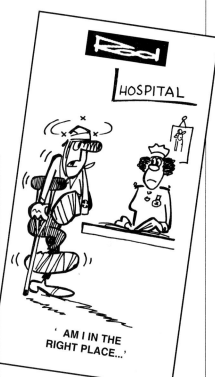

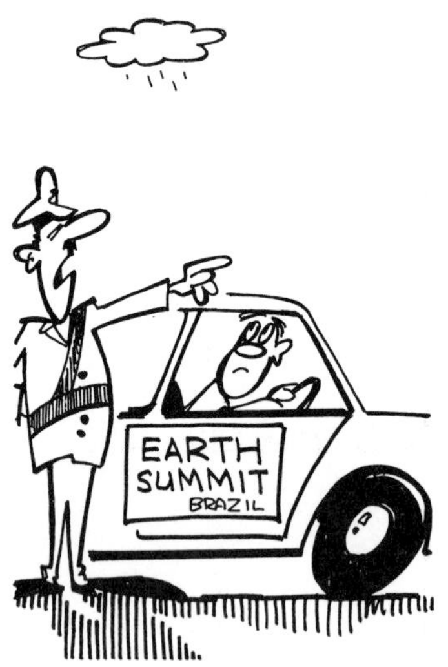
EARTH
SUMMIT
BRAZIL

' FOLLOW WHAT USED TO BE THE RAIN FORREST..'

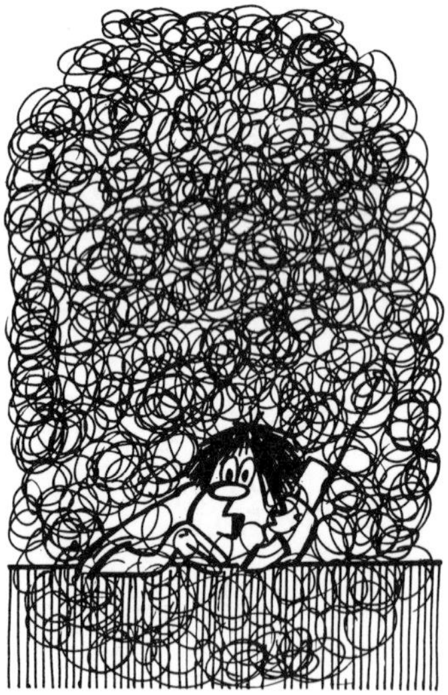

' I honestely don't know how many a day --- I'm a passive smoker ... '

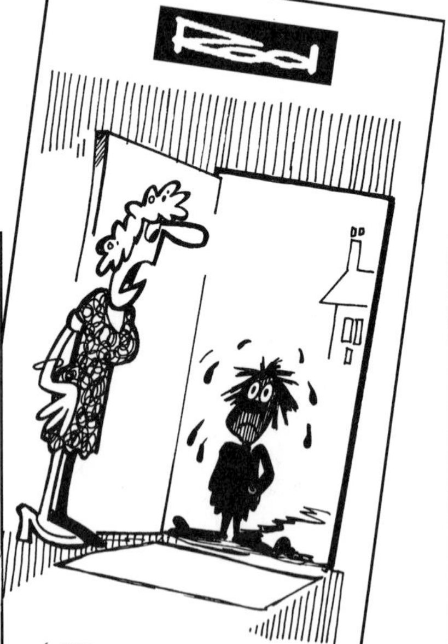

' YOU'VE BEEN AT THE BEACH AGAIN... '

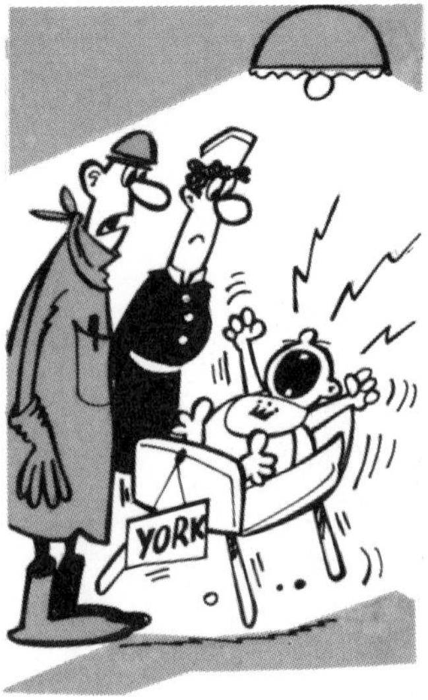
YORK

' SHE LOOKS MORE LIKE A PRIME MINISTER THAN A QUEEN...'

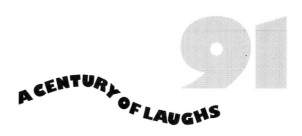

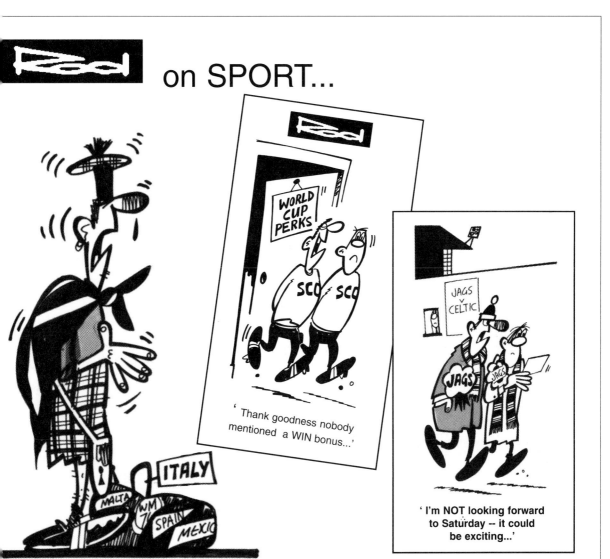

Rod on SPORT...

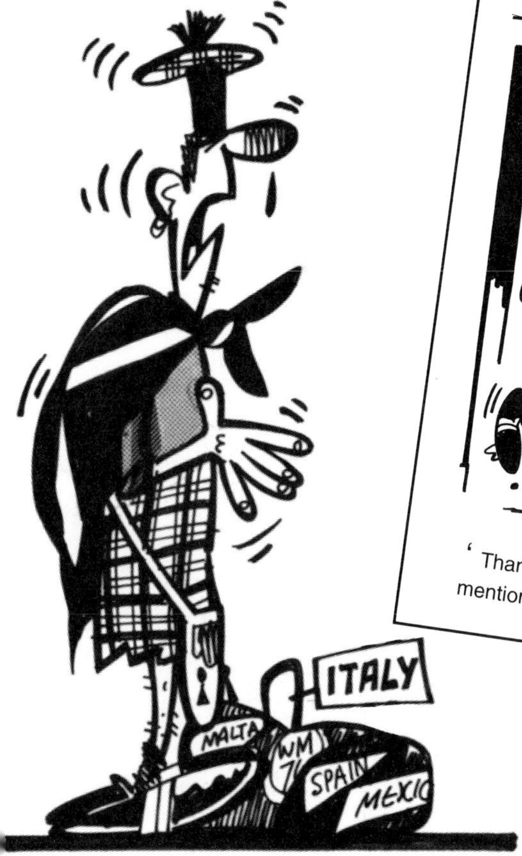
ITALY
MALTA
SPAIN
MEXIC

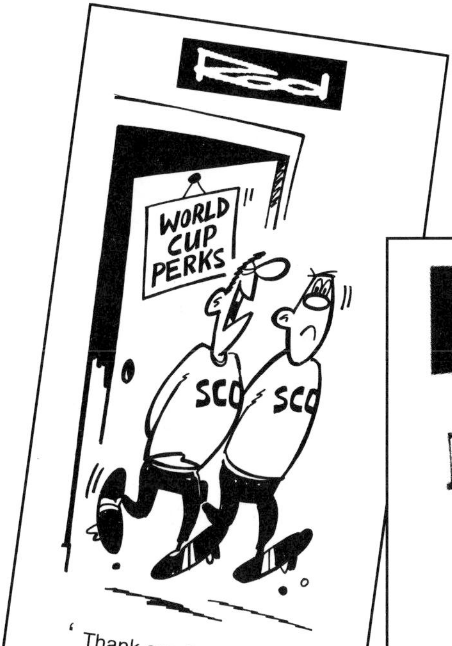
WORLD CUP PERKS
SCO
SCO

'Thank goodness nobody mentioned a WIN bonus...'

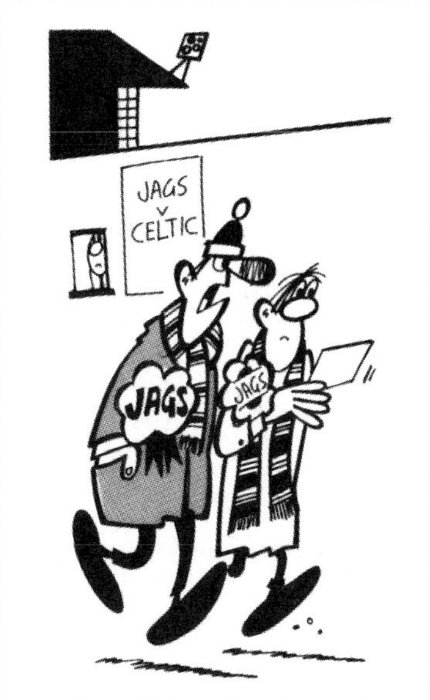
JAGS v CELTIC
JAGS
JAGS

'I'm NOT looking forward to Saturday -- it could be exciting...'

100M
STARTER

SCOTTISH TENNIS

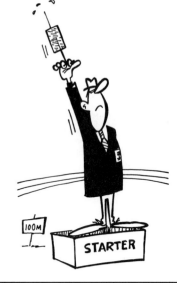

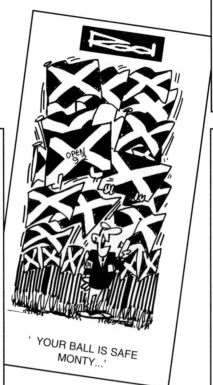

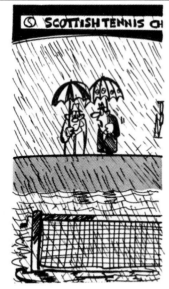

' WE'VE HAD A LATE ENTRY -- DAVID WILKIE... '

OPEN 92

' YOUR BALL IS SAFE MONTY...'

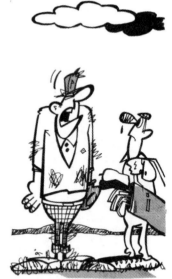

' If I play as badly again -- I'm going to fire you...'

SAUDI

‘ Just think -- in 20 years he’ll be able to play for the under 16 team... ‘

YOB
EN
ENG

‘ ... DISAPPOINTED --- I EVEN FORGOT TO MUG SOMEBODY... ‘

‘ But ref - what evidence do you have...’

ACTOR OF THE YEAR

GENOVA
TYSON KO
MANDELA FREE

' Wullie - we could win the World Cup..."

' CAN I BORROW THE SHEET AFTER YOU...'

The JUNGLE

" ITS GOIN' TO THE HALL OF FAME..."

USA 94

' DON'T WORRY, YOU'LL GET USED TO IT...'

But let's return to that Hebridean hooligan, Angus Og, unofficial laird of Drambeg...

ANGUS OG

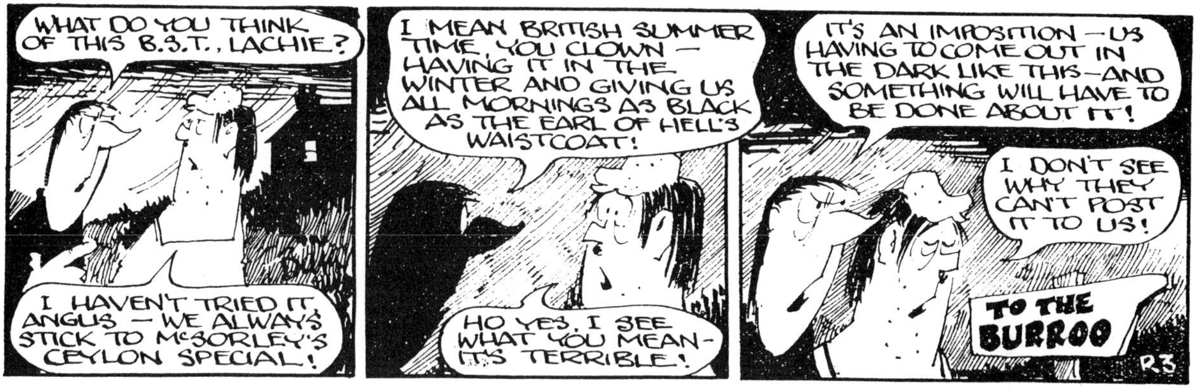
WHAT DO YOU THINK OF THIS B.S.T., LACHIE?
I HAVEN'T TRIED IT, ANGUS – WE ALWAYS STICK TO McSORLEY'S CEYLON SPECIAL!
I MEAN BRITISH SUMMER TIME, YOU CLOWN – HAVING IT IN THE WINTER AND GIVING US ALL MORNINGS AS BLACK AS THE EARL OF HELL'S WAISTCOAT!
HO YES, I SEE WHAT YOU MEAN – IT'S TERRIBLE!
IT'S AN IMPOSITION – US HAVING TO COME OUT IN THE DARK LIKE THIS – AND SOMETHING WILL HAVE TO BE DONE ABOUT IT!
I DON'T SEE WHY THEY CAN'T POST IT TO US!
TO THE BURROO

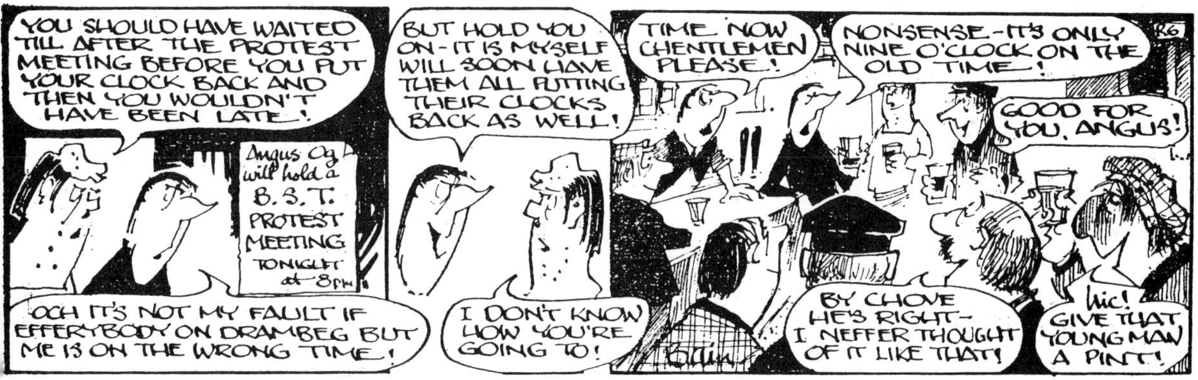
YOU SHOULD HAVE WAITED TILL AFTER THE PROTEST MEETING BEFORE YOU PUT YOUR CLOCK BACK AND THEN YOU WOULDN'T HAVE BEEN LATE!
Angus Og will hold a B.S.T. PROTEST MEETING TONIGHT at 8pm
OCH IT'S NOT MY FAULT IF EFFERYBODY ON DRAMBEG BUT ME IS ON THE WRONG TIME!
BUT HOLD YOU ON – IT IS MYSELF WILL SOON HAVE THEM ALL PUTTING THEIR CLOCKS BACK AS WELL!
I DON'T KNOW HOW YOU'RE GOING TO!
TIME NOW CHENTLEMEN PLEASE!
NONSENSE – IT'S ONLY NINE O'CLOCK ON THE OLD TIME!
GOOD FOR YOU, ANGUS!
BY CHOVE HE'S RIGHT – I NEFFER THOUGHT OF IT LIKE THAT!
hic! GIVE THAT YOUNG MAN A PINT!

Angus, it was, who first made that bold step into glorious technicolour!

So now enjoy an early Angus Og adventure, with the bonus of today's colour stalwarts . . . 'Shuggie and Duggie', Tom Bullimore and Kev White's adventures over a wall; 'Prince of the Palace' by Michael Atkinson – corgi tales from inside Buck House; Bryan Walker's 'Grandad and the Lad', the problems of a grandad with a grand lad; and 'A Man Called Horace' from Andrew Christine and Roger Kettle featuring a bear, a snake, and other assorted animals including cowboys and indians.

Proof, if any were needed, that every age produces men and women able to make us laugh at ourselves. Who knows where the cartoonists of the next century will come from? The only safe bet is that if they're good enough, and funny enough, you'll find them in the pages of the *Daily Record.*

LOOKING FOR ANGUS?

He's in our new colour cartoon section on Page 37

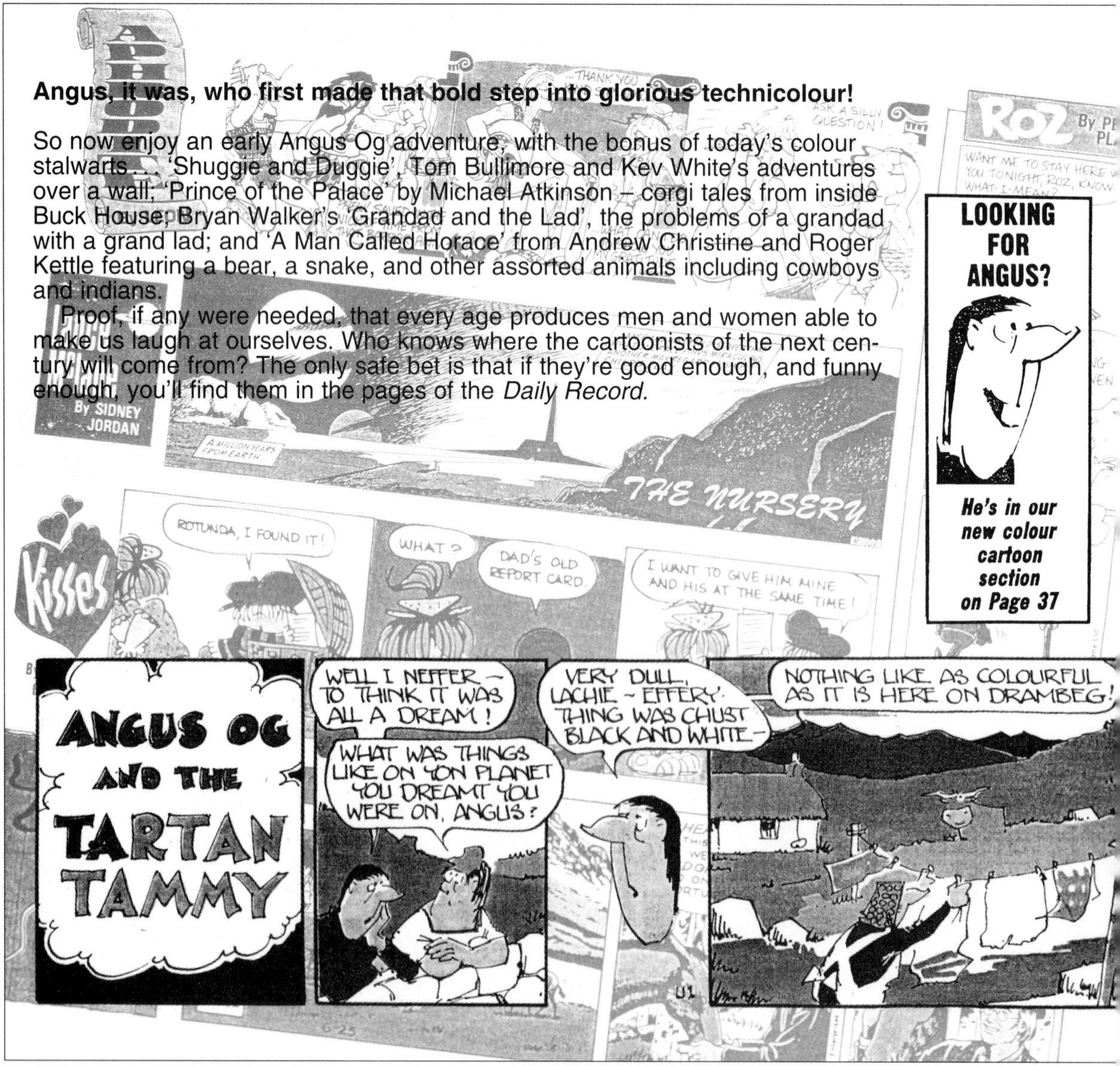
THE NURSERY
ROTUNDA, I FOUND IT!
WHAT?
DAD'S OLD REPORT CARD.
I WANT TO GIVE HIM MINE AND HIS AT THE SAME TIME!
ANGUS OG AND THE TARTAN TAMMY
WELL I NEFFER — TO THINK IT WAS ALL A DREAM!
WHAT WAS THINGS LIKE ON YON PLANET YOU DREAMT YOU WERE ON, ANGUS?
VERY DULL, LACHIE – EFFERY THING WAS CHUST BLACK AND WHITE –
NOTHING LIKE AS COLOURFUL AS IT IS HERE ON DRAMBEG!

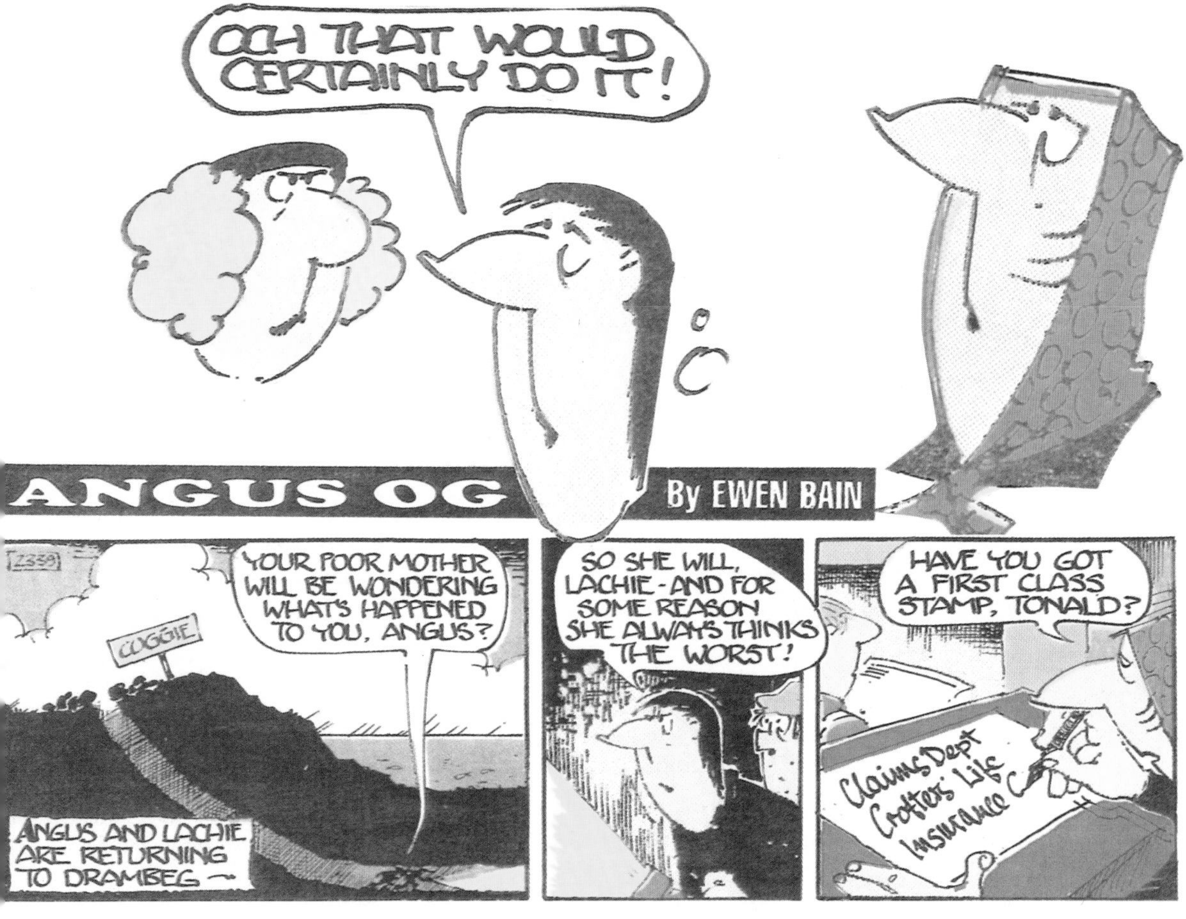
OCH THAT WOULD CERTAINLY DO IT!
ANGUS OG
By EWEN BAIN
YOUR POOR MOTHER WILL BE WONDERING WHAT'S HAPPENED TO YOU, ANGUS?
CUGGIE
ANGUS AND LACHIE ARE RETURNING TO DRAMBEG —
SO SHE WILL, LACHIE - AND FOR SOME REASON SHE ALWAYS THINKS THE WORST!
HAVE YOU GOT A FIRST CLASS STAMP, TONALD?
Claims Dept Crofters' Life Insurance C

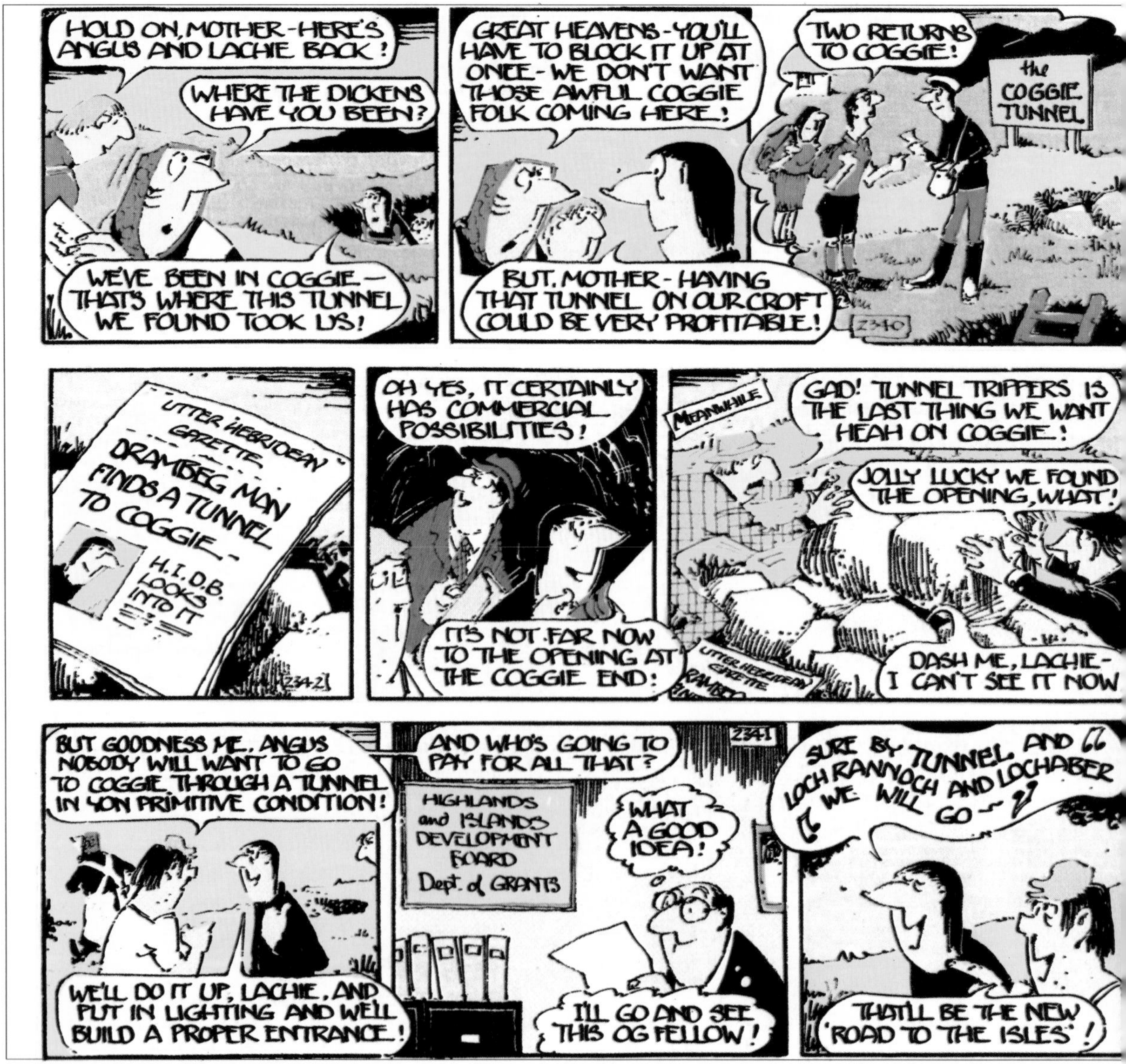
HOLD ON, MOTHER - HERE'S ANGUS AND LACHIE BACK!
WHERE THE DICKENS HAVE YOU BEEN?
WE'VE BEEN IN COGGIE - THAT'S WHERE THIS TUNNEL WE FOUND TOOK US!
GREAT HEAVENS - YOU'LL HAVE TO BLOCK IT UP AT ONCE - WE DON'T WANT THOSE AWFUL COGGIE FOLK COMING HERE!
BUT, MOTHER - HAVING THAT TUNNEL ON OUR CROFT COULD BE VERY PROFITABLE!
TWO RETURNS TO COGGIE!
the COGGIE TUNNEL
2340
UTTER HEBRIDEAN GAZETTE
DRAMBEG MAN FINDS A TUNNEL TO COGGIE
H.I.D.B. LOOKS INTO IT
2342
OH YES, IT CERTAINLY HAS COMMERCIAL POSSIBILITIES!
IT'S NOT FAR NOW TO THE OPENING AT THE COGGIE END!
MEANWHILE
GAD! TUNNEL TRIPPERS IS THE LAST THING WE WANT HEAH ON COGGIE!
JOLLY LUCKY WE FOUND THE OPENING, WHAT!
DASH ME, LACHIE - I CAN'T SEE IT NOW
UTTER HEBRIDEAN GAZETTE
BUT GOODNESS ME, ANGUS NOBODY WILL WANT TO GO TO COGGIE THROUGH A TUNNEL IN YON PRIMITIVE CONDITION!
WE'LL DO IT UP, LACHIE, AND PUT IN LIGHTING AND WE'LL BUILD A PROPER ENTRANCE!
AND WHO'S GOING TO PAY FOR ALL THAT?
2341
HIGHLANDS and ISLANDS DEVELOPMENT BOARD Dept. of GRANTS
WHAT A GOOD IDEA!
I'LL GO AND SEE THIS OG FELLOW!
"SURE BY TUNNEL AND LOCH RANNOCH AND LOCHABER WE WILL GO -"
THAT'LL BE THE NEW 'ROAD TO THE ISLES'!

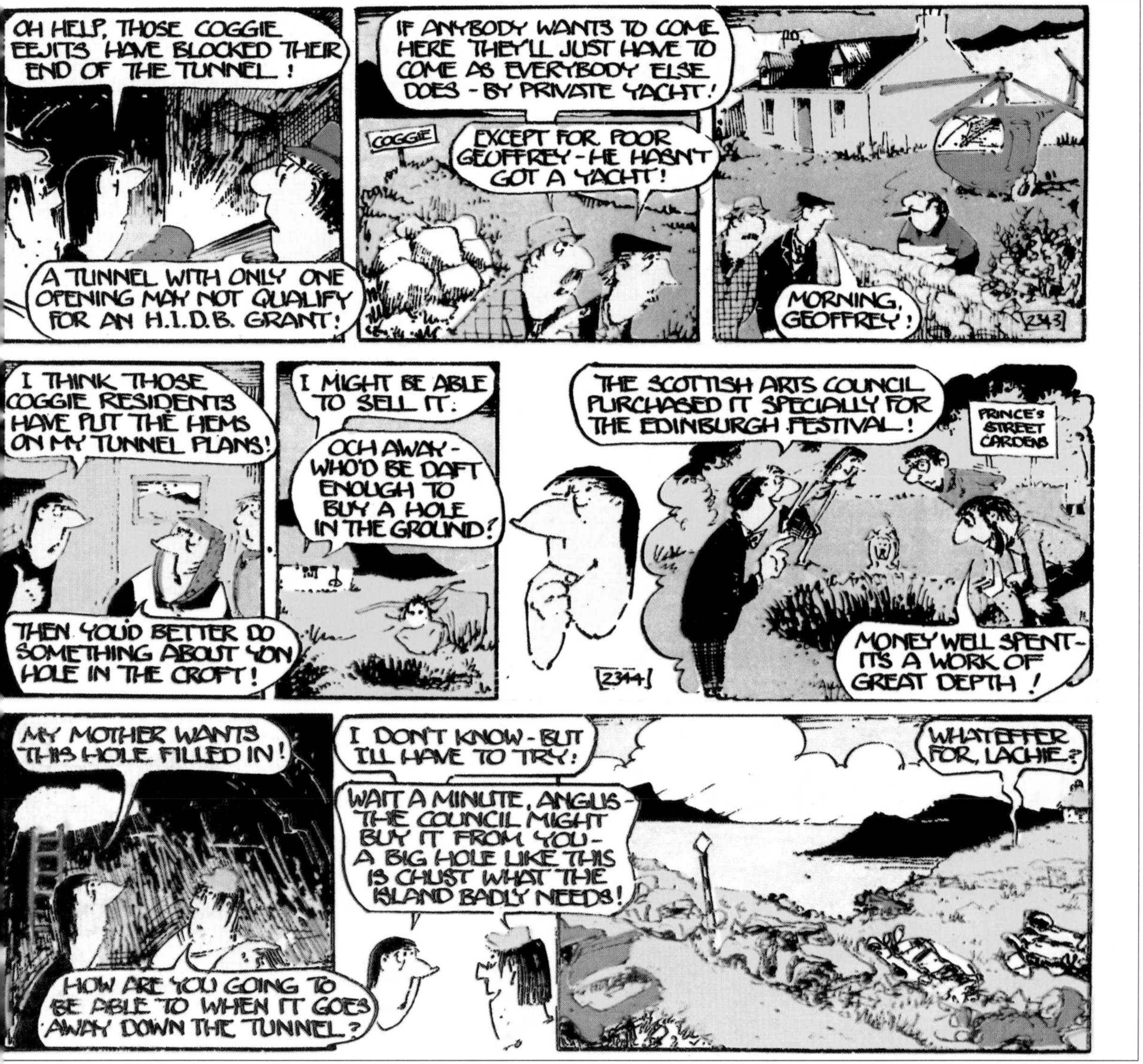
OH HELP, THOSE COGGIE EEJITS HAVE BLOCKED THEIR END OF THE TUNNEL!
A TUNNEL WITH ONLY ONE OPENING MAY NOT QUALIFY FOR AN H.I.D.B. GRANT!
IF ANYBODY WANTS TO COME HERE THEY'LL JUST HAVE TO COME AS EVERYBODY ELSE DOES - BY PRIVATE YACHT!
COGGIE
EXCEPT FOR POOR GEOFFREY - HE HASN'T GOT A YACHT!
MORNING, GEOFFREY!
2343
I THINK THOSE COGGIE RESIDENTS HAVE PUT THE HEMS ON MY TUNNEL PLANS!
THEN YOU'D BETTER DO SOMETHING ABOUT YON HOLE IN THE CROFT!
I MIGHT BE ABLE TO SELL IT.
OCH AWAY - WHO'D BE DAFT ENOUGH TO BUY A HOLE IN THE GROUND?
2344
THE SCOTTISH ARTS COUNCIL PURCHASED IT SPECIALLY FOR THE EDINBURGH FESTIVAL!
PRINCE'S STREET GARDENS
MONEY WELL SPENT - IT'S A WORK OF GREAT DEPTH!
MY MOTHER WANTS THIS HOLE FILLED IN!
HOW ARE YOU GOING TO BE ABLE TO WHEN IT GOES AWAY DOWN THE TUNNEL?
I DON'T KNOW - BUT I'LL HAVE TO TRY!
WAIT A MINUTE, ANGUS - THE COUNCIL MIGHT BUY IT FROM YOU - A BIG HOLE LIKE THIS IS CHUST WHAT THE ISLAND BADLY NEEDS!
WHATEFFER FOR, LACHIE?

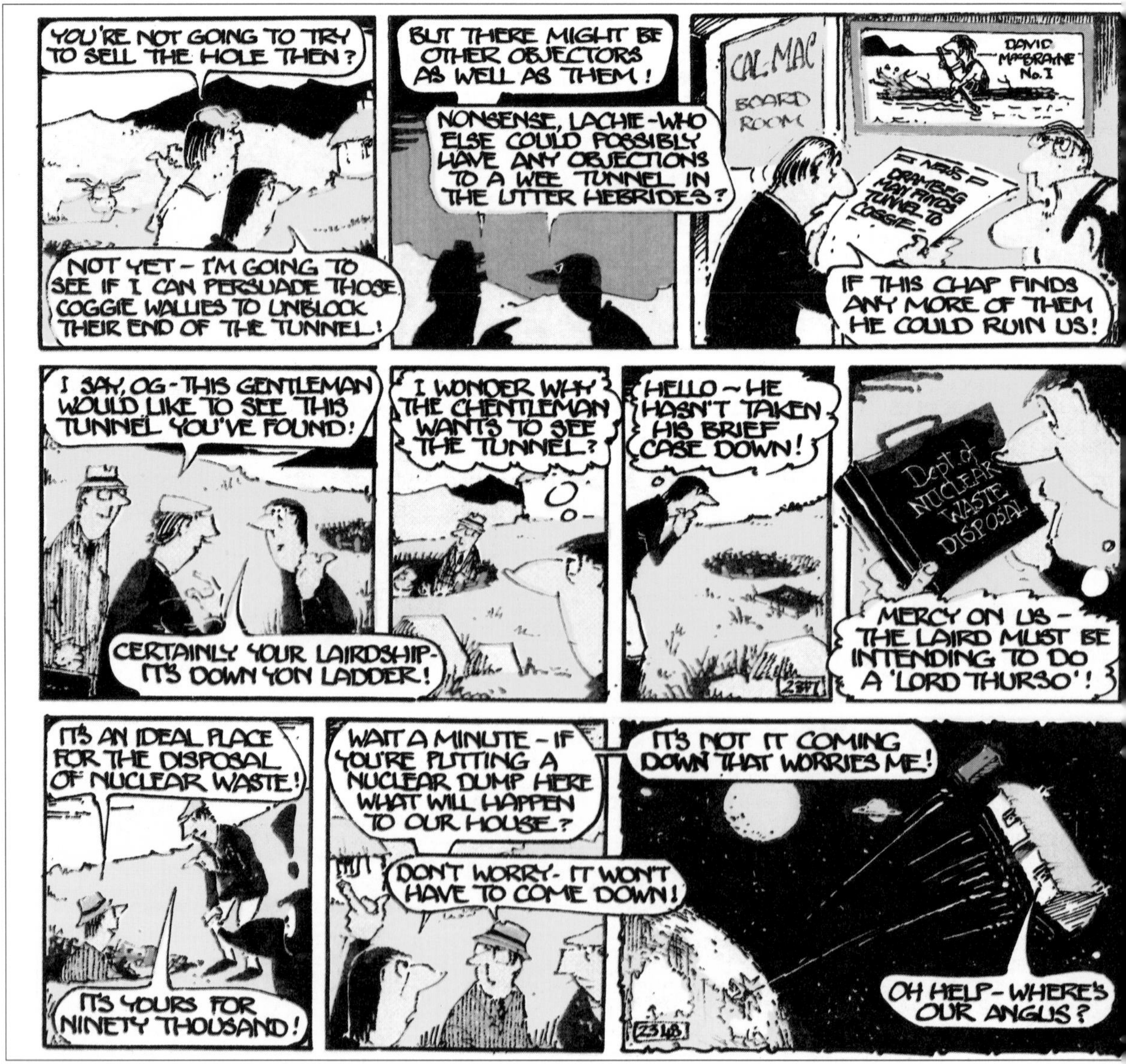
YOU'RE NOT GOING TO TRY TO SELL THE HOLE THEN?
NOT YET – I'M GOING TO SEE IF I CAN PERSUADE THOSE COGGIE WALLIES TO UNBLOCK THEIR END OF THE TUNNEL!
BUT THERE MIGHT BE OTHER OBJECTORS AS WELL AS THEM!
NONSENSE, LACHIE – WHO ELSE COULD POSSIBLY HAVE ANY OBJECTIONS TO A WEE TUNNEL IN THE UTTER HEBRIDES?
CAL-MAC
BOARD ROOM
DAVID MacBRAYNE No. I
NEWS
DRAMBEG MAN FINDS TUNNEL TO COGGIE
IF THIS CHAP FINDS ANY MORE OF THEM HE COULD RUIN US!
I SAY, OG – THIS GENTLEMAN WOULD LIKE TO SEE THIS TUNNEL YOU'VE FOUND!
CERTAINLY YOUR LAIRDSHIP – IT'S DOWN YON LADDER!
I WONDER WHY THE CHENTLEMAN WANTS TO SEE THE TUNNEL?
HELLO – HE HASN'T TAKEN HIS BRIEF CASE DOWN!
Dept of NUCLEAR WASTE DISPOSAL
MERCY ON US – THE LAIRD MUST BE INTENDING TO DO A 'LORD THURSO'!
IT'S AN IDEAL PLACE FOR THE DISPOSAL OF NUCLEAR WASTE!
IT'S YOURS FOR NINETY THOUSAND!
WAIT A MINUTE – IF YOU'RE PUTTING A NUCLEAR DUMP HERE WHAT WILL HAPPEN TO OUR HOUSE?
DON'T WORRY – IT WON'T HAVE TO COME DOWN!
IT'S NOT IT COMING DOWN THAT WORRIES ME!
OH HELP – WHERE'S OUR ANGUS?

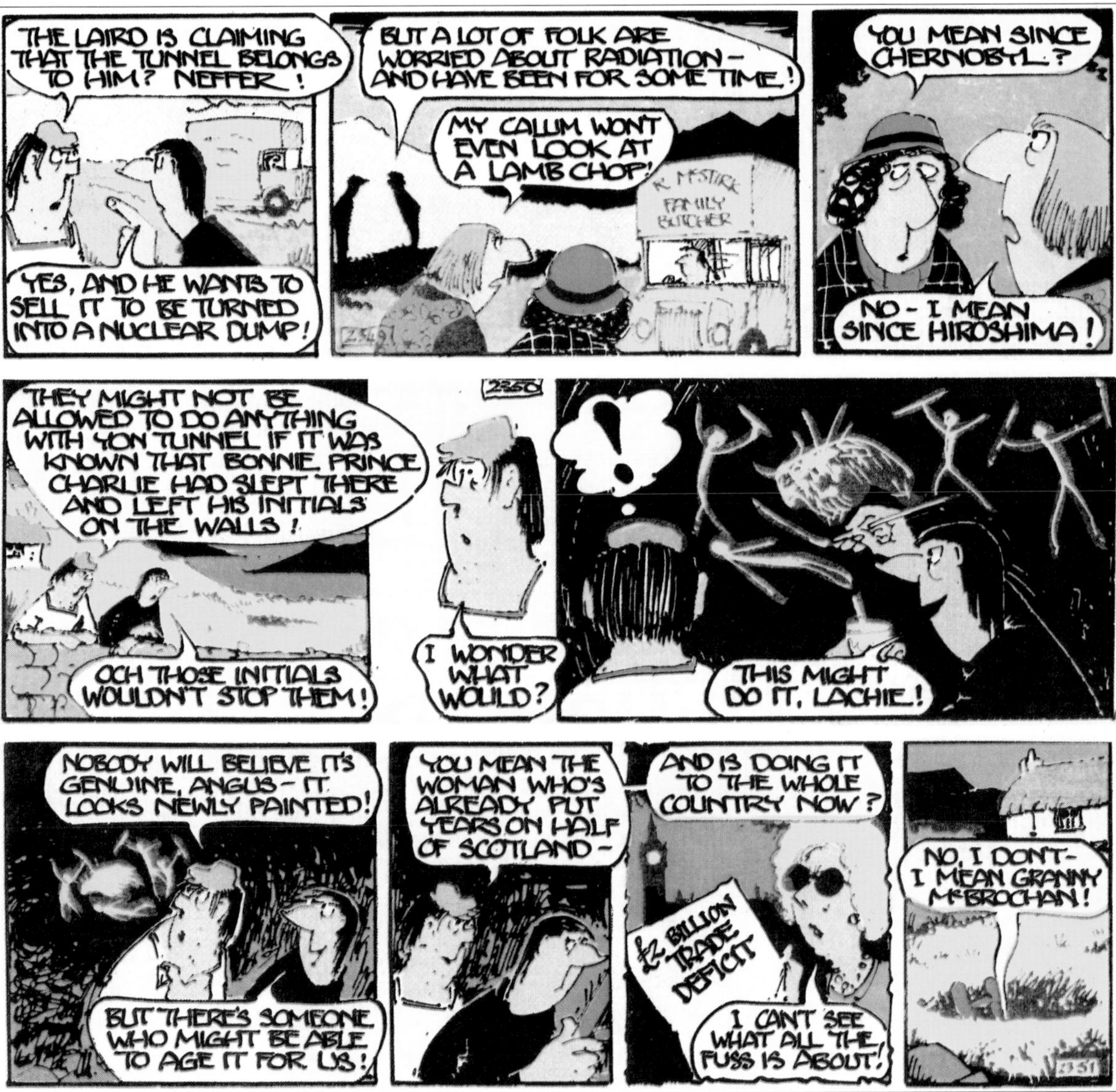
THE LAIRD IS CLAIMING THAT THE TUNNEL BELONGS TO HIM? NEFFER!
YES, AND HE WANTS TO SELL IT TO BE TURNED INTO A NUCLEAR DUMP!
BUT A LOT OF FOLK ARE WORRIED ABOUT RADIATION – AND HAVE BEEN FOR SOME TIME!
MY CALUM WON'T EVEN LOOK AT A LAMB CHOP!
FAMILY BUTCHER
2349
YOU MEAN SINCE CHERNOBYL?
NO – I MEAN SINCE HIROSHIMA!
THEY MIGHT NOT BE ALLOWED TO DO ANYTHING WITH YON TUNNEL IF IT WAS KNOWN THAT BONNIE PRINCE CHARLIE HAD SLEPT THERE AND LEFT HIS INITIALS ON THE WALLS!
OCH THOSE INITIALS WOULDN'T STOP THEM!
2350
I WONDER WHAT WOULD?
!
THIS MIGHT DO IT, LACHIE!
NOBODY WILL BELIEVE IT'S GENUINE, ANGUS – IT LOOKS NEWLY PAINTED!
BUT THERE'S SOMEONE WHO MIGHT BE ABLE TO AGE IT FOR US!
YOU MEAN THE WOMAN WHO'S ALREADY PUT YEARS ON HALF OF SCOTLAND –
AND IS DOING IT TO THE WHOLE COUNTRY NOW?
£2 BILLION TRADE DEFICIT
I CAN'T SEE WHAT ALL THE FUSS IS ABOUT!
NO, I DON'T – I MEAN GRANNY McBROCHAN!
2351

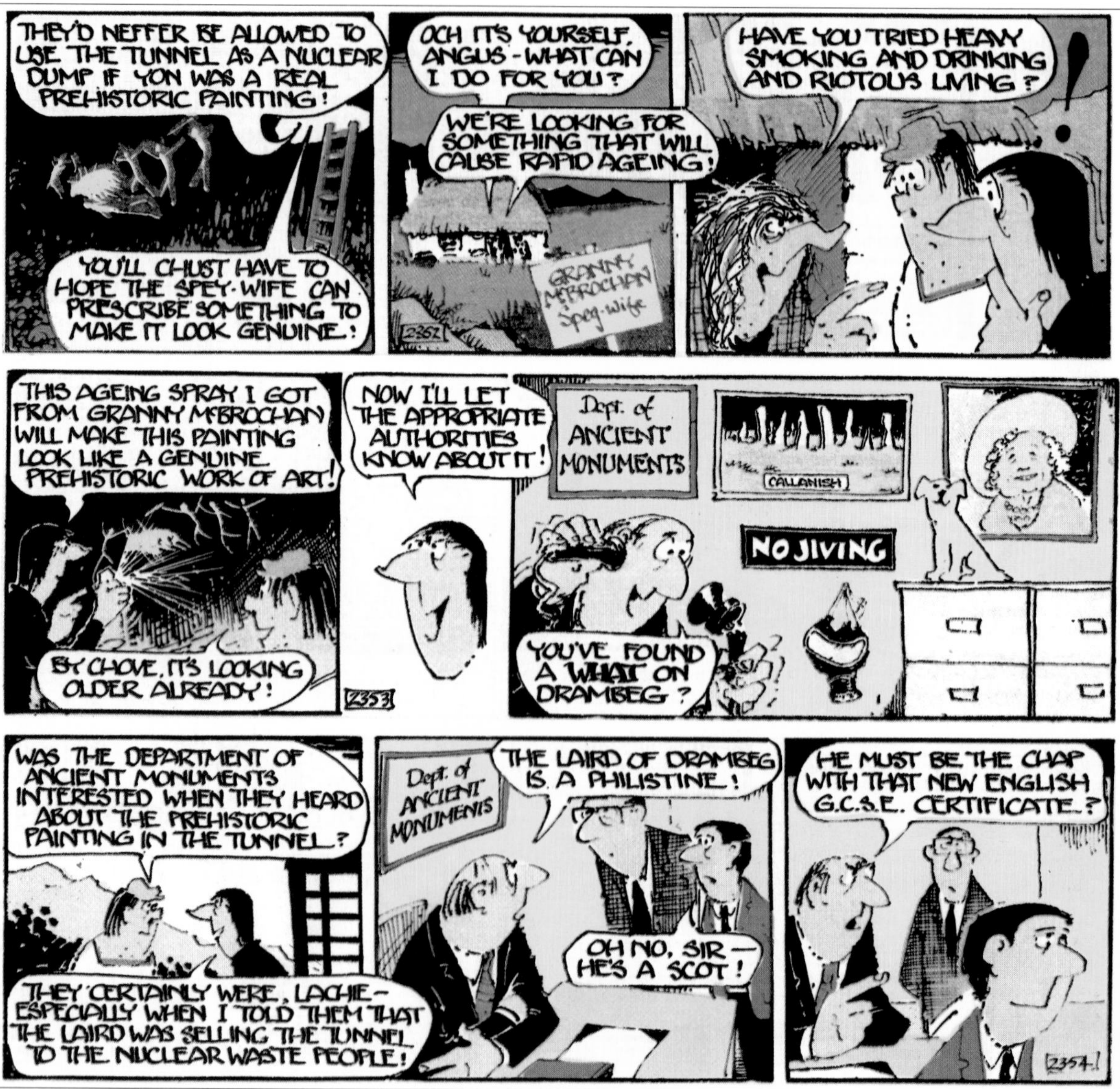
THEY'D NEFFER BE ALLOWED TO USE THE TUNNEL AS A NUCLEAR DUMP IF YON WAS A REAL PREHISTORIC PAINTING!
YOU'LL CHUST HAVE TO HOPE THE SPEY-WIFE CAN PRESCRIBE SOMETHING TO MAKE IT LOOK GENUINE!
OCH IT'S YOURSELF, ANGUS - WHAT CAN I DO FOR YOU?
WE'RE LOOKING FOR SOMETHING THAT WILL CAUSE RAPID AGEING!
GRANNY McBROCHAN Spey-wife
2352
HAVE YOU TRIED HEAVY SMOKING AND DRINKING AND RIOTOUS LIVING?
!
THIS AGEING SPRAY I GOT FROM GRANNY McBROCHAN WILL MAKE THIS PAINTING LOOK LIKE A GENUINE PREHISTORIC WORK OF ART!
BY CHOVE, IT'S LOOKING OLDER ALREADY!
2353
NOW I'LL LET THE APPROPRIATE AUTHORITIES KNOW ABOUT IT!
Dept. of ANCIENT MONUMENTS
CALLANISH
NO JIVING
YOU'VE FOUND A WHAT ON DRAMBEG?
WAS THE DEPARTMENT OF ANCIENT MONUMENTS INTERESTED WHEN THEY HEARD ABOUT THE PREHISTORIC PAINTING IN THE TUNNEL?
THEY CERTAINLY WERE, LACHIE - ESPECIALLY WHEN I TOLD THEM THAT THE LAIRD WAS SELLING THE TUNNEL TO THE NUCLEAR WASTE PEOPLE!
Dept. of ANCIENT MONUMENTS
THE LAIRD OF DRAMBEG IS A PHILISTINE!
OH NO, SIR - HE'S A SCOT!
HE MUST BE THE CHAP WITH THAT NEW ENGLISH G.C.S.E. CERTIFICATE?
2354

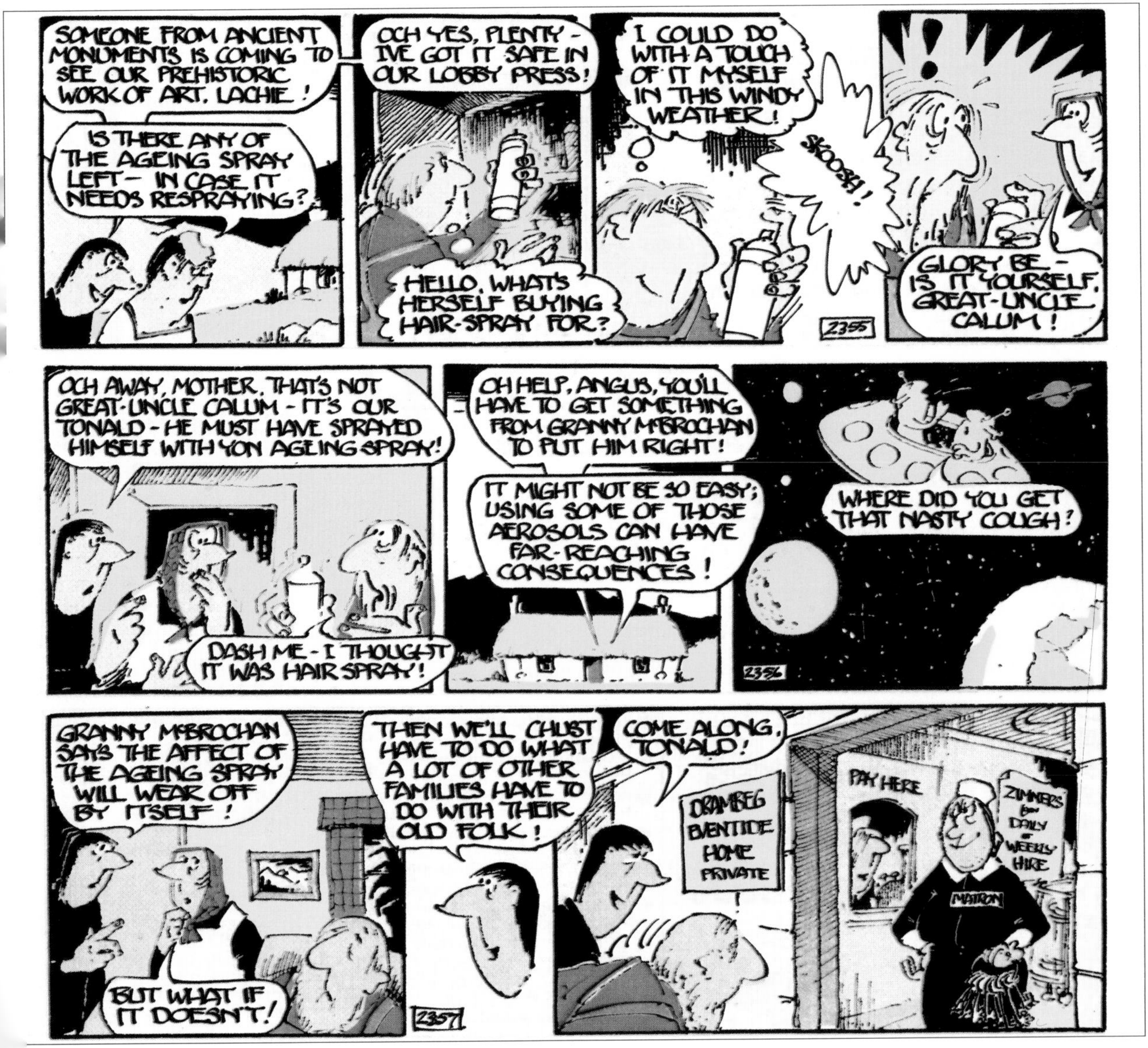
SOMEONE FROM ANCIENT MONUMENTS IS COMING TO SEE OUR PREHISTORIC WORK OF ART, LACHIE!
IS THERE ANY OF THE AGEING SPRAY LEFT– IN CASE IT NEEDS RESPRAYING?
OCH YES, PLENTY – I'VE GOT IT SAFE IN OUR LOBBY PRESS!
HELLO, WHAT'S HERSELF BUYING HAIR-SPRAY FOR?
I COULD DO WITH A TOUCH OF IT MYSELF IN THIS WINDY WEATHER!
SKOOSH!
GLORY BE – IS IT YOURSELF, GREAT-UNCLE CALUM!
2355
OCH AWAY, MOTHER, THAT'S NOT GREAT-UNCLE CALUM – IT'S OUR TONALD – HE MUST HAVE SPRAYED HIMSELF WITH YON AGEING SPRAY!
DASH ME – I THOUGHT IT WAS HAIR SPRAY!
OH HELP, ANGUS, YOU'LL HAVE TO GET SOMETHING FROM GRANNY McBROCHAN TO PUT HIM RIGHT!
IT MIGHT NOT BE SO EASY; USING SOME OF THOSE AEROSOLS CAN HAVE FAR-REACHING CONSEQUENCES!
WHERE DID YOU GET THAT NASTY COUGH?
2356
GRANNY McBROCHAN SAYS THE AFFECT OF THE AGEING SPRAY WILL WEAR OFF BY ITSELF!
BUT WHAT IF IT DOESN'T!
THEN WE'LL CHUST HAVE TO DO WHAT A LOT OF OTHER FAMILIES HAVE TO DO WITH THEIR OLD FOLK!
2357
COME ALONG, TONALD!
DRAMBEG EVENTIDE HOME PRIVATE
PAY HERE
ZIMMERS for DAILY or WEEKLY HIRE
MATRON

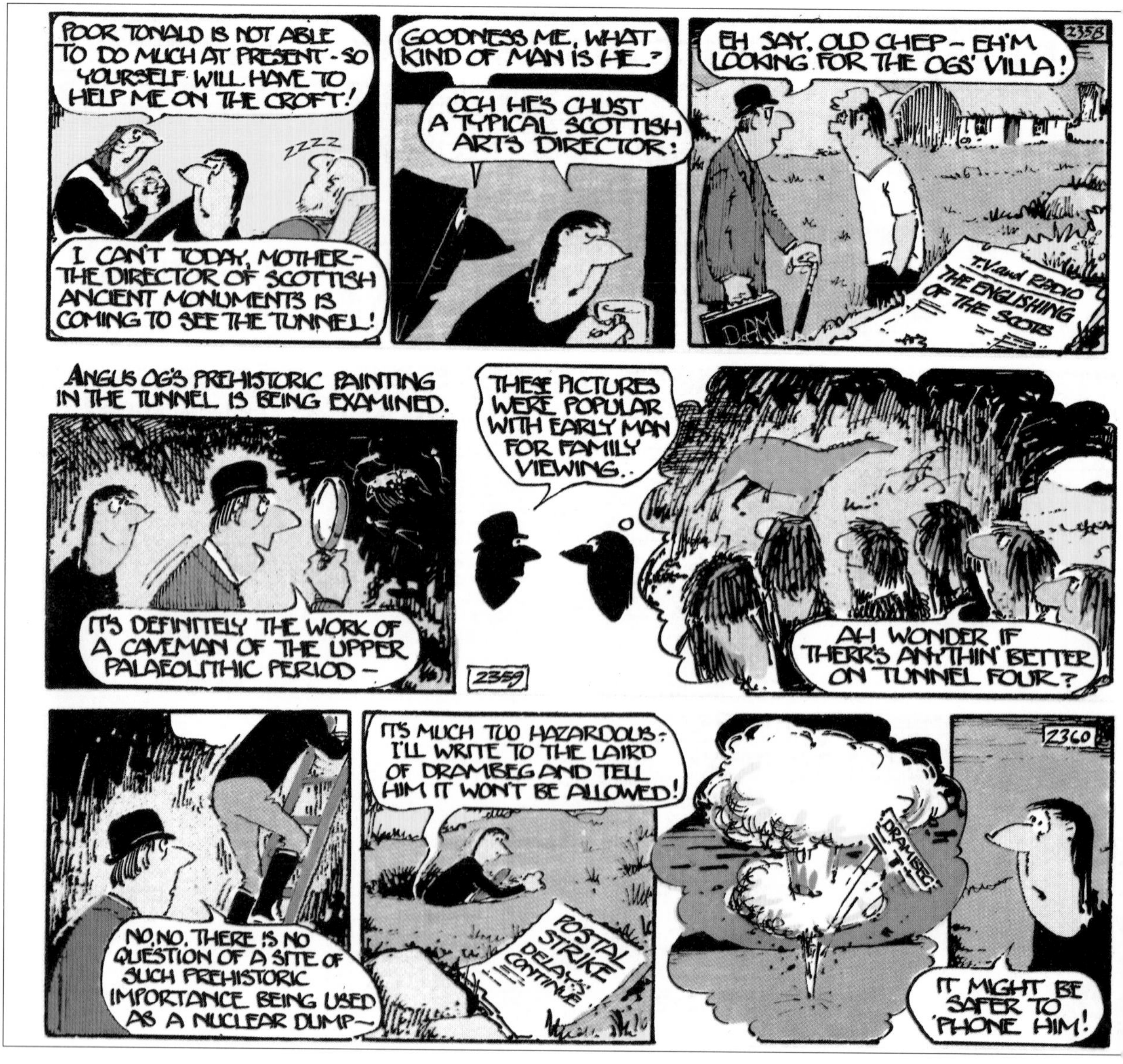
POOR TONALD IS NOT ABLE TO DO MUCH AT PRESENT - SO YOURSELF WILL HAVE TO HELP ME ON THE CROFT!
ZZZZ
I CAN'T TODAY, MOTHER- THE DIRECTOR OF SCOTTISH ANCIENT MONUMENTS IS COMING TO SEE THE TUNNEL!
GOODNESS ME, WHAT KIND OF MAN IS HE?
OCH HE'S CHUST A TYPICAL SCOTTISH ARTS DIRECTOR!
2358
EH SAY, OLD CHEP - EH'M LOOKING FOR THE OGS' VILLA!
T.V. and RADIO
THE ENGLISHING OF THE SCOTS
ANGUS OG'S PREHISTORIC PAINTING IN THE TUNNEL IS BEING EXAMINED.
IT'S DEFINITELY THE WORK OF A CAVEMAN OF THE UPPER PALAEOLITHIC PERIOD -
2359
THESE PICTURES WERE POPULAR WITH EARLY MAN FOR FAMILY VIEWING.
AH WONDER IF THERR'S ANYTHIN' BETTER ON TUNNEL FOUR?
NO, NO, THERE IS NO QUESTION OF A SITE OF SUCH PREHISTORIC IMPORTANCE BEING USED AS A NUCLEAR DUMP-
IT'S MUCH TOO HAZARDOUS- I'LL WRITE TO THE LAIRD OF DRAMBEG AND TELL HIM IT WON'T BE ALLOWED!
POSTAL STRIKE DELAYS CONTINUE
2360
DRAMBEG
IT MIGHT BE SAFER TO 'PHONE HIM!

A MAN CALLED HORACE
by ANDREW CHRISTINE and ROGER KETTLE

THE ARMY'S REALLY SCRAPING THE BARREL THIS TIME.

THEY'VE JUST RELEASED A STATEMENT EXPLAINING WHY CUSTER LOST THE BATTLE OF THE LITTLE BIGHORN.

"CRAZY HORSE WAS OFFSIDE."

KETTLE & CHRISTINE
YOU'VE DONE TWO THINGS A POKER PLAYER SHOULDN'T.
WHAT'S THE OTHER?
ONE IS SHOW EMOTION.
GROW A STUPID MOUSTACHE.
KETTLE & CHRISTINE
WANTED
$500
LOOK AT THIS!
WHAT A BRILLIANT WAY TO MAKE SOME EASY MONEY!
WE'LL START A POSTER-PRINTING COMPANY!
KETTLE & CHRISTINE
I'M OFF TO DO A BIT OF SHOOTING PRACTICE.
DO YOU HAVE ANY OLD CANS?
NOT BARN-DOOR SIZE.

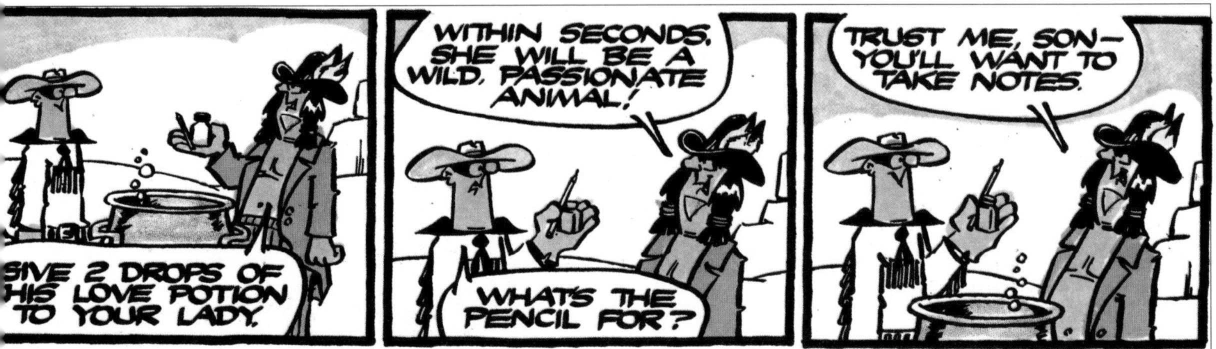
IVE 2 DROPS OF HIS LOVE POTION TO YOUR LADY.
WITHIN SECONDS, SHE WILL BE A WILD, PASSIONATE ANIMAL!
WHAT'S THE PENCIL FOR?
TRUST ME, SON— YOU'LL WANT TO TAKE NOTES.

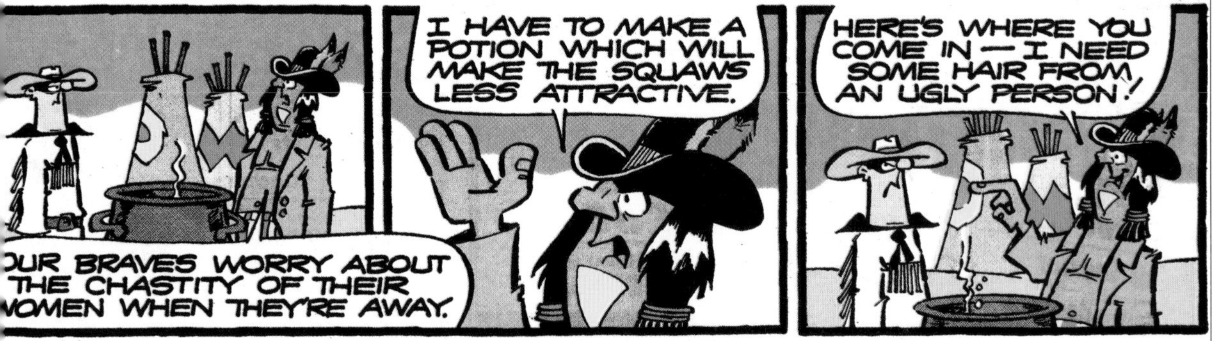
OUR BRAVES WORRY ABOUT THE CHASTITY OF THEIR WOMEN WHEN THEY'RE AWAY.
I HAVE TO MAKE A POTION WHICH WILL MAKE THE SQUAWS LESS ATTRACTIVE.
HERE'S WHERE YOU COME IN — I NEED SOME HAIR FROM AN UGLY PERSON!

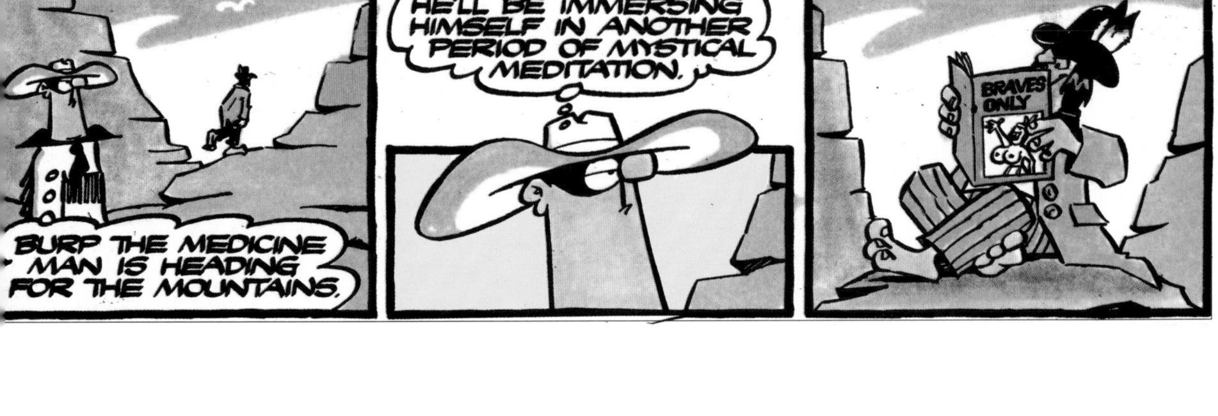
BURP THE MEDICINE MAN IS HEADING FOR THE MOUNTAINS.
HE'LL BE IMMERSING HIMSELF IN ANOTHER PERIOD OF MYSTICAL MEDITATION.
BRAVES ONLY

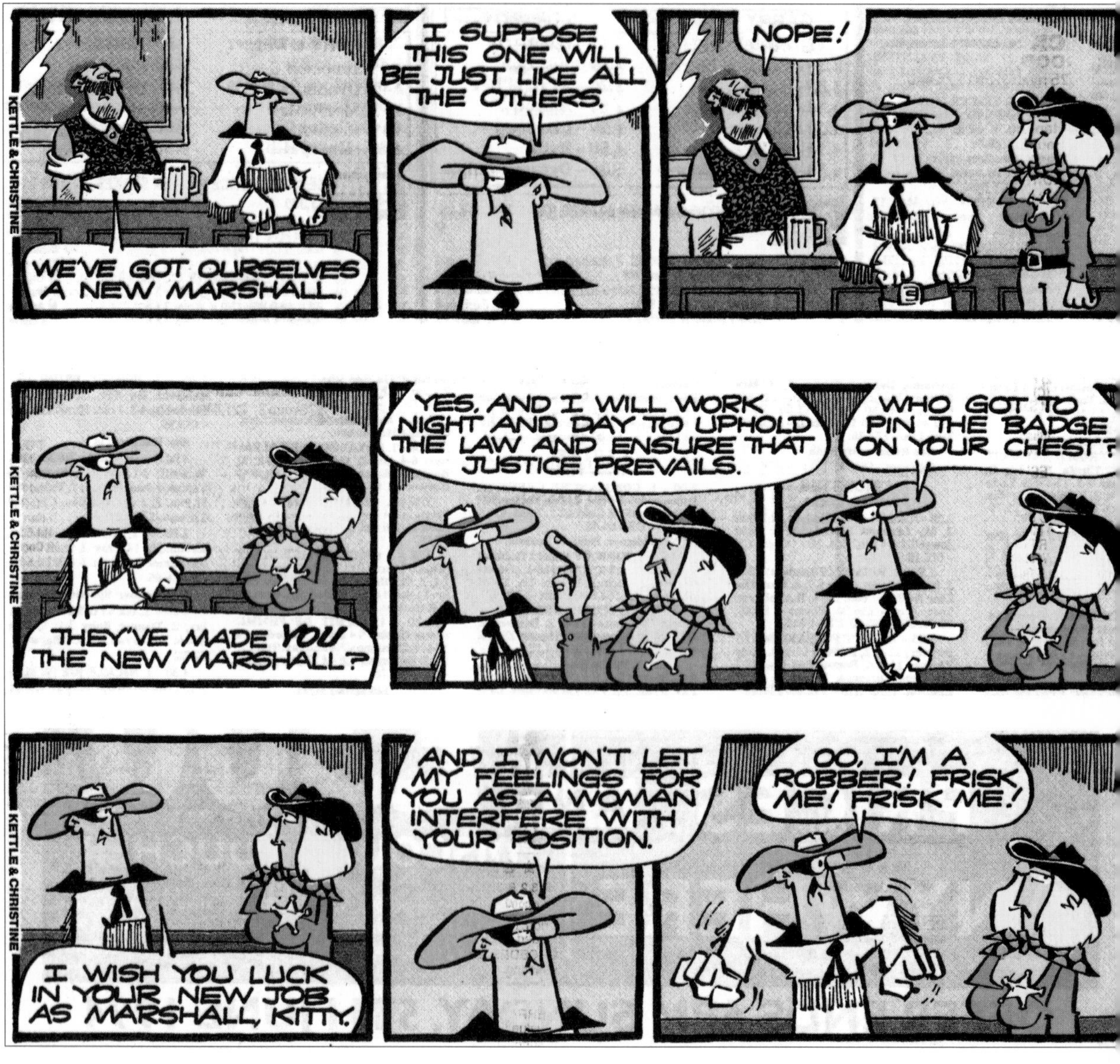
KETTLE & CHRISTINE
WE'VE GOT OURSELVES A NEW MARSHALL.
I SUPPOSE THIS ONE WILL BE JUST LIKE ALL THE OTHERS.
NOPE!
KETTLE & CHRISTINE
THEY'VE MADE *YOU* THE NEW MARSHALL?
YES, AND I WILL WORK NIGHT AND DAY TO UPHOLD THE LAW AND ENSURE THAT JUSTICE PREVAILS.
WHO GOT TO PIN THE BADGE ON YOUR CHEST?
KETTLE & CHRISTINE
I WISH YOU LUCK IN YOUR NEW JOB AS MARSHALL, KITTY.
AND I WON'T LET MY FEELINGS FOR YOU AS A WOMAN INTERFERE WITH YOUR POSITION.
OO, I'M A ROBBER! FRISK ME! FRISK ME!

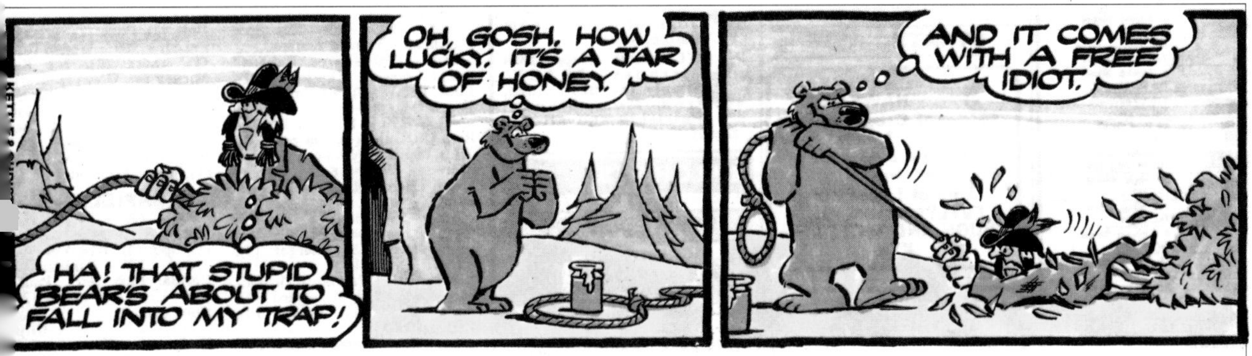
HA! THAT STUPID BEAR'S ABOUT TO FALL INTO MY TRAP!
OH, GOSH, HOW LUCKY. IT'S A JAR OF HONEY.
AND IT COMES WITH A FREE IDIOT.

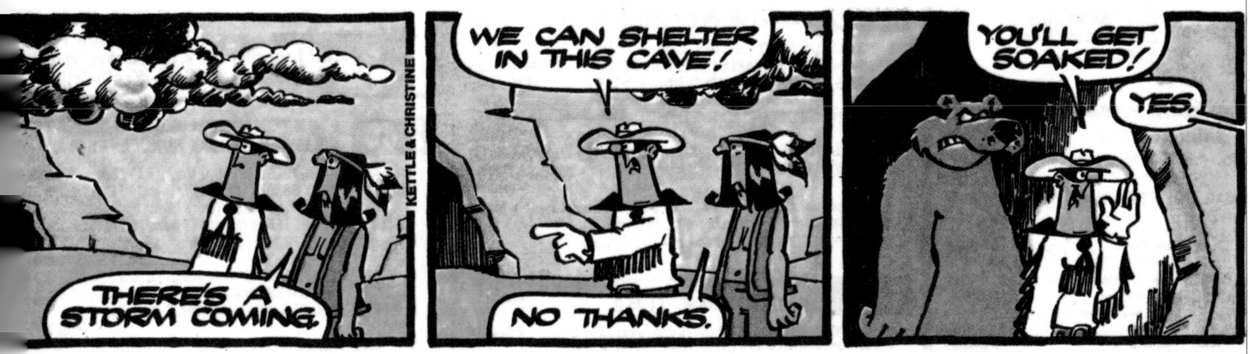
THERE'S A STORM COMING.
KETTLE & CHRISTINE
WE CAN SHELTER IN THIS CAVE!
NO THANKS.
YOU'LL GET SOAKED!
YES.

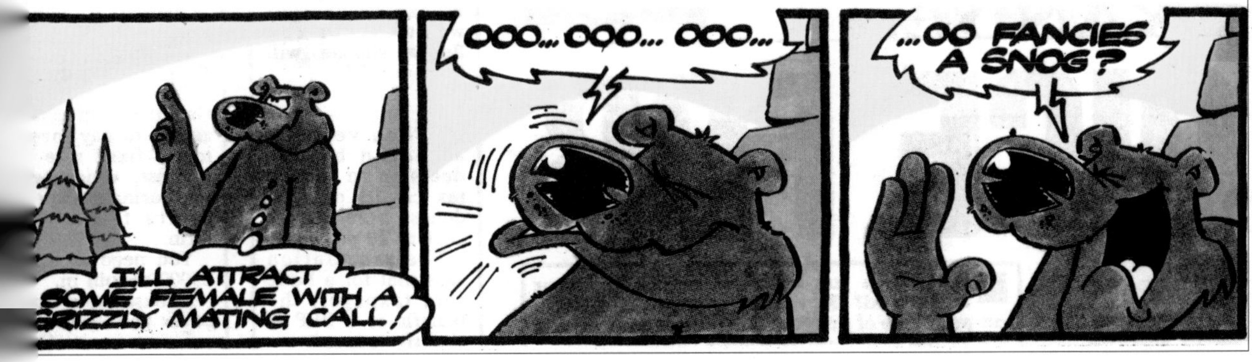
I'LL ATTRACT SOME FEMALE WITH A GRIZZLY MATING CALL!
OOO... OOO... OOO...
...OO FANCIES A SNOG?

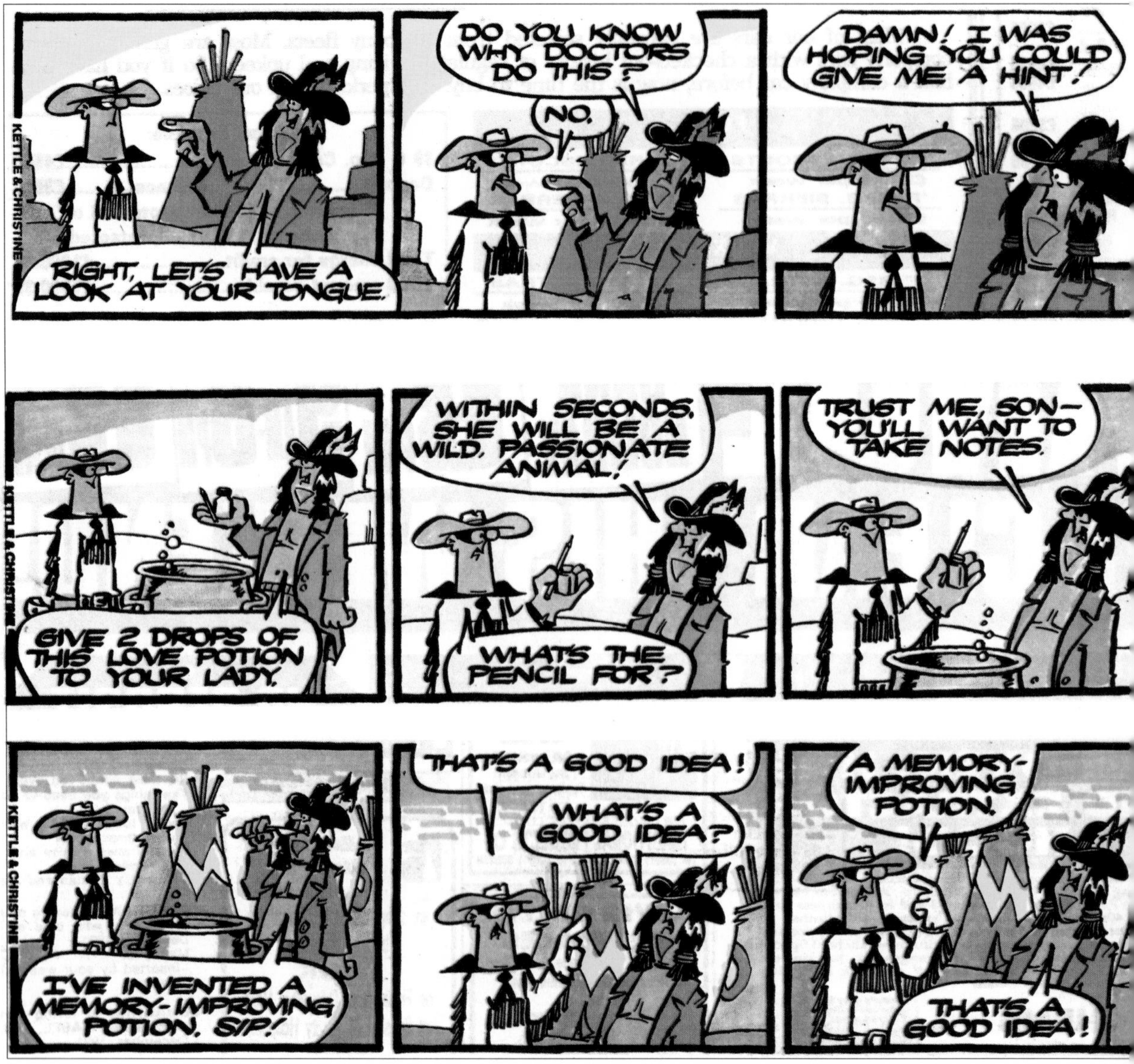
KETTLE & CHRISTINE
RIGHT, LET'S HAVE A LOOK AT YOUR TONGUE.
DO YOU KNOW WHY DOCTORS DO THIS?
NO.
DAMN! I WAS HOPING YOU COULD GIVE ME A HINT!
KETTLE & CHRISTINE
GIVE 2 DROPS OF THIS LOVE POTION TO YOUR LADY.
WITHIN SECONDS, SHE WILL BE A WILD, PASSIONATE ANIMAL!
WHAT'S THE PENCIL FOR?
TRUST ME, SON— YOU'LL WANT TO TAKE NOTES.
KETTLE & CHRISTINE
I'VE INVENTED A MEMORY-IMPROVING POTION. SIP!
THAT'S A GOOD IDEA!
WHAT'S A GOOD IDEA?
A MEMORY-IMPROVING POTION.
THAT'S A GOOD IDEA!

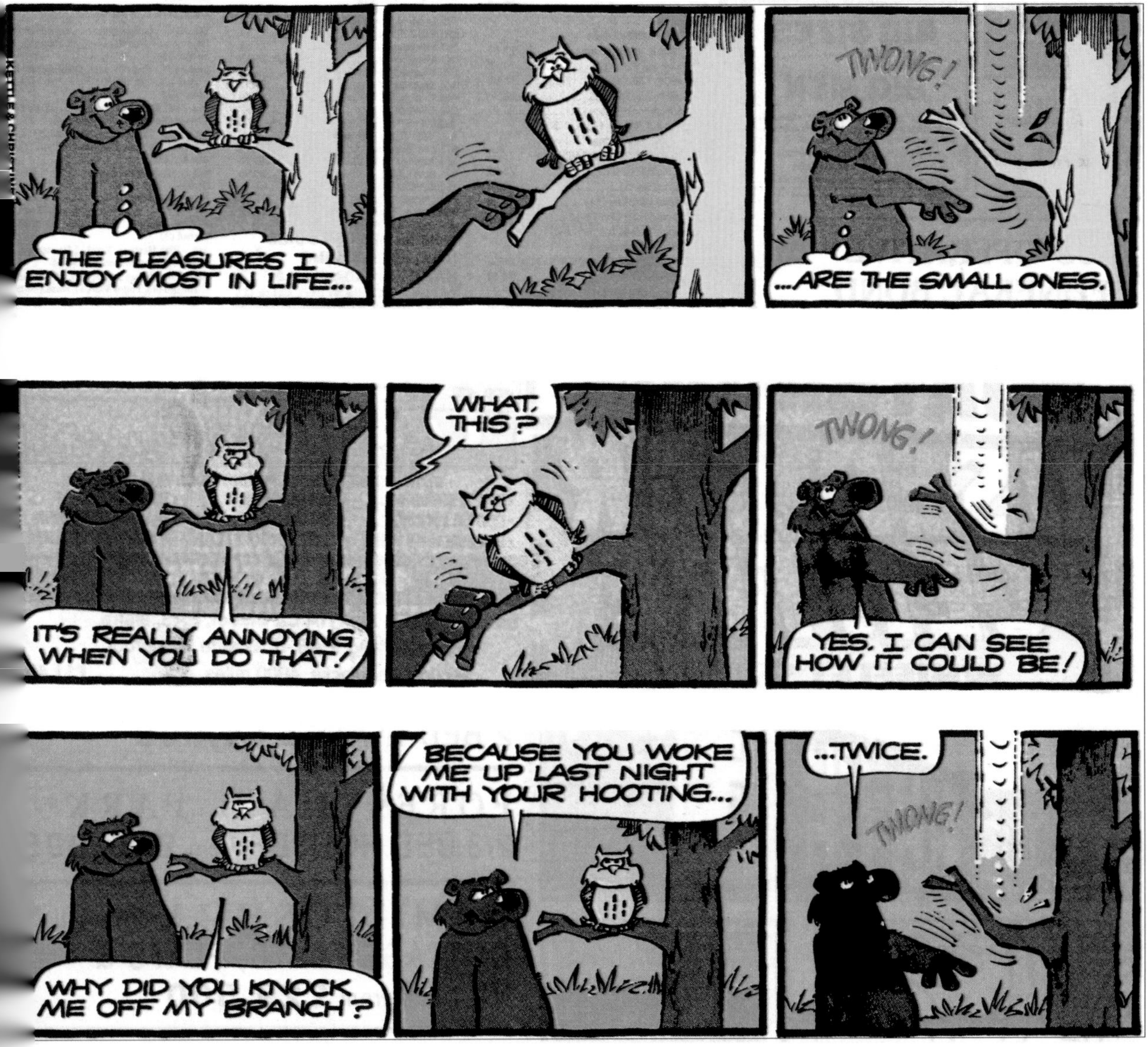
THE PLEASURES I ENJOY MOST IN LIFE...
TWONG!
...ARE THE SMALL ONES.
IT'S REALLY ANNOYING WHEN YOU DO THAT!
WHAT, THIS?
TWONG!
YES. I CAN SEE HOW IT COULD BE!
WHY DID YOU KNOCK ME OFF MY BRANCH?
BECAUSE YOU WOKE ME UP LAST NIGHT WITH YOUR HOOTING...
...TWICE.
TWONG!

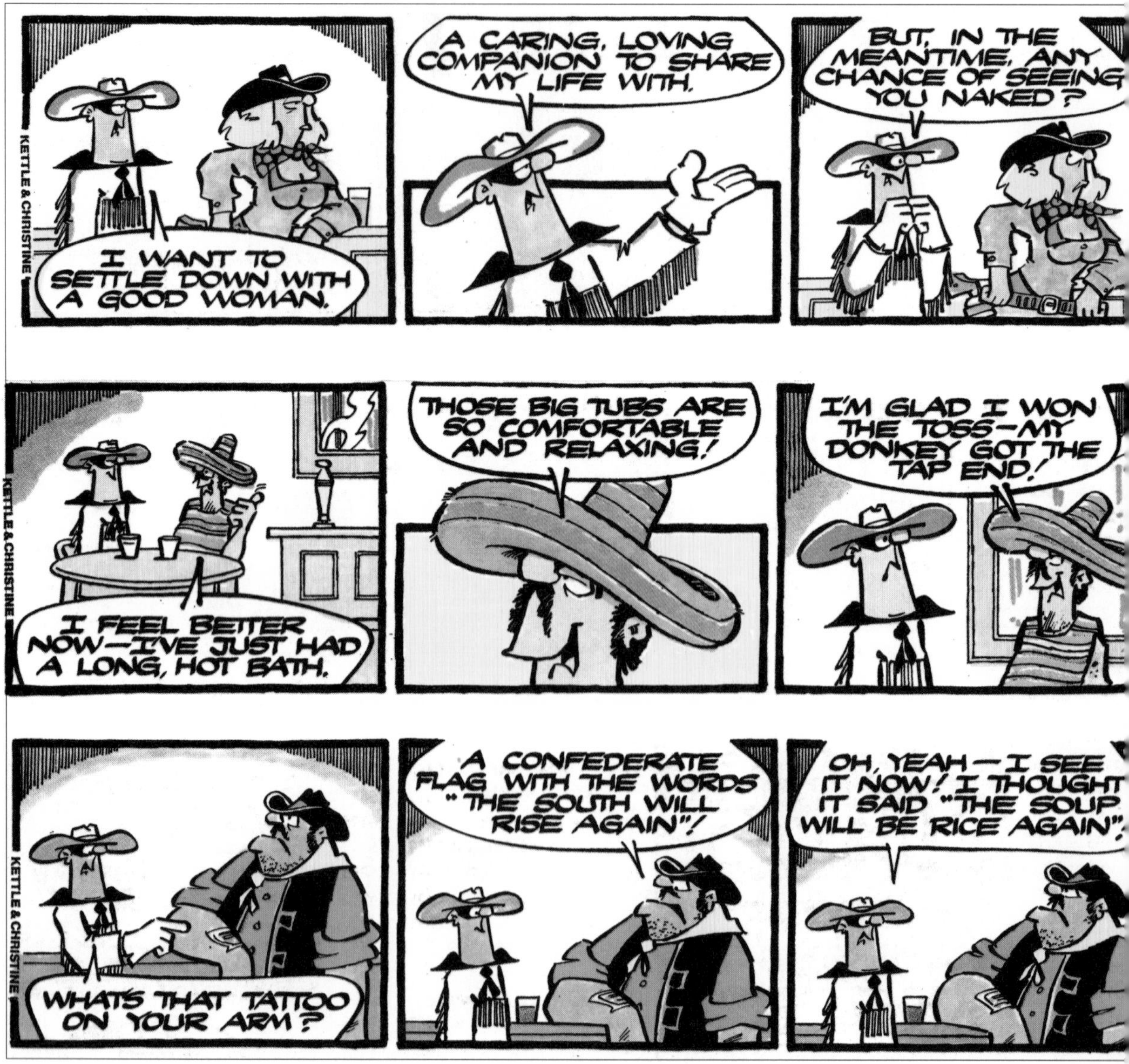
KETTLE & CHRISTINE
I WANT TO SETTLE DOWN WITH A GOOD WOMAN.
A CARING, LOVING COMPANION TO SHARE MY LIFE WITH.
BUT, IN THE MEANTIME, ANY CHANCE OF SEEING YOU NAKED?
KETTLE & CHRISTINE
I FEEL BETTER NOW—I'VE JUST HAD A LONG, HOT BATH.
THOSE BIG TUBS ARE SO COMFORTABLE AND RELAXING!
I'M GLAD I WON THE TOSS—MY DONKEY GOT THE TAP END!
KETTLE & CHRISTINE
WHAT'S THAT TATTOO ON YOUR ARM?
A CONFEDERATE FLAG WITH THE WORDS "THE SOUTH WILL RISE AGAIN"!
OH, YEAH—I SEE IT NOW! I THOUGHT IT SAID "THE SOUP WILL BE RICE AGAIN"!

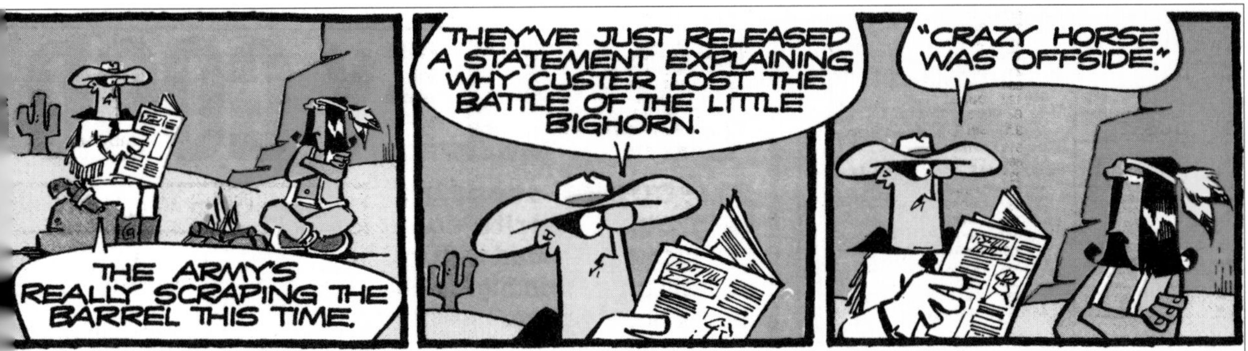
THE ARMY'S REALLY SCRAPING THE BARREL THIS TIME.
THEY'VE JUST RELEASED A STATEMENT EXPLAINING WHY CUSTER LOST THE BATTLE OF THE LITTLE BIGHORN.
"CRAZY HORSE WAS OFFSIDE."

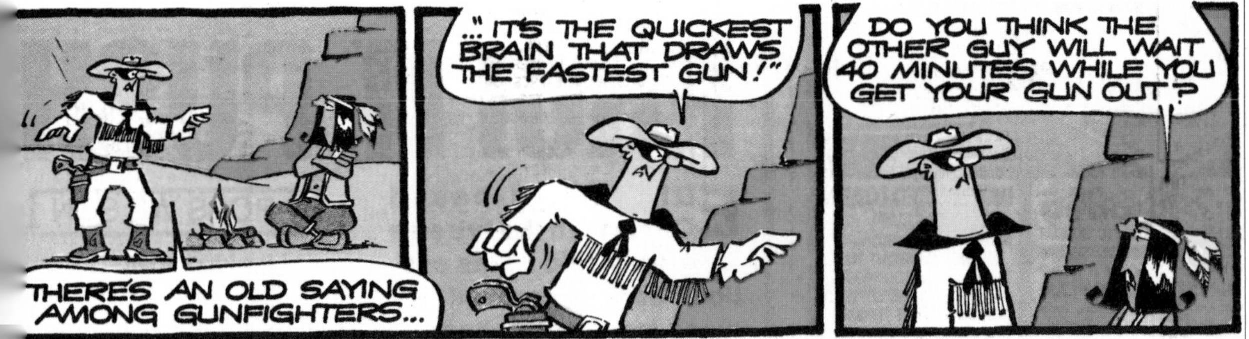
THERE'S AN OLD SAYING AMONG GUNFIGHTERS...
..." IT'S THE QUICKEST BRAIN THAT DRAWS THE FASTEST GUN!"
DO YOU THINK THE OTHER GUY WILL WAIT 40 MINUTES WHILE YOU GET YOUR GUN OUT?

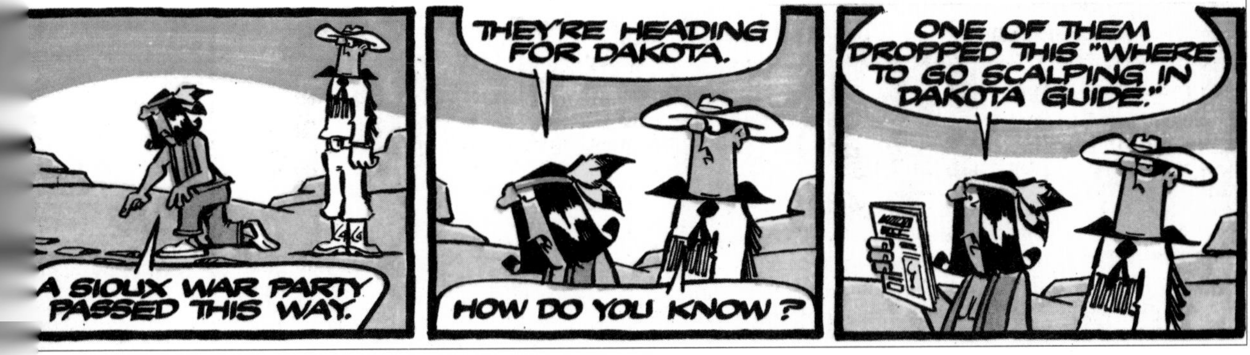
A SIOUX WAR PARTY PASSED THIS WAY.
HOW DO YOU KNOW?
THEY'RE HEADING FOR DAKOTA.
ONE OF THEM DROPPED THIS "WHERE TO GO SCALPING IN DAKOTA GUIDE."

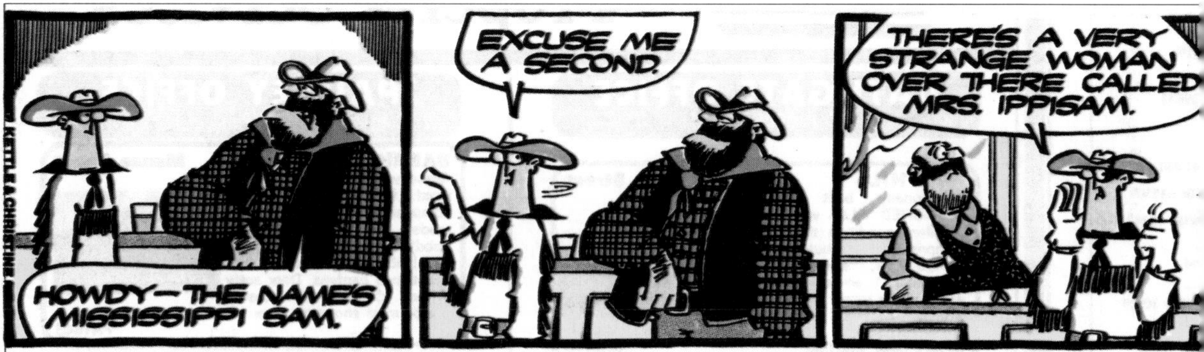
KETTLE & CHRISTINE
HOWDY—THE NAME'S MISSISSIPPI SAM.
EXCUSE ME A SECOND.
THERE'S A VERY STRANGE WOMAN OVER THERE CALLED MRS. IPPISAM.

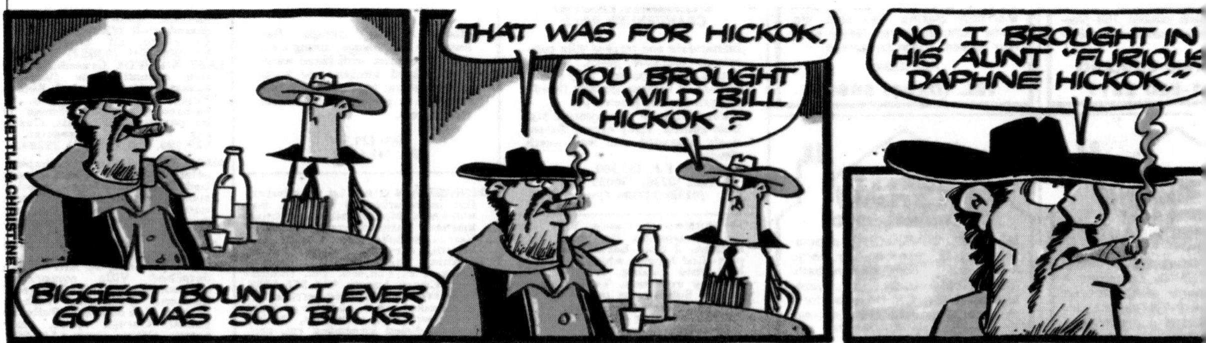
KETTLE & CHRISTINE
BIGGEST BOUNTY I EVER GOT WAS 500 BUCKS.
YOU BROUGHT IN WILD BILL HICKOK?
THAT WAS FOR HICKOK.
NO, I BROUGHT IN HIS AUNT "FURIOUS DAPHNE HICKOK."

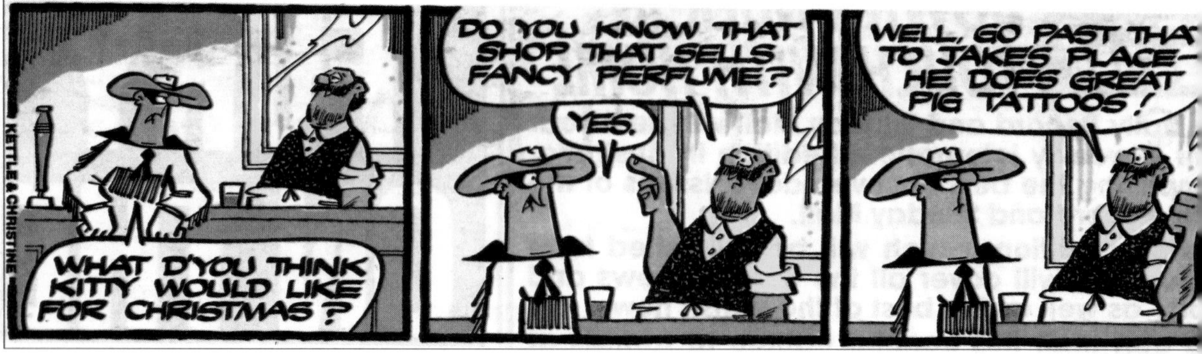
KETTLE & CHRISTINE
WHAT D'YOU THINK KITTY WOULD LIKE FOR CHRISTMAS?
DO YOU KNOW THAT SHOP THAT SELLS FANCY PERFUME?
YES.
WELL, GO PAST THAT TO JAKE'S PLACE—HE DOES GREAT PIG TATTOOS!

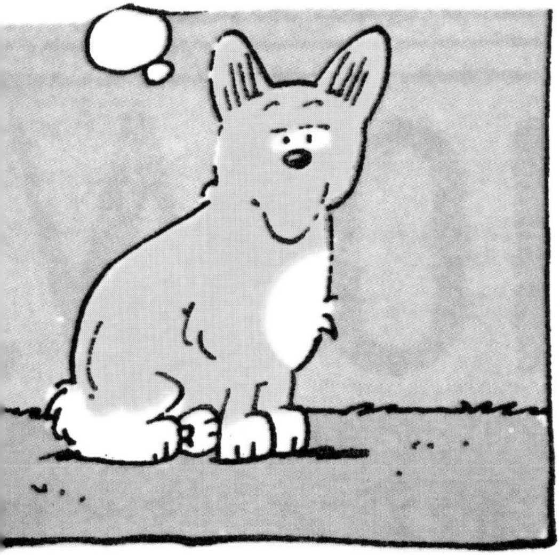

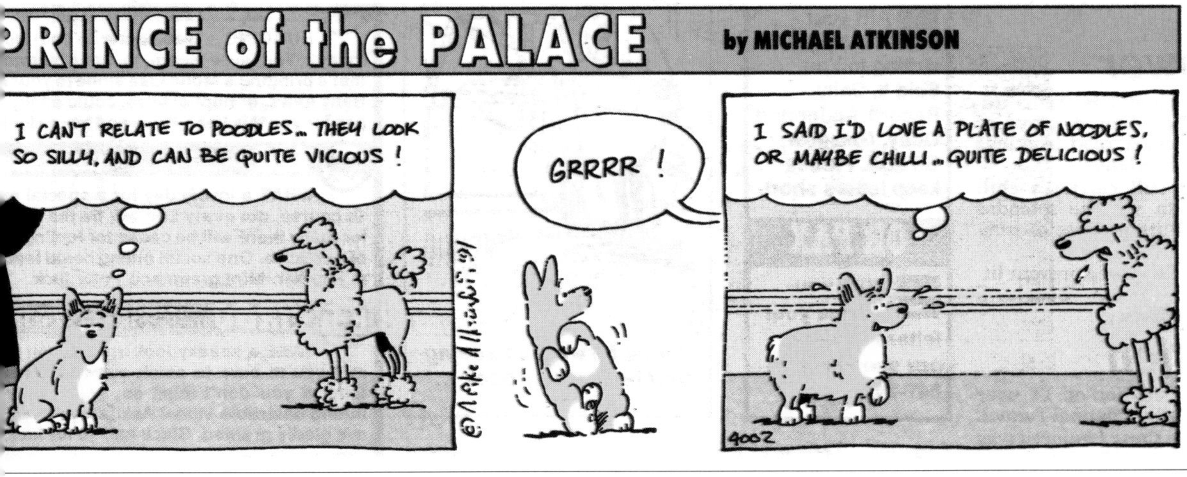
PRINCE of the PALACE
by MICHAEL ATKINSON
I CAN'T RELATE TO POODLES... THEY LOOK SO SILLY, AND CAN BE QUITE VICIOUS !
GRRRR !
I SAID I'D LOVE A PLATE OF NOODLES, OR MAYBE CHILLI... QUITE DELICIOUS !

WHO WROTE IT?

ALOYSIUS SNIKPMIS.

CORGIS IN CRISIS — ALOYSIUS SNIKPMIS

SNIKPMIS... SNIKPMIS... WAIT A MINUTE, THAT'S SIMPKINS BACKWARDS!

YOU DON'T THINK...?!?

I DON'T BELIEVE IT! I DON'T BELIEVE SIMPKINS IS REALLY CALLED ALOYSIUS!

YOUR NUTS MA'AM!

YOUR CRACKERS MA'AM!

THIS IS OUTRAGEOUS...

THANK YOU... PUT THEM ON THE TABLE WOULD YOU.

WE ROYALS ARE ILL-EQUIPPED TO HANDLE THE EMOTIONAL ROLLER COASTER THAT IS MODERN MARRIAGE PRINCE.

CHARLES IS IN A REFLECTIVE MOOD TODAY.

WE'RE TRAINED FROM BIRTH NOT TO SHOW OUR FEELINGS IN PUBLIC.

I REMEMBER WHEN I WAS QUITE YOUNG, NOT EVEN BEING ALLOWED TO CRY WHEN WE WENT TO SEE 'DUMBO'!

SAD!

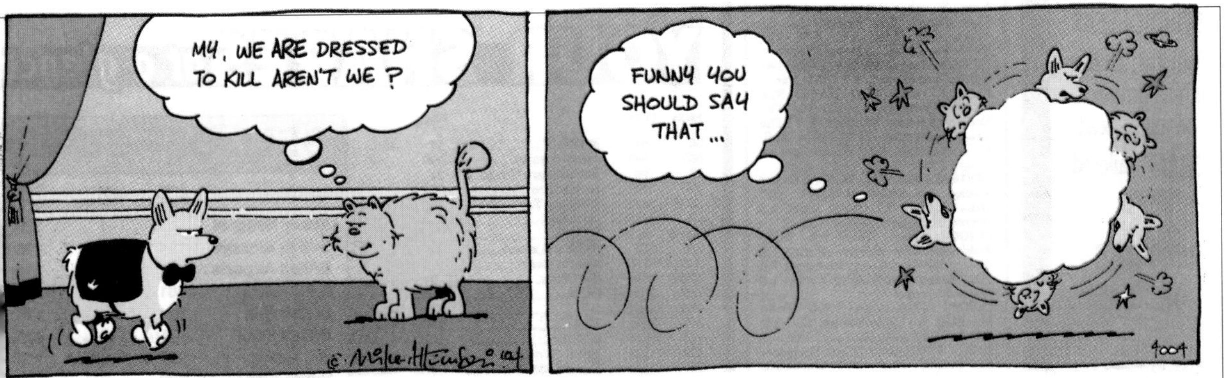
MY, WE ARE DRESSED TO KILL AREN'T WE ?
FUNNY YOU SHOULD SAY THAT ...
4004

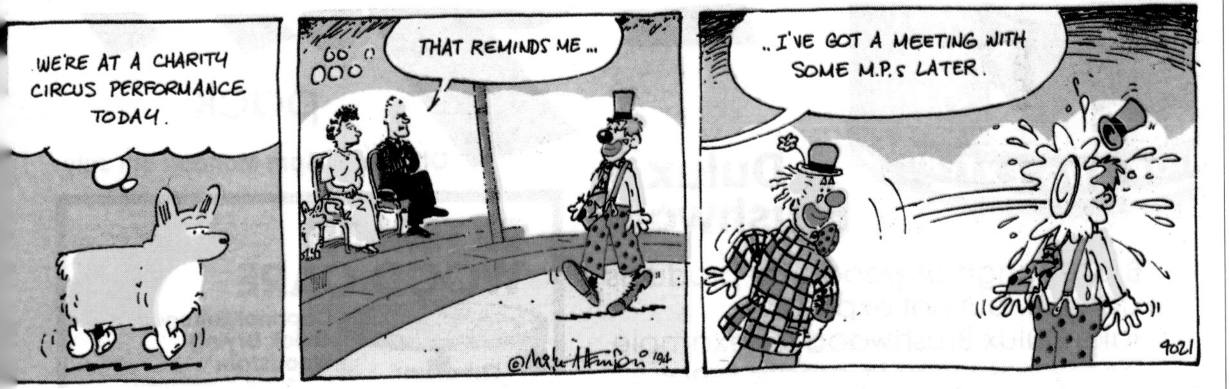
WE'RE AT A CHARITY CIRCUS PERFORMANCE TODAY.
THAT REMINDS ME ...
.. I'VE GOT A MEETING WITH SOME M.P.s LATER.
4021

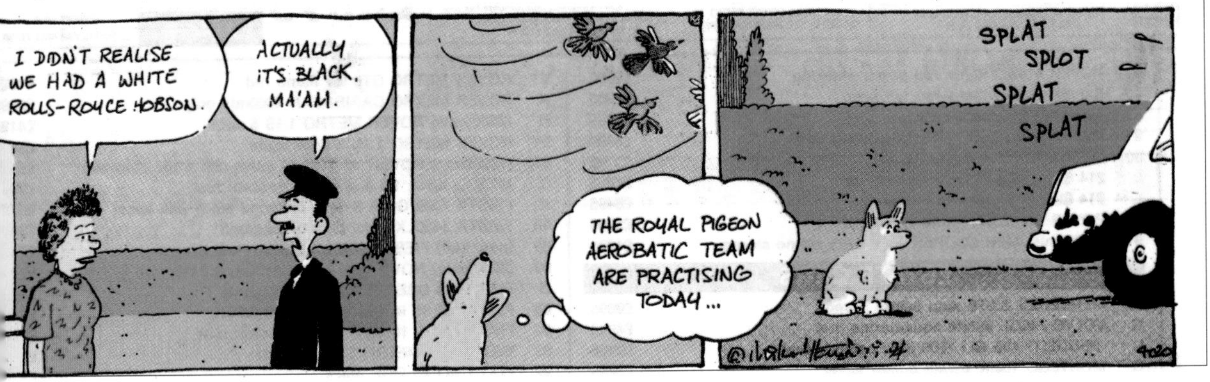
I DIDN'T REALISE WE HAD A WHITE ROLLS-ROYCE HOBSON.
ACTUALLY IT'S BLACK, MA'AM.
THE ROYAL PIGEON AEROBATIC TEAM ARE PRACTISING TODAY...
SPLAT
SPLOT
SPLAT
SPLAT

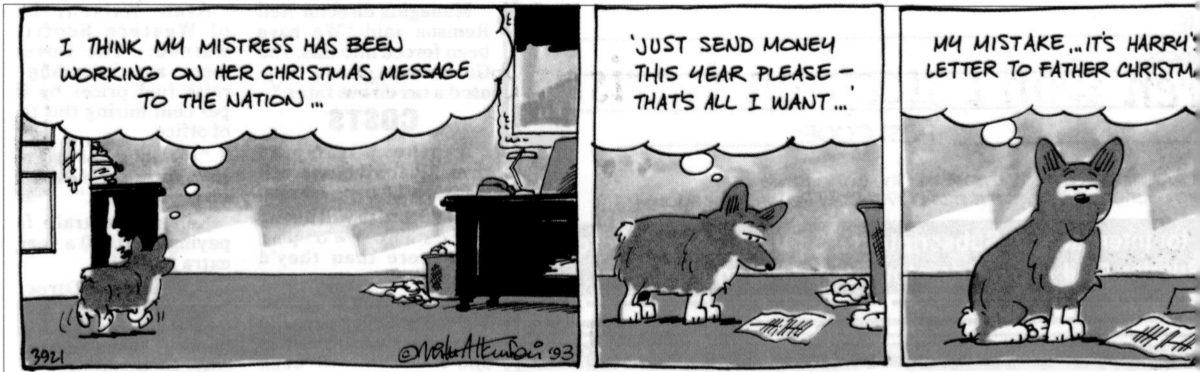
I THINK MY MISTRESS HAS BEEN WORKING ON HER CHRISTMAS MESSAGE TO THE NATION ...
'JUST SEND MONEY THIS YEAR PLEASE – THAT'S ALL I WANT ...'
MY MISTAKE ... IT'S HARRY'S LETTER TO FATHER CHRISTMA
3921

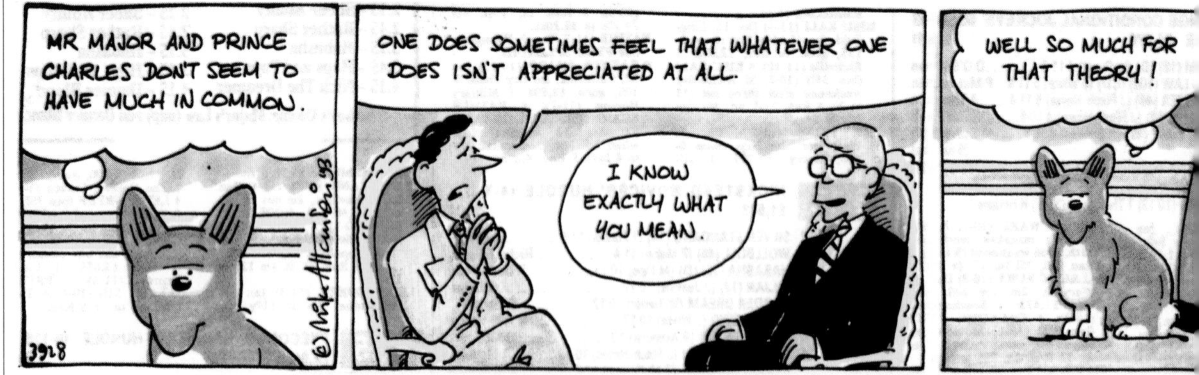
MR MAJOR AND PRINCE CHARLES DON'T SEEM TO HAVE MUCH IN COMMON.
ONE DOES SOMETIMES FEEL THAT WHATEVER ONE DOES ISN'T APPRECIATED AT ALL.
I KNOW EXACTLY WHAT YOU MEAN.
WELL SO MUCH FOR THAT THEORY!
3928

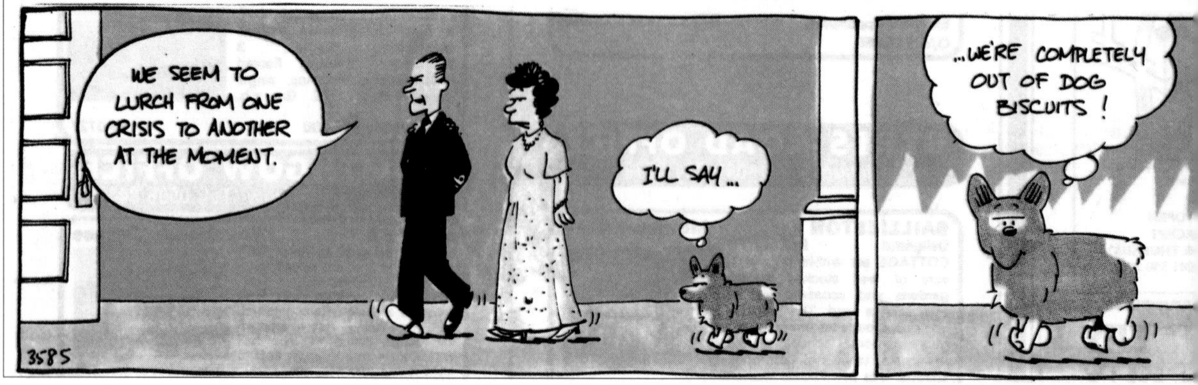
WE SEEM TO LURCH FROM ONE CRISIS TO ANOTHER AT THE MOMENT.
I'LL SAY ...
... WE'RE COMPLETELY OUT OF DOG BISCUITS!
3585

GRANDAD and the LAD by BRYAN WALKER

YPICAL !. MILES FROM HOME
ND IT HAS TO RAIN !

IT'S ONLY A SHOWER GRANDAD

I PUT THIS HAT ON TO KEEP THE *SUN* OFF MY HEAD !!

WELL.. IT SEEMS TO BE WORKING

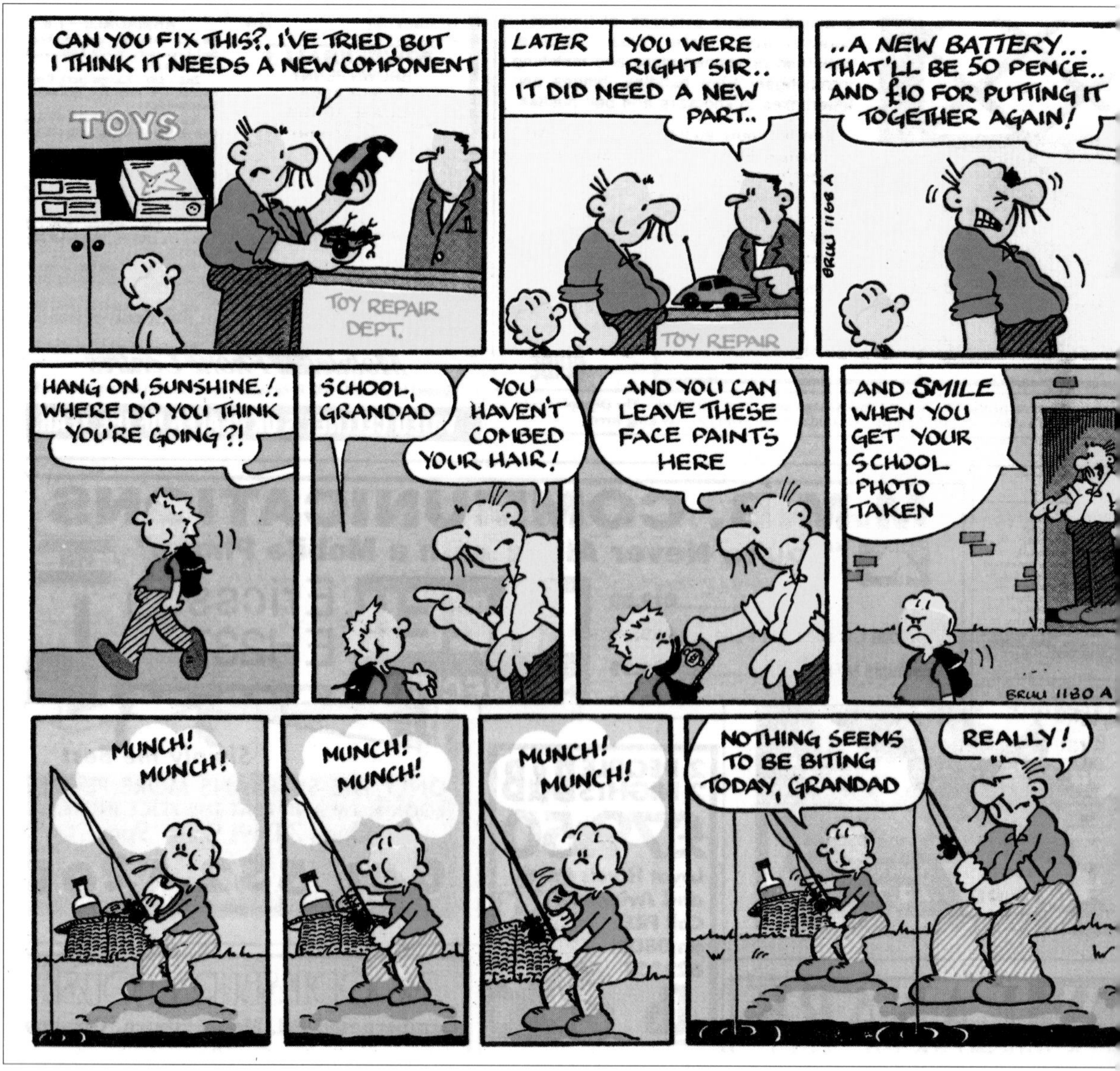
CAN YOU FIX THIS?. I'VE TRIED, BUT I THINK IT NEEDS A NEW COMPONENT
TOYS
TOY REPAIR DEPT.
LATER
YOU WERE RIGHT SIR.. IT DID NEED A NEW PART..
TOY REPAIR
..A NEW BATTERY... THAT'LL BE 50 PENCE.. AND £10 FOR PUTTING IT TOGETHER AGAIN!
HANG ON, SUNSHINE!. WHERE DO YOU THINK YOU'RE GOING?!
SCHOOL, GRANDAD
YOU HAVEN'T COMBED YOUR HAIR!
AND YOU CAN LEAVE THESE FACE PAINTS HERE
AND SMILE WHEN YOU GET YOUR SCHOOL PHOTO TAKEN
BRUU 1180 A
MUNCH! MUNCH!
MUNCH! MUNCH!
MUNCH! MUNCH!
NOTHING SEEMS TO BE BITING TODAY, GRANDAD
REALLY!

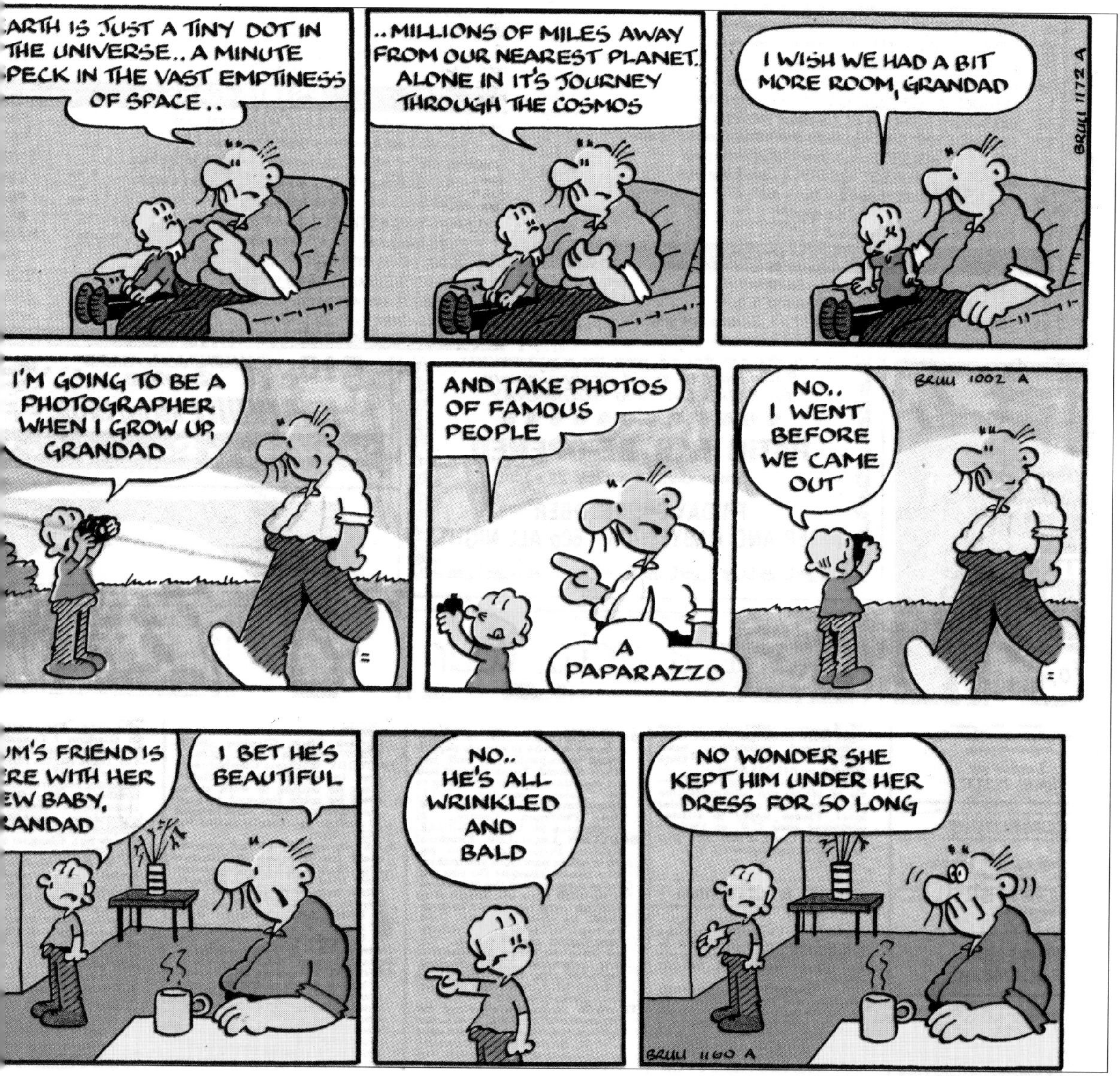
ARTH IS JUST A TINY DOT IN THE UNIVERSE.. A MINUTE PECK IN THE VAST EMPTINESS OF SPACE..
..MILLIONS OF MILES AWAY FROM OUR NEAREST PLANET. ALONE IN IT'S JOURNEY THROUGH THE COSMOS
I WISH WE HAD A BIT MORE ROOM, GRANDAD
BRUU 1172 A
I'M GOING TO BE A PHOTOGRAPHER WHEN I GROW UP, GRANDAD
AND TAKE PHOTOS OF FAMOUS PEOPLE
A PAPARAZZO
NO.. I WENT BEFORE WE CAME OUT
BRUU 1002 A
UM'S FRIEND IS ERE WITH HER EW BABY, RANDAD
I BET HE'S BEAUTIFUL
NO.. HE'S ALL WRINKLED AND BALD
NO WONDER SHE KEPT HIM UNDER HER DRESS FOR SO LONG
BRUU 1160 A

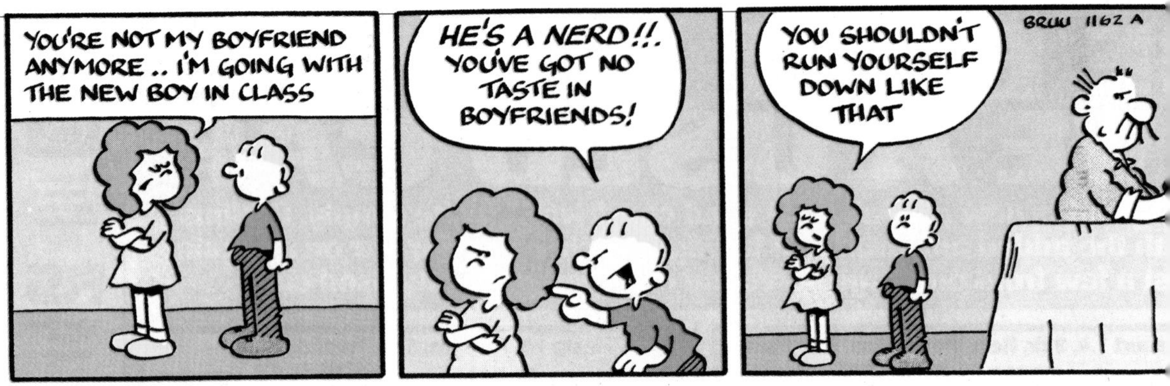
YOU'RE NOT MY BOYFRIEND ANYMORE .. I'M GOING WITH THE NEW BOY IN CLASS
HE'S A NERD!!. YOU'VE GOT NO TASTE IN BOYFRIENDS!
YOU SHOULDN'T RUN YOURSELF DOWN LIKE THAT
BRUU 1162 A

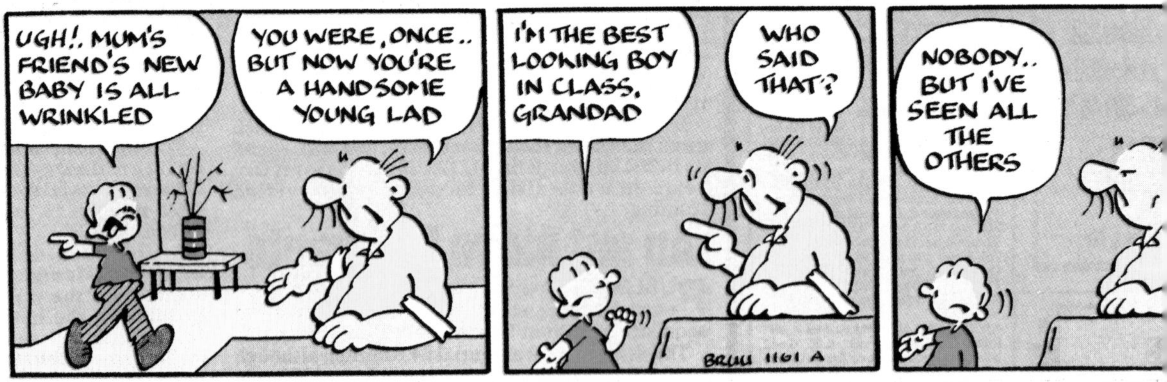
UGH!. MUM'S FRIEND'S NEW BABY IS ALL WRINKLED
YOU WERE, ONCE.. BUT NOW YOU'RE A HANDSOME YOUNG LAD
I'M THE BEST LOOKING BOY IN CLASS, GRANDAD
WHO SAID THAT?
BRUU 1161 A
NOBODY.. BUT I'VE SEEN ALL THE OTHERS

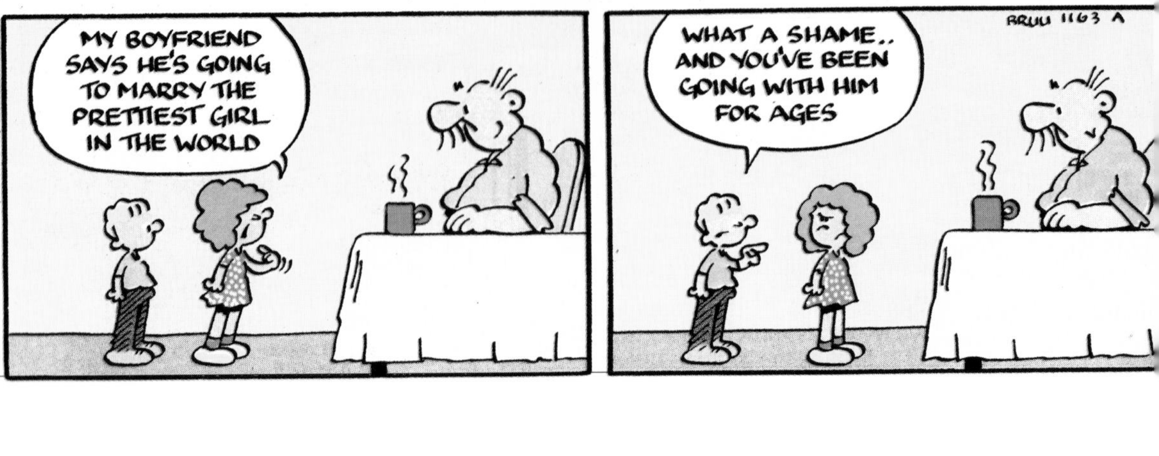
MY BOYFRIEND SAYS HE'S GOING TO MARRY THE PRETTIEST GIRL IN THE WORLD
WHAT A SHAME.. AND YOU'VE BEEN GOING WITH HIM FOR AGES
BRUU 1163 A

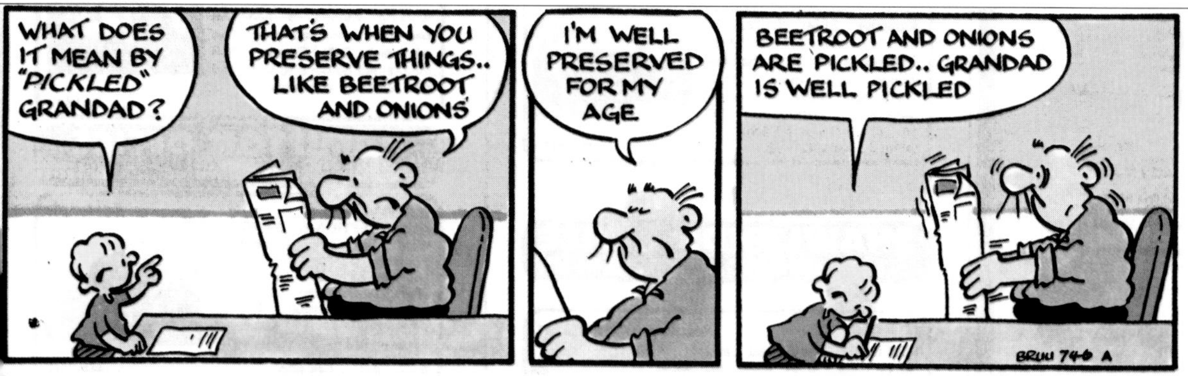
WHAT DOES IT MEAN BY "PICKLED" GRANDAD?
THAT'S WHEN YOU PRESERVE THINGS.. LIKE BEETROOT AND ONIONS
I'M WELL PRESERVED FOR MY AGE
BEETROOT AND ONIONS ARE PICKLED.. GRANDAD IS WELL PICKLED
BRUU 746 A

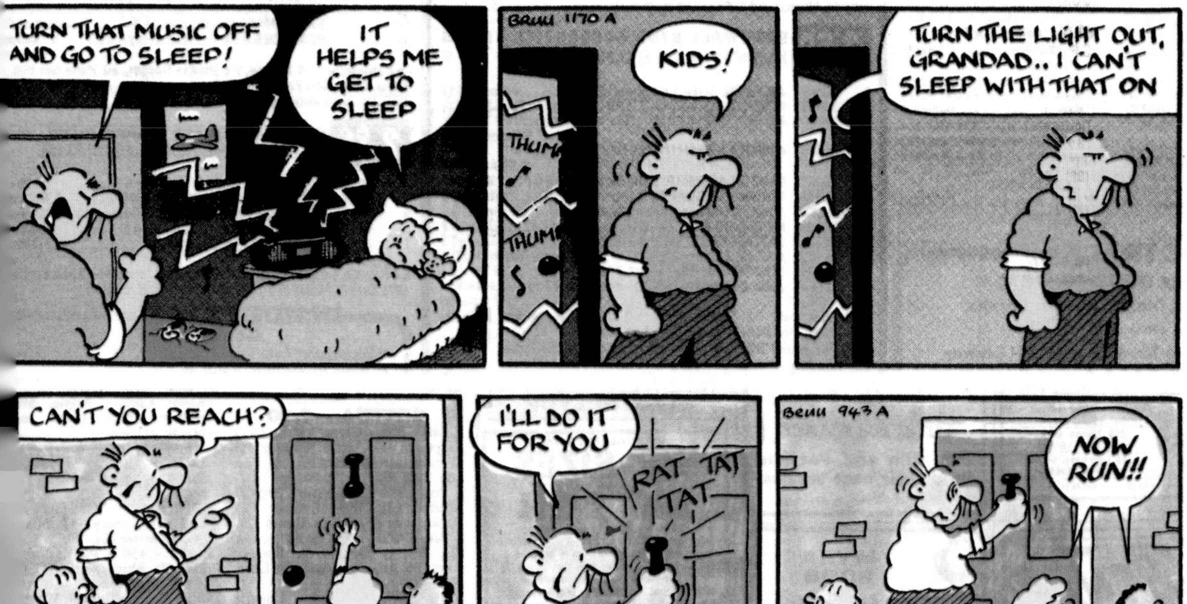
TURN THAT MUSIC OFF AND GO TO SLEEP!
IT HELPS ME GET TO SLEEP
BRUU 1170 A
KIDS!
THUM
THUM
TURN THE LIGHT OUT, GRANDAD.. I CAN'T SLEEP WITH THAT ON

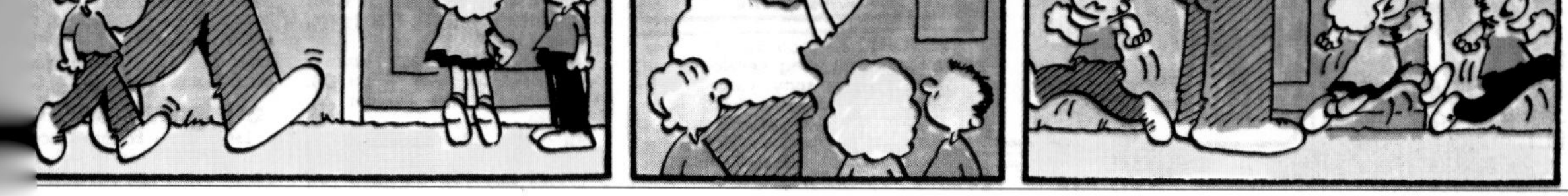
CAN'T YOU REACH?
I'LL DO IT FOR YOU
RAT TAT TAT
BRUU 943 A
NOW RUN!!

WELL HERE IT COMES!

SHUGGIE and DUGGIE

by TOM BULLIMORE and KEV WHITE

LISTEN, TREVOR...DAVE'S AGREED TO LEAVE YOU ALONE PROVIDING YOU DON'T ANTAGONISE HIM. DO YOU AGREE?
OF COURSE I AGREE, DO YOU THINK I'M THICK OR SOMETHING?!...
...BY THE WAY, WHAT DOES ANTAGONISE MEAN?

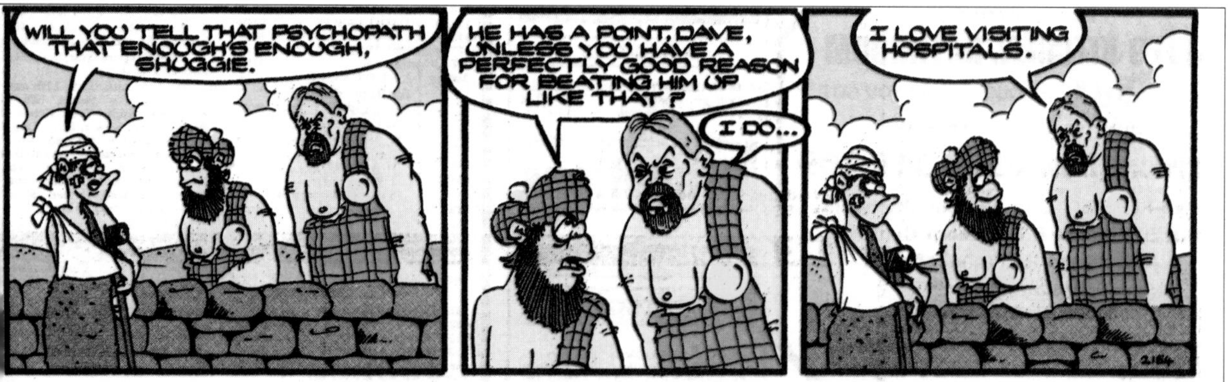
WILL YOU TELL THAT PSYCHOPATH THAT ENOUGH'S ENOUGH, SHUGGIE.
HE HAS A POINT, DAVE, UNLESS YOU HAVE A PERFECTLY GOOD REASON FOR BEATING HIM UP LIKE THAT ?
I DO...
I LOVE VISITING HOSPITALS.
2154

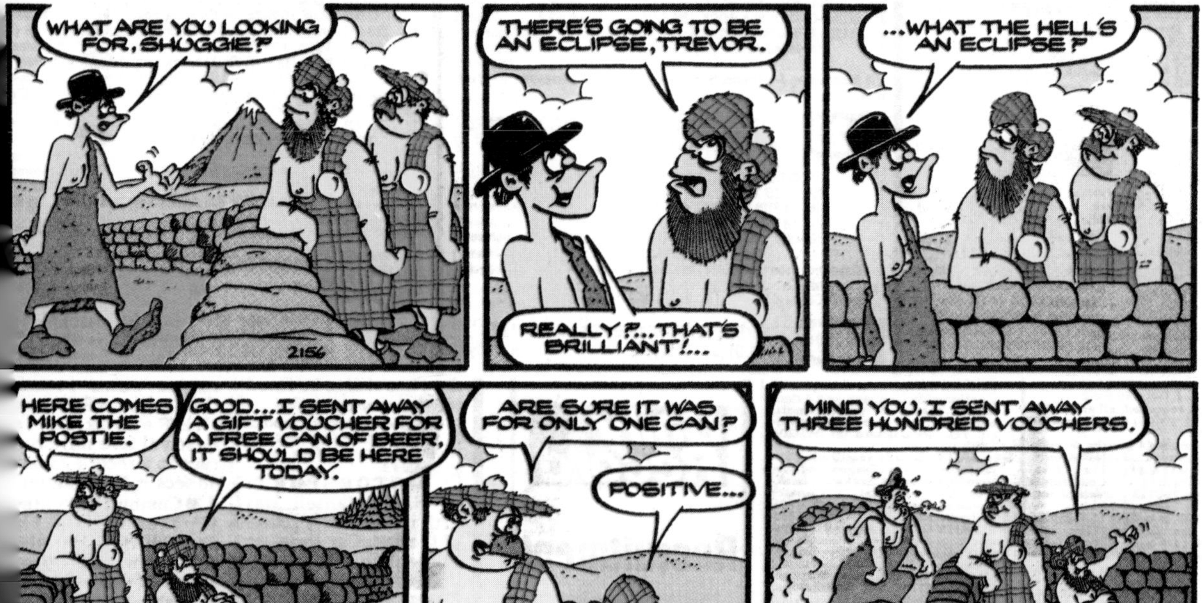
WHAT ARE YOU LOOKING FOR, SHUGGIE ?
2156
THERE'S GOING TO BE AN ECLIPSE, TREVOR.
REALLY ?...THAT'S BRILLIANT !...
...WHAT THE HELL'S AN ECLIPSE ?

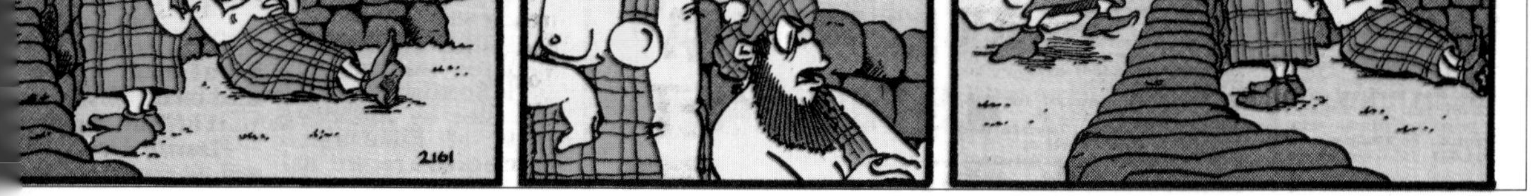
HERE COMES MIKE THE POSTIE.
GOOD...I SENT AWAY A GIFT VOUCHER FOR A FREE CAN OF BEER, IT SHOULD BE HERE TODAY.
2161
ARE SURE IT WAS FOR ONLY ONE CAN ?
POSITIVE...
MIND YOU, I SENT AWAY THREE HUNDRED VOUCHERS.

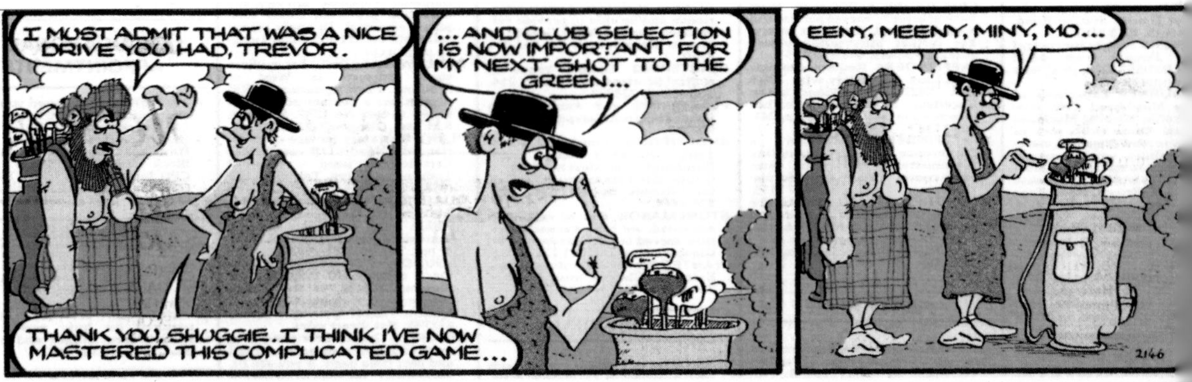
I MUST ADMIT THAT WAS A NICE DRIVE YOU HAD, TREVOR.
THANK YOU, SHUGGIE. I THINK I'VE NOW MASTERED THIS COMPLICATED GAME...
...AND CLUB SELECTION IS NOW IMPORTANT FOR MY NEXT SHOT TO THE GREEN...
EENY, MEENY, MINY, MO...
2146

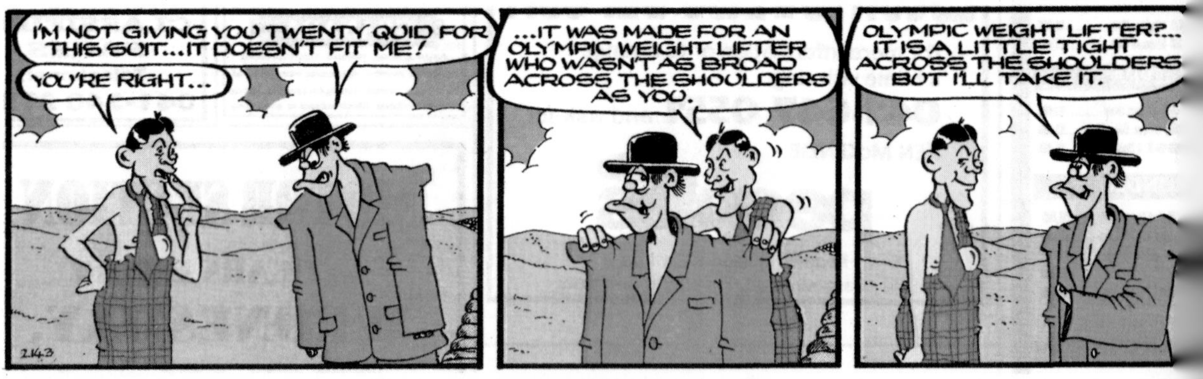
I'M NOT GIVING YOU TWENTY QUID FOR THIS SUIT...IT DOESN'T FIT ME!
YOU'RE RIGHT...
2143
...IT WAS MADE FOR AN OLYMPIC WEIGHT LIFTER WHO WASN'T AS BROAD ACROSS THE SHOULDERS AS YOU.
OLYMPIC WEIGHT LIFTER?... IT IS A LITTLE TIGHT ACROSS THE SHOULDERS BUT I'LL TAKE IT.

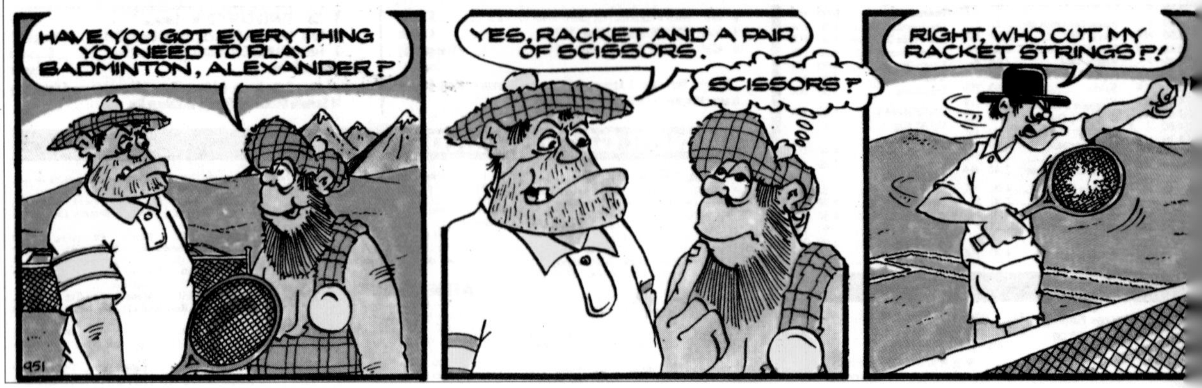
HAVE YOU GOT EVERYTHING YOU NEED TO PLAY BADMINTON, ALEXANDER?
951
YES, RACKET AND A PAIR OF SCISSORS.
SCISSORS?
RIGHT, WHO CUT MY RACKET STRINGS?!

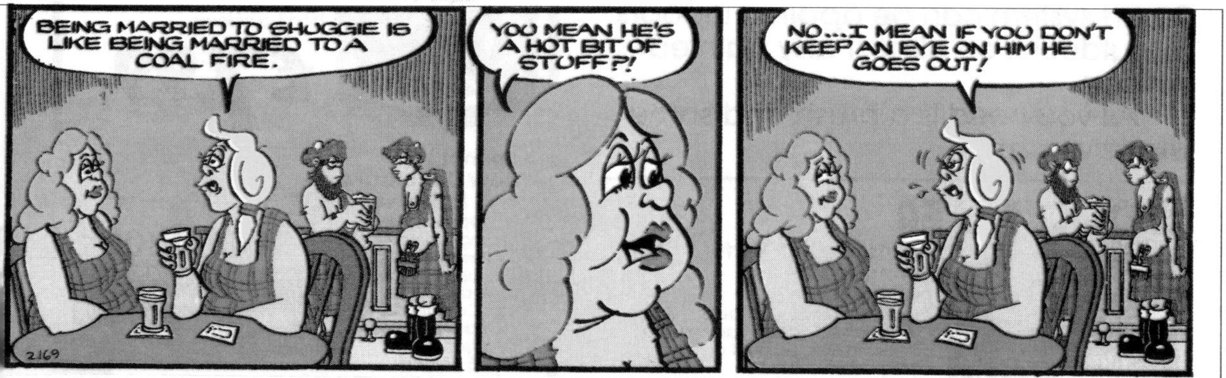
BEING MARRIED TO SHUGGIE IS LIKE BEING MARRIED TO A COAL FIRE.
2169
YOU MEAN HE'S A HOT BIT OF STUFF?!
NO...I MEAN IF YOU DON'T KEEP AN EYE ON HIM HE GOES OUT!

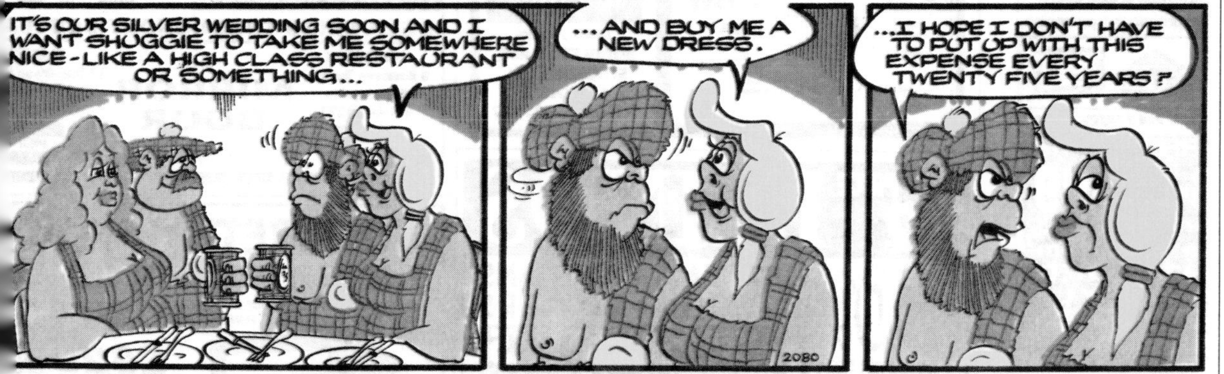
IT'S OUR SILVER WEDDING SOON AND I WANT SHUGGIE TO TAKE ME SOMEWHERE NICE - LIKE A HIGH CLASS RESTAURANT OR SOMETHING...
...AND BUY ME A NEW DRESS.
2080
...I HOPE I DON'T HAVE TO PUT UP WITH THIS EXPENSE EVERY TWENTY FIVE YEARS?

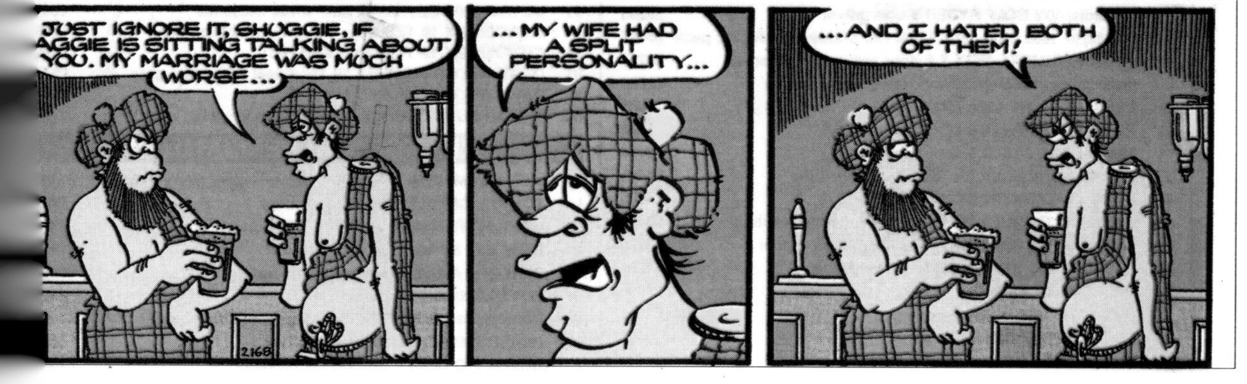
JUST IGNORE IT, SHUGGIE, IF AGGIE IS SITTING TALKING ABOUT YOU. MY MARRIAGE WAS MUCH WORSE...
2168
...MY WIFE HAD A SPLIT PERSONALITY...
...AND I HATED BOTH OF THEM!

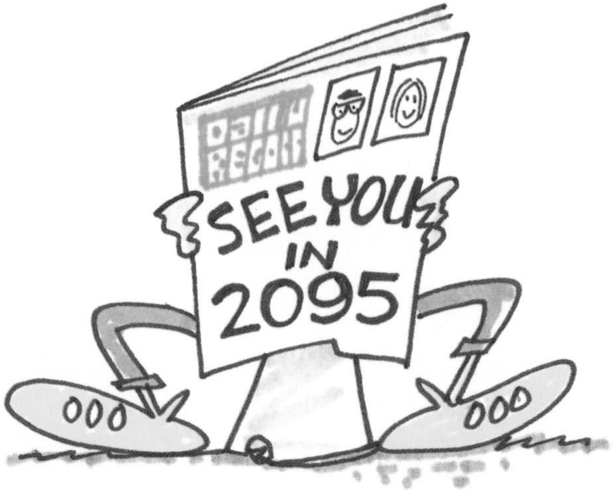
SEE YOU
IN
2095